RACIAL BAGGAGE

Racial Baggage

MEXICAN IMMIGRANTS AND RACE ACROSS THE BORDER

Sylvia Zamora

Stanford University Press
STANFORD, CALIFORNIA

STANFORD UNIVERSITY PRESS
Stanford, California

Printed in the United States of America on acid-free, archival-quality paper

Library of Congress Cataloging-in-Publication Data

Names: Zamora, Sylvia, author.

Title: Racial baggage : Mexican immigrants and race across the border / Sylvia Zamora.

Description: Stanford, California : Stanford University Press, 2022. | Includes bibliographical references and index.

Identifiers: LCCN 2021052396 (print) | LCCN 2021052397 (ebook) | ISBN 9781503628526 (cloth) | ISBN 9781503632240 (paperback) | ISBN 9781503632257 (ebook)

Subjects: LCSH: Mexicans—Race identity—United States. | Mexicans—United States—Social conditions. | Immigrants—United States—Social conditions. | Racism—United States. | Racism—Mexico. | United States—Race relations. | Mexico—Race relations. | United States—Emigration and immigration—Social aspects. | Mexico—Emigration and immigration—Social aspects.

Classification: LCC E184.M5 Z36 2022 (print) | LCC E184.M5 (ebook) | DDC 305.868/72073—dc23/eng/20211029

LC record available at https://lccn.loc.gov/2021052396

LC ebook record available at https://lccn.loc.gov/2021052397

Cover design: George Kirkpatrick

Cover art: AAA map of Los Angeles and vicinity, 1957. Tom Hilton

Typeset by Motto Publishing Services in 11/15 Arno Pro

Contents

Preface

I was born and raised and still live in South Gate, a working-class Latino immigrant community one block from Watts. This was the 1980s and early 1990s, when Watts was predominantly Black and being ravaged by the crack epidemic and ensuing violence, drug addiction, poverty, and hyper police surveillance—a landscape famously depicted in classic films like *Boyz n the Hood* and *Menace II Society*. Even though our neighborhoods were physically close to each other, they were a world apart socially. The messages I received from my Latino friends and family growing up were clear: do not cross the intersection. It all began to change in the 1990s, when immigrants from Mexico and Central America began arriving in large numbers and settling in Watts and the surrounding areas, eventually turning South L.A. majority Latino.

It was during this demographic transition, when I was in high school, that I got to know Watts more intimately and came to see the similarities between our communities. I visited often with a friend, a fellow Mexican American whose family had been living in Watts for two years. They were one of the only Latino families on her block. We would spend hours on her front porch watching passersby and occasionally walking to the corner liquor store to buy candy. During that time, I took a Chicano/a Studies course (it was the first time being offered in my public high school) and began to develop the language and tools to observe the parallels with my own community: underfunded schools, overcrowded housing, heavy police surveillance, vacant and graffitied storefronts, more liquor stores than healthy food options, and a lot of Black and Brown people struggling to make ends meet. Sure, in Watts I witnessed the occasional conflict between longtime African American residents and Latino immigrant newcomers, but I wondered why such a racial divide existed when, to my budding sociological eye, it seemed as if our social conditions were more similar than different.

One October day, my childhood best friend, Jessica, asked if I wanted to go to a police brutality march in downtown L.A. Wanting to make an adventure of taking public transit on our own, I decided to join her. We left school early—unbeknownst to our parents—and arrived to join a large gathering of protesters. Family members of those unjustly killed at the hands of police held posters displaying photos of their loved ones, chanting, "No justice, no peace!" I couldn't help but notice that all of the faces on the posters were Black and Brown, and mostly young. I was moved by the collective expression of rage and noticed it bubbling up in me too. I was also inspired by the powerful act of Black and Brown solidarity that I was witnessing.

This was the turning point in my political development.

I have since become fascinated by Black and Brown solidarity movements across time and place. In graduate school, I explored this very topic in my first research study, which examined African American and Latino grassroots coalition-building within a South L.A. nonprofit community organization. I wanted to understand why and how these groups—who always seemed to be pitted against each other in popular discourse—could create *and sustain* cross-racial coalitions. I found that the framing strategies deployed by coalition leaders were critical to fostering a strong sense of collective identity based on race and place. But in the process of interviewing coalition members, I also discovered that African Americans and Latinos alike held unconscious biases toward each other. Both groups believed these prejudices needed to be dealt with head-on, not despite racial solidarity but for the sake of it.

That same year, news reports of so-called race wars between African Americans and Latinos began to make national headlines. One *Los Angeles Times* article addressed an incident involving a Latino gang shooting of a fourteen-year-old African American girl in Highland Park, an L.A. neighborhood undergoing dramatic demographic change. The author, a law professor at a prestigious university, went so far as to refer to the shooting as "a manifestation of an increasingly common trend: Latino ethnic cleansing of African Americans from multiracial neighborhoods." It was a sweeping generalization of Latinos' racial attitudes toward African Americans. Through my involvement with Black and Brown coalition-building, I knew this characterization was misleading and ran the danger of pandering to White audiences who might come to believe that people of color can be equally racist, thereby absolving themselves of any accountability for dismantling White supremacy.

I knew that if I wanted to understand the complexity and nuances of African American and Latino relations, I would need to take immigrant racial attitudes—and their origins—seriously. I enrolled in courses on race, ethnicity, and immigration and delved into sociological literature on race relations to better understand what I was seeing on the ground in South L.A. The traditional frameworks and theories I came across, such as racial threat theory, which centers Black-White relations, did not apply to immigrant attitudes toward groups who also experience racial marginalization. As I thought about the ways that Mexican immigrants learn about the U.S. racial stratification system, I realized that I needed to first go back to the roots of their racial thinking: Mexico. That was when this book was born.

Racial attitudes are messy, especially when they involve people of color who carry the weight of European colonialism and U.S. imperialism. More often than not, our views and opinions about different racial and ethnic groups run the spectrum from favorable to unfavorable and everything in between. Our racial perceptions can change over time and can be contradictory. As the daughter of Mexican immigrants, I was attuned to the anti-Black narratives that run rampant in our communities. I observed how much family members and others in my immigrant community coveted light skin and eyes. The ideology of *blanqueamiento* (Whitening) is embedded deep in our psyches. My own mother, who has beautiful dark skin, full lips, and thick wavy hair, would warn me to stay out of the sun lest I turn "*negra*." Even as a kid, I thought that these warnings didn't sit well. When I made my way from predominantly Brown South Gate to predominantly White Smith College, my resistance against Whiteness was amplified: I deliberately got as much sun as possible, to see just how dark my skin could get. (I get pretty dark, it turns out!).

When I started this research a decade ago, I was specifically interested in Mexican immigrants' racial perceptions of African Americans. As I engaged more deeply with this book project, it became clear that I could not disentangle Mexicans' constructions of Blackness from hegemonic ideologies of Whiteness, *mestizaje*, Indigeneity, and race more broadly. Nor could I treat racial formation in the Mexican context as analytically distinct from racial formations in the U.S. To this end, I drew great insight from the conceptual and empirical work of scholars who pioneered comparative social science research on race across the Americas—Jorge Duany, Jose Itzigsohn, and Anani Dzidzienyo; and including my own mentors, Ginetta Candelario, Edward E. Telles, and the late Mark Q. Sawyer, among others—who shaped my own theorization of Mexican transnational experiences of race. In the end, I learned that the immigration experience itself transforms how migrants come to see race, identity, and their group position within overlapping and evolving U.S. and Mexican racial hierarchies. This is the personal, political, and intellectual point of departure from which my book *Racial Baggage* begins.

Acknowledgments

It has been quite a long journey to complete this book, and I could not have done it without the love and support of my family, friends, and mentors along the way. As the only person in my family to graduate from college, I am aware that writing and publishing a book is no small feat. I was fortunate in my youth to come across inspiring teachers who gave me the tools to think critically about the social conditions I was witnessing in my working-class neighborhood. I am grateful to my middle school teacher, the late Bob Tanner, for introducing me to the writings of Howard Zinn and Karl Marx and for nurturing my budding political and intellectual curiosity—even well into my college years. I still have the pin he gifted me in eighth grade that read "Rebel Looking for a Cause." I think I finally found my cause. I also want to thank Jesus Martinez, my high school Chicano/a Studies teacher and neighbor, for opening my eyes to the history of conquest and resilience in the Americas and inspiring me to be an agent of social change.

I arrived at Smith College with very limited knowledge of sociology. Ginetta Candelario, the first Latina professor and sociologist I ever met, taught me to fall in love with sociology and, although I was unaware of it then, planted the intellectual seeds for this research. Your brilliant seminar "Blackness in the Americas" first challenged me to see race from a hemispheric perspective and forever changed my thinking. You encouraged me to apply for the Mellon Mays Undergraduate Fellowship program and cheered me on during my very first research presentation. Thank you for inspiring me to become a sociologist.

When I arrived at UCLA, I had even less knowledge about what a career in academia entailed. I am forever indebted to my closest mentors and role models, Vilma Ortiz and Edward E. Telles, who took this first-generation working-class student under their wing and turned her into a trained scholar. Your guidance, generosity, intellectual rigor, and occasional much-needed nudge during and after my time at UCLA are the reason this book exists. Thank you for providing me with a strong foundation for my life and career.

My deepest thanks also extend to the late Mark Q. Sawyer. His unique global perspective on race relations will always be fundamental to my understanding of race. Mark, you were a fierce advocate for graduate students of color, and it meant a lot to know you were always there for me personally and professionally. I also thank Ruben Hernandez-Leon for welcoming me to the department the very first time I visited UCLA. Your expertise on Mexican migration helped me sharpen my analytical senses, and your sense of humor is always appreciated. I would also like to acknowledge Rebecca Emigh, Mignon Moore, Roger Waldinger, and Gaspar Rivera-Salgado for their intellectual support. I thank the wonderful students who took my "Blackness in Mexico" and "African American and Latino Relations" courses taught my last year at UCLA. Their genuine curiosity, personal experiences, and new approaches to these subjects challenged my own thinking and inspired me to continue this work.

I have many people to thank for the success of my fieldwork in Mexico. A special thank you to my *tia* Irma Zamora Magaña, *tio*

Lorenzo Viera Santillan, and *primas* in Guadalajara, who graciously put me up until I could find housing and took time out of their busy lives to make sure I was OK. I am grateful to Miguel Valladolid for helping me navigate the city and recruit respondents. Dr. Mercedes González de la Rocha and staff at the *Centro de Investigaciones y Estudios Superiores en Antropologia Social en Occidente* provided me with a welcoming academic home during my time in Guadalajara. This research was made possible with generous funding and support. At UCLA, the Eugene Cota-Robles Fellowship, the Diversity Initiative for Graduate Study in the Social Sciences Research Mentorship Grant, the Latin American Institute, and the Institute for American Cultures Chicana/o Studies Research Center Grant provided funds for several summers of research. Grants from the Social Science Research Council, the UC Center for New Racial Studies, and the UC Institute for Mexico and the U.S. (UC MEXUS) helped with data collection and interview transcriptions. I was also supported by the Woodrow Wilson National Fellowship Foundation and the John Randolph Haynes and Dora Haynes Foundation. This book was completed with support from Loyola Marymount University's Bellarmine College of Letters and Arts College Fellowship and the Faculty Summer Research and Writing Grant, as well as a Career Enhancement Fellowship from the Institute for Citizens & Scholars (formerly the Woodrow Wilson Foundation).

I thank all of the individuals interviewed for this study whose names remain anonymous. I am especially indebted to the undocumented immigrants, who, despite having legitimate fears and concerns about participating in a study of this kind, trusted me with their stories and opened up their lives and homes to me.

This book was a decade in the making. Over the years, and across academic institutions, I have leaned on the support of many amazingly smart, funny, and kind people. At UCLA, Marisa Gerstein Pineau, Nazgol Ghandnoosh, Christina Chin, Nancy Yuen, Laura Orrico, Forrest Stuart, Anup Sheth, Wes Hiers, Laura Bekes, Iddo Tavory, Chinyere Osuji, Elena Shih, Leisy Abrego, David Cort, Veronica Terriquez, Kjerstin Gruys, John O'Brien, Matt Jackson, Tina Beyene, and others, thank you for the small and big ways in which you made my time at UCLA more enjoyable. To my Raza Graduate Student Association crew, Alfonso Gonzales, Lorena Alvarado, Alex Garcia, Alexandro Hernandez, Lupe Escobar, Nolan Cabrera, Revel Sims, and Marek Cabrera, thank you for being comrades in struggle. I am so proud of all of our accomplishments. My deepest gratitude is reserved for Anthony Ocampo, Indara Suarez, Erica Morales, Amada Armenta, and Anthony Alvarez. Thank you for being there during my lowest moments in this academic grind, reminding me that I—we—got this. I also thank my closest sister-friends, Yesenia Ramirez, Mienah Sharif, Claudia Sandoval, Jessica Espinoza, Johanna Gutierrez, Vanessa Guzmán, Celia Lacayo, Caitlin Patler, Gretel Rosas, and Amreen Karmali, whose wise words, company, laughter, and moral support have sustained me over the years. I look forward to a lifetime of sisterhood.

I thank everyone who read chapters and provided critical feedback on earlier drafts, especially the *mujeres* of Vilma's working group, Vilma Ortiz, Celia Lacayo, Ariana Valle, Irene Vega, Deisy Del Real, Cassandra Salgado, Rocío García, Laura Enriquez, Karina Chavarria, Carla Salazar Gonzalez, Miriam Martinez-Aranda, and Laura Orrico. I also thank Glenda Flores, Rocío Rosales, Amada Armenta, Edward E. Telles, Tiffany Joseph, Theo Greene, Michael Rodríguez-Muñiz, and Anthony Ocampo for being generous with their time. Many others shaped the book through informal conversations about the research and the book publishing process, as well as offering general moral support: Tanya Golash-Boza, Ayu Saraswati, Jennifer A. Jones, Tianna Paschel, Neda Magbouleh, Shannon Gleeson, Chris Zepeda-Millán, Pierrette Hondagneu-Sotelo, Jessica Vasquez, Julie Dowling, Christina Sue, Cristina Mora, Tyrone Forman, David Embrick, Cynthia Feliciano, Helen Marrow, Lorrie Frasure, Joanna Perez, Walter Thompson-Hernández, Kency Cornejo, and Rudy Mondragón.

This book has also benefited from the insightful questions and comments I have received over the years when I have presented this work. I thank audiences at UCLA; the University of Chicago; the University of Notre Dame; Stanford University; the University of Illinois Chicago; the University of Delaware; Bryn Mawr College; UC Irvine; Loyola Marymount University; the American Sociological Association; the Latinx Studies Association; the Association of Black Sociologists; the Pacific Sociological Association; the Latin American Studies Association's Section on Ethnicity, Race, and Indigenous Peoples (LASA-ERIP); the Politics of Race, Immigration, and Ethnicity Consortium (PRIEC); the Mellon Mays Fellowship Summer Conferences; and the Institute for Citizens & Scholars Career Enhancement Fellows Retreat. Many thanks to the award committees of the American Sociological Association's 2019 Distinguished Contribution to Research Article of the Latina/o Sociology section, the 2012 James E. Blackwell Distinguished Graduate Student Paper of the Racial and Ethnic Minorities section, and the 2012 Best Student Paper of the International Migration section. I am honored to receive this recognition from my sociology peers.

My time as a Provost's Postdoctoral Fellow at the University of Chicago was critical in my career as an academic. I am grateful to the Department of Sociology for hosting me, especially Omar McRoberts, Forrest Stuart, Elizabeth Clemens, and Kimberly K.

Hoang for supporting my research. I thank Tracye Matthews, Dara Epison, and Michael Dawson for providing a warm and welcoming space at the Center for the Study of Race, Politics, and Culture. A special thank you to Tianna Paschel, Lorena Garcia, Cathy Cohen, Jennifer A. Jones, Michael Rodríguez-Muñiz, Ainsely LeSure, Marcelle Medford, Julius Jones, Alfredo Gonzalez, Stephanie Hair, Judith Camacho, Amanda Lewis, Connie Wun, and Gabriel Cortez. There were times I did not think I could make it through my time in Chicago, but your friendship and kindness carried me through.

Thank you to my colleagues in the Sociology Department at Loyola Marymount University, who have been wonderful and provided me with a supportive environment in which to complete this book, especially Anna Muraco, Rachel Washburn, and Ravaris Moore, and Nadia Kim, Rebecca Sager, and Stephanie Lemoncelli. Thank you also to my colleagues in the Chicana/o Studies Department for making me feel at home.

I want to express my sincerest appreciation to my editor, Marcela Maxfield, at Stanford University Press for guiding me through the manuscript preparation process with patience and kindness. I have also benefited enormously from the anonymous reviewers' careful reading, critical feedback, and enthusiastic support of this research. Thank you also to Kate Epstein for helping to make my arguments more concise and convincing.

I finished writing this book while raising my toddler, Mateo, as a single mother during the COVID-19 pandemic. This would have been impossible without the practical and emotional support of my mother, Guadalupe Zamora. Although she never had the opportunity to pursue an education beyond the fourth grade, she has taught me far more about life and resilience than any book or university ever could. *Gracias por tu amistad y apoyo incondicional, mamá.* I am also grateful for my smart and loving nephew Sergio, and to my sister, Veronica, for treating Mateo like her own and helping out in all the ways that only a sister could. I also owe much to my father, Sergio Zamora, for supporting everything I set my mind to and whose passion for debate has shaped me into the woman I am today—one who knows the value of her voice.

I am most grateful for Mateo, the light of my life. Thank you for bringing me so much joy and for giving purpose to all of this. Someday you will understand what it means that Mom finished a book while you were still running around in diapers, and I hope you take pride in it as much as I take pride in the curious, funny, smart, and caring individual that you are becoming. This book—and everything I do—is for you, love.

Immigration and
Racial Transformation in America

MARTIN, A FIFTY-TWO-YEAR-OLD Mexican immigrant with thirty-two years of experience living in Los Angeles, recounts a life in Mexico where racism, according to him, did not exist. "Racism in Mexico? Personally, I don't think so," he retorted to my question about whether he had ever felt discriminated against in his home country. "Racism is when you don't like somebody because they're Black or White or from another country. But why wouldn't you be friends with everyone [in Mexico]? We are all Mexican."

In stark contrast to Martin's description of Mexico as a country free of racial conflict is American society, which he came to see as rife with racism. Growing up in a small town on the outskirts of Guadalajara, Mexico, Martin was fascinated by the stories of the United States that his *padrino* (godfather), Jose, would tell. Now in his seventies, Jose left Mexico as a young boy to start a new life in San Bernardino, California, when Martin was just a baby. During one of his padrino's many visits to Jalisco, Martin overheard him talking with his compadre about the rigid racial divide in 1960s Jim Crow America:

> He [Jose] would say that there are major differences between the races. There are Mexicans, African Americans, and Anglos.

Back in those days, they [Anglos] didn't want the races to mix. Not even on buses, restaurants, or anywhere. They would even designate separate spaces for themselves. On the bus, half was for them and the other half for everyone else. African Americans couldn't go into the nice restaurants, much less us Mexicans. There was a lot of racism.

Over the years, Martin's padrino would relay countless stories of the American race system. Racial segregation and the idea that race determined where people could live or dine especially intrigued Martin. Back then, he had not yet ventured outside his racially homogenous town, as he saw it, much less crossed the border to *el norte*. "These stories," he remembered, "planted a seed [in me]. They never left me."

The United States Martin encountered in 1982 was in the midst of dramatic racial and political transformation. Economic restructuring, growing unemployment, gang violence, and heavy police surveillance made life in Los Angeles particularly challenging for new arrivals.

When I first got here . . . I would just sleep and go to work and back. There were lots of Black people in the neighborhood. My uncle would tell me, "Be careful with the [Black] neighbors. It's best if you keep your head down and avoid any problems." I didn't want to bring any attention to myself because I didn't have papers and was afraid of getting pulled over by the police, so I did what he told me and avoided contact with Black people. . . .When my uncle told me to watch out for the Mexican neighbors, I didn't understand. I would ask him, "But why, *tio*? They're the same race as us." Yeah, they were Mexican, but they were born here, and in those days there were

lots of gangs. Instead of helping us out, gang members would
try to mess with anybody who had just arrived from Mexico.

Martin is one of the seventy-five Mexicans I interviewed who,
over the course of their lives and migration experiences, learned
to navigate race, identity, and illegality within a transnational social space. Given that Mexican immigrants—one of the oldest and
largest streams of migrants to the U.S.—have long maintained
strong transnational ties, this book explores how the immigration
experience changes not only immigrants themselves but also those
who remain in Mexico. Or, to put it another way, how does migration to the U.S.—a nation long defined by chattel slavery, Jim Crow
segregation, anti-immigrant nativist xenophobia, and race riots—
transform Mexicans' understanding of race and inequality in both
home and host countries? How are immigrants influenced by U.S.
racial ideologies even before they migrate? And what are the implications of the racial baggage they bring with them to the U.S. for
evolving race relations in their communities of settlement? Based
on the experiences and perspectives of Mexicans in Guadalajara,
Jalisco, and Los Angeles, California, this book brings attention to
a transnational theorization of race that considers how racial ideas
and practices travel across geopolitical borders to influence the racial thinking and practices of individuals "here and there" and, in
the process, generate new experiences of racial difference, belonging, and citizenship for those who migrate. In doing so, it aims to
counter the "methodological nationalism"—that is, the idea that
the nation-state is the natural container of analysis—that permeates much of the American sociological literature on race and immigration (Wimmer and Glick-Schiller 2002, 302).

In our highly globalized world, people, capital, and technologies move across borders with unprecedented ease, but so do

sociocultural values, ideas, and customs—all of which are highly racialized. American notions of race regularly make their way into millions of Mexican households via Hollywood film and television and depictions of life in America as portrayed by immigrants during phone calls and social media messaging. *Racial Baggage* is a story of cross-border movement not only in terms of individuals' physical migration but also of racial migration—that is, the back-and-forth of racial ideologies, images, discourses, and practices across time and place. My interviews with Mexican non-migrants in Guadalajara and Mexican immigrants in Los Angeles reveal that they are regularly exposed to dominant U.S. racial ideologies in Mexico long before they migrate. As such, this book reflects the understanding that migrants' "racial baggage" affects how they navigate the American racial system and come to understand their place within it.

Mexico and the United States have been profoundly intertwined economically, politically, and socially for more than a century. Mexican transnational migration, as well as return migration, precedes the existence of a physical border, giving way to a long-established and rich transnational connection. Many immigrants who settle across the U.S. maintain strong ties to hometown associations and churches, sending economic remittances to loved ones and returning to visit their homelands for annual fiestas. While we know that these transnational endeavors have a powerful impact on the economic, political, and social landscape of the communities the migrants leave behind (see, for example, Duquette-Rury 2019), we know less about how migrants' social ties to home facilitate racial remittances and, in the process, refashion the meaning of race in the sending community. We know even less about how the racial baggage that immigrant newcomers bring with them to the U.S. affects how Mexicans perceive racial "others" in their new society and their own place within the country's racialized strat-ification system. Throughout this book, I argue that any consid-eration of immigrants' transnational lives must take seriously the way this racial baggage may shape how they see their place in the U.S. socioracial hierarchy.

Race in Mexico and the U.S. has manifested itself quite differ-ently in policies and everyday life, yet most Americans know lit-tle about race in Mexico and even less about how Mexican immi-grant newcomers reconcile the vastly different racial contexts of their home and host countries upon migration to the U.S. (Moreno Figueroa 2008; Moreno Figueroa and Saldívar Tanaka 2016). The U.S. is historically defined by its long-standing Black-White color line rooted in a racial ideology of hypodescent, or the one-drop rule, in which the White category was deemed pure and racially mixed individuals were relegated to a lesser status. In contrast, Mexican society is dominated by *mestizaje* ideology and social practices that hail a particular racial mixture and work to mask ra-cial difference and discrimination. Simply put, to many Mexicans, the U.S. epitomizes a racist nation, while Mexico is (falsely) seen as a nation free of racism.

When Mexicans leave their country for the U.S., they leave be-hind their mestizo privilege, one defined by a strong sense of na-tional belonging rooted in their citizenship and racial embodi-ment of the "ideal" Mexican. Upon arrival, newcomers undergo a uniquely American process of racialization. Those who arrived in Los Angeles, where my fieldwork took place, found that their Mexicanness instantly cast them as simultaneously a racialized minority and legal outcast. Relegated to the bottom rungs of the racial hierarchy, migrants encountered a newly subordinated sta-tus they did not contend with in Mexico. Indeed, it is precisely their mestizaje—that which conferred privilege in the Mexican context—that has historically deemed them an inferior "mongrel" race in America (Gómez 2015). They are criminalized as "illegal" and are subject to devastating effects of legal violence and political exclusion (Menjívar and Abrego 2012). Almost overnight, Mexican newcomers arguably become among the most vulnerable and exploitable underclass in their new society (Massey 2014). The Mexico-U.S. border, then, effectively becomes the site where, upon entry, newcomers take on this newfound racialized subjectivity.

Over time, immigrants attempt to make sense of how their new society sees them and, in turn, how they see themselves. The Mexican migrants I spoke with came to understand their "new" racial and legal status in relation not only to White Americans but to other subordinated groups, like Black Americans and U.S.-born Latinos, whom they come into greater contact with in their neighborhoods and workplaces. In this book, I argue that immigrant newcomers learn to define race in a way distinct from both the color-conscious hierarchy of Mexican society and the Black-White binary prevalent for much of U.S. history. In the process, their stories demonstrate that race is not static but rather an evolving social phenomenon forever altered by immigration.

Rethinking Race Through a Transnational Lens

The phenomenon of racial ideas and practices traveling across geopolitical borders to influence racial thinking and practices across multiple contexts is not new (Hooker 2017; Katzew 2005; Stepan 1991). Ideas about race have crossed borders since European colonizers landed in the Americas, but the rise of neoliberal globalization—the integration of the world economy—over the past three decades has significantly sped up what feels like the unstoppable circulation of new technologies of communication, facilitating the spread of U.S. culture worldwide. Yet race and processes of racialization have not always been central to scholarly discussions of global transformation and mass migration (Thomas and Clarke 2006; Kim 2008).

In our era of globalized media, in which ideas and information move across borders with unprecedented ease, widely televised events in the U.S.—like the election of Barack Obama, Trump's anti-immigrant campaign to "build the wall," or racial justice movements expressing outrage over police brutality—can powerfully shape the way global audiences view American race relations. In particular, the growing speed at which people in Mexico and throughout Latin America can access American primetime television through cable networks and the internet means that Latino immigrants in the U.S. are only a click away from communication with loved ones back home. The widespread use of smartphones and more recent social media advancements like Facebook, WhatsApp, Instagram, and TikTok have only enabled American popular culture—and the racial ideologies it carries with it—to flow ever more quickly across a much wider scale (Orgad 2012; Rodriguez 2018). The transnational flow of ideas and information is a two-way street; Mexican notions of race and identity, such as those found in widely popular telenovelas, also make their way to U.S. audiences.

In addition to global media, a number of scholars have examined the ways that migrants stay socially and politically connected to their homelands, even many years after settling in their new country (Basch, Schiller, and Szanton Blanc 1994; Waldinger 2013; Portes and Rumbaut 2006; Levitt 1998). The foundational sociological framework for studying immigrants' maintenance of social ties and loyalties to their home countries is transnationalism, traditionally conceptualized as the process by which immigrants maintain "social relations that link together their societies of origin and settlement" (Basch, Schiller, and Szanton Blanc 1994, 7).[1] A main focus of this vast body of literature has been on global economic remittances. Yet the same social relationships that facilitate economic remittances facilitate the flow of racial—and sometimes racist—ideas across borders (Levitt 2001).

Everyday migrants, like those featured in this study, play an important role in creating and disseminating racial ideas across borders. In her classic study of Dominican migration to the U.S., sociologist Peggy Levitt (2001, 54) coined the term "social remittances" to underscore how sociocultural transnational exchanges, such as political ideas, gendered behaviors, and social capital, are instrumental in exporting American culture abroad. Levitt shows how immigrant women in New York City picked up "Americanized" ideals about gender equality and relayed these messages back to their mothers, sisters, and friends in the Dominican Republic, who then adopted these "new" gender norms into their own lives, even though they never migrated themselves.

Given that ordinary individuals, much like state institutions and global media, have the power to "create global culture at the local level" (Levitt 2001, 11), scholars have called for a "transnationalism from below," which pays attention to how the social worlds and everyday behavior of individuals help to create—and sustain—transnational social spaces. This book is an attempt to answer that call. Indeed, the same way that articulations of gender and sexuality are exchanged in migrant transnational social spaces, so too are ideas about race (Duany 1998; Itzigsohn et al. 1999; Candelario 2007; Kim 2008; Roth 2012; Jones 2013; Joseph 2015; Zamora 2016). Drawing inspiration from Levitt's "social remittances," in this book I elaborate on the term "racial remittances" in order to highlight how ordinary migrants, and the everyday transnational lives they maintain, are a key mechanism for the diffusion of hegemonic U.S.

8

racial ideologies, discourses, stereotypes, schemas, and practices across national boundaries.

The past two decades have seen an emergent scholarly literature on transnational migration and race. For example, in her book *Imperial Citizens: Koreans and Race from Seoul to LA.*, sociologist Nadia Kim (2008) documents how American ideologies of White superiority were introduced to Korean society through U.S. military occupation and global media. Among other things, she shows compelling evidence for how Korean media coverage of the 1992 Los Angeles unrest, particularly images of the violence directed at Korean-owned businesses, shaped Koreans' perceptions of African Americans as criminal and violent, exposing would-be migrants to U.S. racist ideologies long before their arrival to the U.S. A similar observation is offered by sociologist Tiffany Joseph (2015), who expanded scholarly understandings of the transnational racial lives of U.S. migrants by examining how Brazilian return migrants negotiate their newly acquired U.S.-based racial views in the context of their Brazilian hometown. Experiencing firsthand overt discrimination in the U.S. shifted returnees' racial attitudes, behaviors, and views of social inequality in Brazil, making them more aware of their country's pervasive anti-Blackness.

To understand how Latin American immigrants contend with vastly different racial systems across the Americas, it is useful to turn to the work of Wendy Roth (2012), a sociologist who examined the experiences of Dominican and Puerto Rican migrants in New York City. Building on the fields of cognitive science and cultural sociology, Roth developed the notion of racial schemas, which she defines as "a bundle of racial categories and the set of rules for what they mean, how they are ordered, and how to apply them to oneself and others." Roth demonstrates that racial schemas are shared by people in a given nation and thus vary across

INTRODUCTION

cultures. However, she poignantly argues, when individuals migrate to a new society, they do not merely shed old racial understandings; they draw on these preexisting schemas to help make sense of their new racial reality, forming new amalgamations along the way that simultaneously shape how race is conceptualized at home and abroad. Empirically, Roth shows that as newly arriving immigrants learned about Latinidad—a distinctly U.S. racial formation—they conveyed this U.S. racial schema to audiences back home, where Dominicans and Puerto Ricans began to embrace a Latino identity from abroad. Given the well-documented fact that Latino identity is "made in the U.S.A." (Suárez-Orozco and Páez 2002; Mora 2014), this finding underscores the powerful ways that transnational migration transforms racialized identities in immigrant-sending and -receiving societies.

Using the case of Mexican migrants to gain insight into the ways that U.S. migration transforms experiences with race for individual Mexicans and broader U.S. society, this book contributes to the emerging study of transnational processes of racialization. *Racial Baggage*, however, differs from previous studies in several important ways. First, unlike Dominicans and Central Americans, for example, who are relatively recent arrivals to the U.S. since the 1980s and 1990s respectively, Mexicans are by far the largest Latino national origin group in the U.S., and they account for nearly 70 percent of all Latinos (Gómez 2020). By comparison, Puerto Ricans, who have, after Mexicans, been in the U.S. the longest of any other Latino group, make up about 10 percent of U.S. Latinos, and Dominicans less than 3 percent (Gómez 2020). The popular phrase "We didn't cross the border, the border crossed us" further points to the unique position of Mexicans in the U.S. as encompassing a range of generational statuses from the most recent arrival to well into the fourth generation (Telles and Sue 2019). Thus, any consideration of how "Latino" newcomers make sense of the U.S. racial stratification system requires a serious understanding of the Mexican immigrant experience.

Yet given the United States' historical emphasis on the Black-White color line, scholars have understandably focused almost exclusively on migrants from countries with a significant Black population (see, for example, Duany 1998; Itzigsohn et al. 1999; Candelario 2007; Roth 2012; Joseph 2015). In contrast, my Mexican respondents hail from a country where, in their lifetimes, the Black population has never exceeded 4 percent of the total population (Telles and PERLA 2014). In fact, it has long been assumed that Afro-Mexicans "disappeared" as a result of racial mixing (Aguirre-Beltrán 1946). In contrast to newcomers from countries like Brazil and Puerto Rico, where African legacies are more readily acknowledged, my respondents were socialized into a racial schema that actively engages in the erasure of all things Black. Indeed, as I discuss in Chapter 1, Mexicans are known to articulate a kind of "racelessness" rooted in mestizaje ideology that sees Blackness and Mexicanness as mutually exclusive.

Moreover, whereas some of the Dominican, Brazilian, and Puerto Rican immigrant respondents in Roth's and Joseph's studies were read as Black American in certain U.S. contexts, the Mexican mestizos I interviewed were rarely if ever perceived as Black. As sociologist Ginetta Candelario (2007, 12) notes, Dominicans with visible Black ancestry are "more likely [than other Latinos] to be treated like native blacks in the public sphere, school system, workplace, and in relations with state authorities." After all, whether Latinos are perceived as Black, White, or Brown matters for how they come to interpret their racialized experience in the U.S., and, even then, there exists in-group variation (Joseph 2015, 8). For example, while Levitt (2001, 109) found that one of the first strategies Dominican immigrants used to navigate race in the U.S. was to disassociate themselves from African Americans by emphasizing their Latino identity, Candelario (2007, 130) found that some Dominicans in Washington, D.C., maintained their Dominican identity but were also incentivized to "go the African American route" and self-identify as Black because it afforded them access to cultural and social capital. This was not the case for the immigrants in my study, who were unambiguously read as "Mexican" and thus did not contend with the potential pros and cons of identifying as Black in the U.S. context.

While previous research has yielded rich data on the experiences of Afro-descendant immigrants, it is based on a relatively small proportion of the Latino population and therefore provides only a snapshot of the Latino immigrant racialized experience. Thus, understanding how migration shapes the racial experiences of Latino immigrants, particularly larger questions about Latinos adopting an identity akin to the African American racialized experience, requires a deeper exploration of the unique experiences of mestizo Mexicans who are neither Black nor White both in terms of how they see themselves and how they are read by others. *Racial Baggage* offers insight from the stories of immigrant newcomers whose relationship to Blackness, in both home and host countries, has yet to be fully explored by scholars concerned mainly with immigrants' relationship to Whiteness.

Latinos and the U.S. Racial Landscape

Demographic projections tell us that the U.S. is on track to become a so-called majority-minority nation, in which people of color make up the majority of the population, by 2040—and Latinos are leading the way. This unprecedented transformation,

which some are calling the "Browning of America," is already evident in states like California, where, as of July 1, 2014, census figures confirmed that Latinos outnumber Whites. Underlying these
narratives are speculations and racial anxieties about which side of
the color line Latinos will be positioned on. Although this demographic shift had been a long time coming, many political pundits
and laypersons were surprised—and perhaps alarmed—that the
largest state in the nation was joining Hawaii and New Mexico as
one of three states with a majority non-White demographic. While
Latino activists celebrated what seemed like a ripe opportunity to
gain Latino political representation, others took to the media to
express concern over what this transformation would mean for a
region already facing fraught race relations amid growing disparities in health care, employment, housing, and the criminal justice
system (Rodríguez-Muñiz 2021). Not surprisingly, anti-immigrant
pundits, fearing that a "Latino takeover" would threaten White supremacy, spewed racist language blaming "illegal" immigrants and
their so-called anchor babies for the end of California's White plu-
rality. What was happening in California, many warned, was a telling sign of what was to come for the rest of the nation. The future
of America's "color lines," therefore, hinged on the fate of the country's Latino, Asian, and Middle Eastern immigrants.

It is therefore no surprise that in recent years scholars, moti-
vated in part by efforts to predict the uncertain future of U.S. race
relations, have given considerable attention to examining the racial trajectory of Latinos (Gans 1999; Yancey 2003; Bonilla-Silva
2004; Lee and Bean 2010; Marrow 2009). Some have cited Latinos' overwhelming propensity to select the "White" or "Other" racial category on the U.S. census as an indication that the group is
moving toward Whiteness and presumably poses no real threat to

the racial status quo (Alba 2020; Bonilla-Silva 2004; Lee and Bean 2010). Likewise, McClain et al. (2006, 573) argue that Latino immigrants will follow in the footsteps of Chinese migrants in Mississippi during the late 1800s, who, despite initially being relegated to the Black category by White plantation owners, actively sought the approval of Whites and soon adopted Whites' negative attitudes toward African Americans (Loewen 1988). They were able to permeate the rigid color line and gain a sort of honorary White status.

In this time of resurgent White nationalism, and with anti-Latino hate crimes on the rise, however, immigrants may no longer see Whitening as a viable strategy for upward mobility.[2] Jones (2019) finds that the rise of exclusionary immigration policies in North Carolina—coupled with a long history of racial tensions between Black and White people—produced a sense of linked fate between Black Americans and immigrants. Whites' anti-Black racism and anti-immigrant prejudice served as the impetus for Black and Latino immigrant racial solidarity that reinforced the racial divide between Whites and non-Whites.

On the other hand, Jones's study is an outlier; many studies have found anti-Black attitudes and social distancing practices among Latino immigrants in particular (Zamora 2016; Hondagneu-Sotelo and Pastor 2021; Marrow 2009; Mindiola, Niemann, and Rodríguez 2002; Oboler and Dzidzienyo 2005; Nteta 2006; Roth 2012). Some scholars have advanced an explanation for this, which I call the post-migration hypothesis: it holds that immigrants learn negative attitudes and behaviors toward Black Americans from living in the United States. One mechanism of such American racial education would be Mexicans' adoption of anti-Black views in an attempt to elevate their social position in a highly stratified U.S. Another would be that they follow the example of White Americans, while a third is that their negative experiences with Black Americans in the U.S. foment their anti-Black prejudices (Marrow 2009; Loewen 1988). Marrow (2009), for example, found that Latino immigrants in the South held favorable views of Whites yet unfavorable views of Black people, who they believed discriminated against Latinos due to perceptions of job competition.

While these studies are important for making sense of Latino racial attitudes, they are based almost exclusively on the U.S. context—the post-migration hypothesis. This is remarkable, given that the U.S. has more immigrants than any other country in the world and Mexicans make up the largest share, at 25 percent of all immigrants (Budiman 2020). Yet we have a limited understanding of the racial baggage they arrive with and how this influences local racial dynamics in their communities of settlement (for some exceptions, see Candelario 2007, Duany 1998, and Roth 2012).

The pre-migration hypothesis, on the other hand, attributes anti-Black attitudes to the historical entrenchment of anti-Blackness in Latin American societies since colonization (Hernandez 2007; McClain et al. 2006). Supporting this notion, studies detecting anti-Black attitudes and social distancing practices among Latino immigrants have shown that the native-born, whose exposure to U.S. culture is more extended, tend to be less racist (Hondagneu-Sotelo and Pastor 2021; Marrow 2009; Mindiola, Niemann, and Rodríguez 2002; Oboler and Dzidzienyo 2005; Nteta 2006; Roth 2012). While there may be other explanations for the comparative tolerance of the second generation, immigrants tend to retain aspects of their culture of origin and its values upon migration, lending credence to the pre-migration hypothesis (Levitt 2001; Zamora 2016). I found, however, that Mexicans' pre-migration understandings of race are not static; they are negotiated and often transformed in the process of migration and incorporation to the host society, rendering claims supporting one hypothesis over the other somewhat questionable.

If Latino immigrants arrive in the U.S. with negative attitudes toward African Americans as part of their racial baggage, this may suggest that factors identified in existing studies, such as social contact, physical proximity, and racial threat or competition for resources, provide only a limited explanation for why Latinos may perceive little commonality with Black Americans. In my interviews, I found that immigrants are highly exposed to U.S. anti-Black ideologies long before they set foot in the country, through global media and contact with those who preceded them to the United States. Over time, they learn the rules of race, so to speak, of their new, multiracial Los Angeles urban landscape. More-established immigrants who served as a direct link between migrants' old and new worlds were often the first ones to welcome new arrivals into Los Angeles and played a pivotal role in migrants' first stages of socialization to U.S. racial norms. My interviews reveal that the racial lessons imparted by these established immigrants—a process I refer to as race brokering—worked to keep some migrants' anti-Black prejudices intact, while others directly challenged them to make room for new racial understandings.

The question still remains, however. Will Mexican immigrants—who stand out among immigrants for experiencing an especially negative context of reception—follow the historical examples of European immigrants who chose racial estrangement from Black Americans as a means of upward mobility? Will they seek alliances with African Americans to combat White racism, as Latino immigrants have done in places like North Carolina, or opt for something else altogether? Given that Mexicans by far make up the largest segment of the Latino population and that a high proportion of Mexicans are foreign-born, I argue in this book that the

[handwritten: ₐ§ what about the state? + its role in fostering racial schemes?]

way in which Mexican immigrants are incorporated into the existing U.S. racialized stratification system will have a good deal of influence on the future of race in the U.S. Understanding how immigrants embrace, reproduce, and sometimes reject hegemonic U.S. racial ideologies and their resulting inequities is central to broader understandings of how the racial status quo can endure—even as that society is rapidly "Browning" (Bonilla-Silva and Dietrich 2008).

Race, Illegality, and Immigrant Incorporation

The sociological study of race and ethnic relations has been central to scholarly understandings of immigrant life in the U.S. Sociologists have long asserted that assimilation—the process of adaptation to a host country—is the inevitable destiny of immigrant groups (Gordon 1964). Yet sociology's most influential theory of immigrant incorporation is limited because it was developed from the U.S. immigration experiences of Southern and Central Europeans, such as Italians, Poles, Jews, and Germans, in the 1890s to 1920s. As history shows us, these European immigrants indeed assimilated into mainstream American culture, largely because they could make claims to whiteness. As sociologist Jessica Vasquez (2011, 8) asserts, assimilation theory assumes Anglo-conformity and is thus "predicated upon an assumption of European superiority." Although classical assimilation theory has provided a foundation for sociologists to examine the impact of immigration on U.S. race relations, it falls short of explaining the social and racial incorporation of today's immigrants, who come mostly from Asia, Latin America, and the Caribbean and face a different set of economic, political, and racial challenges. Assimilation theory also largely leaves out of the equation African Americans, whose involuntary migration was the direct result of enslavement and who, after many

17

generations in the U.S., continue to endure marked discrimination and marginalization (Morris 2015).

Sociologist Milton Gordon argued in the 1960s that immigrant assimilation was not automatic. He maintained that assimilation could be achieved only through high rates of intermarriage with and residential proximity to the White majority, the shedding of one's ethnic identity, and Whites' full acceptance of immigrant groups (Gordon 1964). Gordon called this process structural assimilation. In line with Gordon, some scholars today suggest that Mexican immigrants are following a similar trajectory of Whitening as Italians, whereby over the course of a generation, they become indistinguishable from the dominant Anglo population (Lee and Bean 2010).

However, a large proportion of the Mexican origin population retains its ethnicity into and even beyond the fourth generation (Telles and Ortiz 2008), a unique feature among immigrant groups that Omi and Winant's (1994) theory of racialization illuminates. Racialization is defined as "the attribution of racial meanings to social groups, practices and relationships," a process that is always evolving and emerges from ideological and discursive constructions. As Julie Dowling (2014, 10) notes, "the roots of [Mexican] racialization in the U.S. can be traced to the Treaty of Guadalupe Hidalgo in 1848, when the current U.S. Southwest was acquired from Mexico. The United States promised citizenship to those Mexicans living in the colonized lands at a time when citizenship and legal rights were still contingent upon whiteness." Because at the time naturalized U.S. citizenship was reserved exclusively for White immigrants, Mexicans who were granted citizenship were deemed White by default. Historians note, however, that although Mexicans became White by law, they were regarded as racially inferior by all other standards (Haney López 2003; Gómez 2007; Almaguer 2008; Menchaca 1995).

In her book *Manifest Destinies: The Making of the Mexican American Race* (2007, 59), Laura Gómez describes the racial logic of White Americans in relation to Mexicans during this period:

> When American settlers and traders first encountered Mexicans in the nineteenth century, it was by no means clear where Mexicans would fit within the American racial hierarchy. . . . Politicians and newspaper editors publicly wondered which fate would await Mexicans: should they be treated like blacks or like Indians? The racial status of Mexicans in the U.S. has always been an ambiguous one; of a racial middle somewhere between Blacks and Whites. There is no doubt, however, that Mexicans have historically been viewed and treated as racially inferior to Whites. Although some Mexicans may be able to pass as "off-white" or "honorary white," Mexicans as a *group* overall have been classified as an inferior "mongrel" race.

The United States as a society is and has always been structured by race. And just as race remains significant in shaping—and constraining—the lives of Mexican and other immigrants of color, so too has illegality. Since 9/11, and significantly accelerated since 2016 when Trump was elected to the presidency, national politics have promoted and reinforced hegemonic ideologies of Latinos as a threat to national security, deeming unauthorized immigrants rapists and criminal invaders, as Trump has publicly done. Coupled with immigration policies that severely restrict undocumented immigrants' ability to attain driver's licenses, medical care, housing, and other social services, these racist tropes about Mexican criminality have cemented ideologies of immigrants as unworthy of citizenship and have served to intensify anti-immigrant violence. Leo Chavez (2008) aptly demonstrates that media discourses and images work to reinforce the notion that Mexicans are unassimilable foreigners, freeloaders, and criminals who threaten the very social and cultural fabric of American society. Although "illegality" is by no means a natural or fixed condition, immigrant groups experience it very differently (Ngai 2004). The persistent imagining of so-called illegal aliens as non-White, poor, and dangerous serves as a political and moral divider between those who belong in the U.S. and those who should remain permanent outsiders (Marciniak 2013).

All too often, Americans' implicit association between Mexican immigration and illegality is taken for granted, as if illegality were an inherent characteristic of Mexicanness. This association is so powerful that its impact extends to immigrants' children, spouses, and family members—even though many were born in this country. Indeed, studies have documented the growing political and racial climate of deep insecurity, suffering, and surveillance of immigrant communities caused by restrictive immigration laws and anti-immigrant police practices (Abrego and Menjívar 2011; Armenta 2017). Illegality—and its intersection with race, class, gender, and other social characteristics—is producing new forms of exclusion from the nation-state (De Genova 2004; Dowling 2014; Ebert and Ovink 2014; Golash-Boza 2006; Golash-Boza and Darity 2008; Telles and Ortiz 2008; Vasquez 2011). The state of "illegality" is an embodied one (De Genova 2004; Ngai 2004). Mexican newcomers who are undocumented become inscribed with illegality the moment they cross into the U.S. The Mexico-U.S. border, then, effectively becomes the site where, upon entry, immigrants take on this distinctly American racialized subjectivity (Zamora 2018). Immigrants' awareness that they are seen and treated as "illegal" foreigners—in some cases by African Americans and U.S.-born Latinos—profoundly shapes how they interpret their place in the U.S. racialized stratification system. This is reflected in the experiences of the immigrants I interviewed and is increasingly informing how people in Mexico come to understand race across the border.

I argue, then, that the making of a racially inferior "illegal" Mexican in the U.S. context is an American brand of racialization that features prominently in the transnational racial journey of immigrant newcomers. The Mexicans featured in this book are aware—at least in theory—that one must have papers to enter the U.S. legally and that many take the risk of migrating without authorization. Illegality, however, is inscribed upon migrant bodies at the point of crossing the Mexico-U.S. border. In other words, illegality is a destination point, so to speak, for millions of Mexican migrants who enter a new racial regime shaped by different social forces, such as draconian immigration laws and a White supremacist ideology that positions immigrants of color as outside the boundaries of national belonging quite literally the minute they set foot on U.S. soil. I also find, however, that the effects of this racialized legal violence reach beyond the U.S. nation-state to influence the racial views of those who remain in Mexico. The non-migrants I interviewed recognize that Mexican immigrants, and Latino immigrants more broadly, are regarded as racially and culturally inferior in the U.S. context, a racial logic that contradicts Mexican racial paradigms of mestizaje and non-racism. As I discuss in Chapter 2, some respondents even come to view these anti-Mexican attacks as an extension of Whites' anti-Blackness, marking a clear departure from how they articulate race in Mexico.

Race(ing) from Guadalajara to Los Angeles

Both Mexico and the United States are defined by a violent history of European conquest and colonization of Indigenous people, and the enslavement of Africans. Both nations have origins that are rooted in the ideology of White supremacy and Spanish and Anglo-American colonialism, and sometimes these racial systems overlap. Similar to many other modern societies, both countries are organized by a socioracial hierarchy in which, broadly speaking, Whiteness is on top, Blackness and Indigeneity at the bottom, and "Brownness"—as well as Asianness—somewhere in the racial middle (O'Brien 2008).

The racial similarities might end there. Racial ideologies and race relations have evolved differently, reflecting each region's distinct sociohistorical processes. U.S. society is best known for its historically Black-White binary rooted in ideologies of hypodescent, White racial purity, and rigid racial categorizations. In Mexico, and in Latin American societies more broadly, the dominant racial paradigm is one of race mixture, or mestizaje. In Mexico, the mestizo—generally regarded as a person of Spanish and Indigenous ancestry—embodies the essence of what it means to be Mexican, much as the Anglo embodies Americanness. Anyone deemed not fully mestizo is cast outside the national imaginary (Moreno Figueroa and Saldívar Tanaka 2016; Jerry 2014).

Demographically, Mexico and the U.S. vary considerably. While demographic changes are rapidly disrupting the White majority in the U.S., it is roughly 60 percent White people (U.S. census 2020). By contrast, the majority group in Mexico are mixed-race mestizos, accounting for 64 percent of the total Mexican population (Telles and PERLA 2014). The U.S. has long had a Black-White racial paradigm, where African Americans were, until recently, the largest non-White group; in Mexico, the main social distinction is between the mestizo majority and the Indigenous, who represent the largest ethnoracial minority, at about 13 percent of the population (Lomnitz 2001; Sue and Golash-Boza 2009 Villarreal 2010). In terms of the Afro-descendant population, only about 3 percent of Mexicans self-identify as Black or *"mulato"* (Telles and PERLA 2014), compared with about 14 percent of Americans who identify as Black (Tamir 2021). Nonetheless, Mexico never adopted racially exclusionary laws upon independence from Spain (Sue 2013; Telles and Paschel 2014).

The Setting

The Mexican state of Jalisco, where a majority of the Mexicans featured in this book hail from, is located in the central-western region of the country and boasts a U.S. migratory history spanning well over a century. In 2010, when data collection for this study began, the state ranked seventh in Mexico for emigration to the U.S. (INEGI 2010). The region, bordering Guanajuato, Michoacán, and Nayarit, largely comprises rancheros of predominantly European descent with relatively low rates of racial mixing. The rural town Los Altos Jalisco is hailed as the "cradle of ranchero society" and is well known for its high concentration of "White" Mexicans with European phenotype (Farr 2006). In many ways, Jalisco epitomizes traditional Mexican culture. Symbols of "Mexicanness" recognized nationally and internationally, such as mariachi music, tequila, and rodeos, originate in this region. There are very few Afro descendants in Jalisco,[3] and although it is home to Indigenous populations, such as Huicholes, the region is largely mestizo and thus demographically reflects what one may call the "Mexican mainstream."

As the second-largest city in Mexico, Guadalajara has greater diversity than other Mexican towns in terms of race and ethnicity, education levels, and socioeconomic status. It is a very cosmopolitan city, with all of the luxuries and amenities one would associate with a global city. It is also a place of stark income inequality and economic residential segregation; upper-class *colonias* (neighborhoods) are found on the outskirts of the central city, often in private communities catering to the elite. The Mexican non-migrants featured in this study were relatively better off than the city's poorest but mainly lived in lower-middle-class neighborhoods and worked blue-collar jobs or in the service industry, such as retail or maintenance. Although their class status could set them apart from wealthy locals, their mestizo appearance, ranging from light to medium-brown skin tone, allowed them to blend in with the majority.

Sociologists have long noted that the places where immigrants settle in the U.S. are a central feature of immigrant life and adaption. It is here where migrants gain nuanced understandings of the local racial hierarchy and their unique place within it. Put simply, if new arrivals are getting schooled on race, the neighborhood is their classroom. Any analysis of immigrant racialization processes, therefore, must take seriously the structural conditions of the neighborhoods into which Latino migrants arrive. Los Angeles is approximately 150 miles from the Mexico-U.S. border and has always been a primary destination for immigrants from Mexico. In 2019, Latinos made up 49 percent of the Los Angeles population, whereas in 1960 they made up only 9 percent (Telles and Ortiz 2008). Like other urban immigrant destinations across the country, Los Angeles has a rich history of ethnic enclaves that define the character of the city. Chinatown, Boyle Heights, and, more recently, Pico Union are unique spaces where new arrivals can feel a sense of familiarity and slowly learn the American way of life alongside co-ethnics. The city is also economically polarized, containing some of the wealthiest zip codes in the nation, including world-famous celebrity hub Beverly Hills 90210. Neighborhood context shapes how migrants live and with whom they interact and thus is instrumental to how individuals make meaning about race, inequality, and where they are situated within the broader socioracial hierarchy. As is typical of Mexican migrants to L.A., the Mexicans featured in this study settled in traditionally low-income Black and Latino communities around Southeast L.A. and the Watts-Florence-Graham region of South Central L.A.

Southeast Los Angeles (SELA) is a collection of cities just a dozen miles southeast of downtown Los Angeles. In the 1950s and 1960s, SELA communities like South Gate and Huntington Park were hailed as "all-American" cities with relatively inexpensive housing, abundant jobs, a booming economy, and a virtually all-White population. Many White residents had migrated during the Dustbowl era and became blue-collar workers in the thriving manufacturing industry. Historian Mike Davis (2001) dubbed SELA the rust belt of Los Angeles. The cities were booming with factory jobs created by manufacturing giants such as Firestone Tire and Rubber Company and General Motors.

Today, SELA is marked by high population density, a declining manufacturing district, working poverty, and a web of major freeways running through it, as well as a toxic cocktail of pollution emitted by industrial plants. It is also a majority-Latino community. Deindustrialization and other economic restructuring that reduced middle-class jobs in the 1980s led to White flight. Racist housing practices dating back to when the cities were incorporated in the 1920s had kept cities like South Gate majority White through the sixties. Black people from "the other side of the tracks" in neighboring Watts who crossed over into SELA were often met with violent harassment by White segregationists. To this day,

Black residents make up less than 1 percent of SELA's population (*Los Angeles Times'* "Mapping L.A." project). Today, Latinos are 96 percent of residents in places like Huntington Park and South Gate (U.S. Census Bureau 2015). Latinos dominate civic life and local schools in this lower-middle-class community where about half the residents are foreign-born homeowners.

By contrast, South Los Angeles, known previously as South Central L.A. and located just west of the Alameda corridor, was long the center of African American pride and culture in Los Angeles. Beginning in the 1920s, tens of thousands of African Americans from the U.S. South migrated to Los Angeles, lured by the promise of union jobs and a Southern California free of Jim Crow apartheid (Flamming 2006). White real estate agents and homeowners determined to keep Black people from moving into their neighborhoods relegated new Black Angelenos to South Central. Many newcomers worked in the industrial plants around South L.A., and by the early 1960s communities like Watts were nearly 100 percent Black. South L.A. was 80 percent Black in 1970 but is now roughly 66 percent Latino (Hondagneu-Sotelo and Pastor 2021). A recent study of Latino integration into South L.A. by sociologists Pierrette Hondagneu-Sotelo and Manuel Pastor (2021) found that many Latino immigrants, even those who expressed anti-Black sentiments, have established a kind of next-door neighbor civility and, in some cases, admiration and respect for their longer-established Black neighbors. The share of Black residents in the region, however, continues to decline steadily as families leave in search of better jobs and affordable housing on the outskirts of Los Angeles, while Latinos continue to settle in the area. This pattern of dramatic racial turnover has been observed in other historically Black communities where Latinos have slowly moved in only to become the majority population in a few short decades—at times leading to tension and hostility between the two groups (Rosas 2019; Hondagneu-Sotelo and Pastor 2021; Rendón 2019).

Among other things that set South L.A. apart from SELA is South L.A.'s poverty and notoriety as the epicenter of the 1992 Los Angeles uprising in the wake of the acquittal of White police offers who brutalized Black motorist Rodney King. Decades of economic neglect, a devastating crack epidemic, and heavy police surveillance and brutality led to pent-up frustration among residents, some of whom were still waiting for city officials to deliver on promises for neighborhood improvement projects made after the 1965 Watts riots. The economic devastation is still evident in Watts and nearby areas today, with vacant lots, boarded-up buildings, a high concentration of liquor stores, and alleyways collecting trash, old furniture, and other items dumped by passersby. More people rent than own their homes, and many immigrants I spoke with, particularly women, perceive the area as potentially dangerous after dark, a distinct change from regular evening strolls enjoyed in their hometown plazas in Mexico.

SELA and South L.A. share important similarities that shape immigrants' experiences with and perceptions of the U.S. racial hierarchy. To start, both regions have virtually no Asian and Anglo residents. Although Korean merchants are common, they do not live in the community, and the overwhelmingly working-class and poor residents view them as economically well-off and upwardly mobile. Both neighborhoods today have a strong Mexican flair to them, characterized by businesses named after Mexican hometowns; street vendors selling *elotes, tamales,* and *raspados;* and shopping centers reminiscent of Mexican plazas—complete with kiosks surrounded by benches. The communities featured in this book in many ways exemplify racially segregated and economically distressed Los Angeles neighborhoods that have been devastated by neoliberal, anti-immigrant, and racist policies; unemployment; drugs; gangs; crime; underfunded schools; and hyper-policing.

Research Methodology and Study Participants

To unpack how transnational migration, and interaction with U.S. racial paradigms, might transform the racial views of immigrant newcomers in the days, years, and decades after arrival to Los Angeles, I conducted a multi-sited, cross-border study designed to examine social processes involving configurations of relations across multiple locations (Burawoy et al. 2000; Desmond 2014). This relational approach moves beyond the more conventional ethnographic focus on either places (e.g., neighborhoods, countries) or groups (e.g., youth, immigrants) and the logic of comparison, which aims to understand how racial attitudes differ across national contexts (Desmond 2014). Rather, this research approach involves collecting qualitative data across geopolitical borders to show how individuals occupying different positions within the transnational social field (e.g., non-migrants, recent and long-term migrants) are bound together by social phenomena such as global migration and nationalist racial projects. In recent decades, the multi-sited and relational approach has been lauded as indispensable to the study of migration, particularly in countering what Wimmer and Schiller (2002) call "methodological nationalism." Yet, despite our increasingly globalized world, many sociological works on immigration and race continue to prioritize the receiving society as the main unit of analysis (Kim 2008, 243).

My research involved intensive fieldwork in Mexico and the United States: Guadalajara, Jalisco, and Los Angeles, California.

Between June 2010 and January 2012, I completed seventy-five interviews with three groups of Mexican individuals: thirty non-
migrants (defined as those who have never lived outside Mexico)
in Jalisco, fifteen recent immigrants (defined as those who have
lived abroad longer than six months), and thirty long-term immigrants (defined as those with ten years or more of experience living in the U.S.).

Study participants were recruited using a snowball sampling
technique. To maximize variation, I interviewed individuals from
different respondent networks and recruited respondents in various neighborhoods, public parks, cafes, and local businesses. Respondents were also referred by personal contacts. To control for
class and educational background, I restricted the sample in both
countries to working-class individuals with less than a college education. Only two non-migrants had visited the U.S. at all, and in
both cases it was for a period of less than four weeks. Understandably, undocumented immigrants were hesitant to give out personal
information to a stranger; therefore, protecting respondents' identities was of critical importance. Each respondent was assigned a
number, and this book uses pseudonyms for them.

Respondents held occupations such as maintenance worker
and groundskeeper, construction worker, factory laborer, dish-
washer, cook, street vendor, and homemaker. Equal numbers of
men and women were included in each group, for a total of thirty-
seven men and thirty-eight women.[4] Ages ranged from twenty-
four to sixty-five, with a median age of thirty-seven. Two thirds of
immigrant respondents were undocumented. Skin tone and phenotype varied across the sample. All but three of the non-migrant
sample were born in Guadalajara, Jalisco, and the others were born
in smaller nearby *pueblos*. The U.S. immigrant sample varied more;

the majority were from larger cities and pueblos in Jalisco and surrounding states in the central-western region of Mexico, and some
individuals were from small, isolated *ranchos.*

The goal of the interviews was to understand Mexican respondents' subjective views of race relations in Mexico and the U.S.,
including their racial attitudes toward "others," their perceptions
of or experiences with discrimination (broadly defined as unequal
treatment based on one's appearance), their motivations for migrating to the U.S., the nature of their transnational engagement
with their origin society, and their encounters with and negotia-
tions of the U.S. racial system upon migration. Interviews lasted
one to two hours; I provided financial compensation for respondents' time. I conducted the majority of the interviews in Spanish; only two respondents opted for English. I tape-recorded and
transcribed all of the interviews, which allowed me to use verba-
tim quotations. Following the interview, respondents filled out
demographic surveys indicating their educational background,
socioeconomic status, occupation, racial and ethnic identity, self-
perceived skin color, and degree of contact with immigrant family
and friends. Immigrant respondents also answered demographic
questions about their lives in Mexico prior to migrating to the U.S.

My Positionality
Throughout the research process, I have remained reflexive about
how my own personal and social characteristics might influence
the study. As the daughter of Mexican immigrants born and raised
in South East Los Angeles, who grew up visiting grandparents,
aunts, uncles, and cousins in Mexico, I have an intimate familiarity
with the culture of migration across the Mexico-U.S. border. Still,
I was not raised in Mexico, nor am I a transnational migrant. In
Jalisco, most people assumed I was native, as my Mexican ancestry,

fluency in Spanish, and phenotype —medium-brown skin, dark eyes, and straight dark-brown hair—allowed me to "pass" as a local, sometimes even after extensive interactions with natives. However, in my role as interviewer, I was simultaneously an insider and outsider, as differences in our accents, experiences, education, and, in some cases, class and legal status became relevant. Revealing my identity as a U.S. citizen and university researcher proved to be both an advantage and disadvantage in discussions of race. While I was able to play the "naive foreigner" who wished to be enlightened about how race functions in Mexican society, I was at times viewed as an "American" who might become offended by respondents' harsh criticism of U.S. society. Similarly, in Los Angeles, I relied on my ability to blend in, speak Spanish, and my deep familiarity with the city's landscape to access highly racialized immigrant spaces in ways that were sensitive to the cultural and social norms of these spaces. Importantly, I took several precautions to put my respondents at ease, particularly the most vulnerable participants—recent undocumented migrants lacking permanent housing, employment, and legal recourse—by dressing casually, using informal conversational Spanish, maintaining a warm rather than professional demeanor, and treating discussions more like casual conversations than research interviews.

Nonetheless, my unique social position enabled me to bring to my work a comparative perspective that is both nuanced and informed by a life's worth of experiences straddling Mexican and American worlds. Although the main argument of this book derived from my interviews with respondents, I complement these data with local and national Mexican and U.S. news stories related to race and ethnicity, current debates regarding Latino immigrants in the U.S., and Latino racialization more broadly that I have been collecting for years.

A Note on Racial Labels

Doing research from a cross-national and relational perspective requires careful attention to how local race discourse—and even racial slang—is used and understood in everyday informal conversation and may differ across the United States, Mexico, and throughout Latin America. For example, race terms often lose their original meaning when translated from Spanish to English, and vice versa, especially when the terms are spoken in street vernacular or used humorously, because they may go unobserved by researchers unfamiliar with the particular culture or history of a place. As several scholars have pointed out, the label "Black" (*negro*) can have many different meanings in Mexican society (Lewis 2000; Sue 2013; Vaughn 2005). While in the U.S. the label "Black" is typically reserved for individuals perceived to be racially Black and is often seen as an immutable characteristic, in Mexico it has a more fluid meaning and can refer descriptively to skin color, such as an Indigenous person with very dark skin—but who would not necessarily be categorized as racially Black. Sue (2013) describes this as the "sun discourse," which refers to Brown mestizo Mexicans who get darker due to a suntan as (temporarily) "Black." Mexicans may say to one another, "Look at you! You stayed out in the sun too long and turned Black!" "*Mirate, estuviste en el sol y quedaste negra.*" The use of the color label "Black" has negative connotations and is often used in a harsh, exaggerated manner to imply that someone's dark skin is undesirable or unattractive. "Black" is also used as a racial category to refer to an individual who is perceived to be racially Black, often based on physical markers including hair texture, phenotype, different shades of skin color, or even accent (e.g., a light-skinned African American visiting Mexico). Often when employing either meaning of the term, Mexicans use the more politically correct term "*moreno*" or "*raza morena*" in place of *"negro"* or *"raza negra"* ("Black race"). "Moreno," which also describes someone with dark Brown skin, can also be used as an intermediary category, somewhere between White and Black. For example, Afro descendants in the Costa Chica region of Mexico have been known to identify as morenos as a way to position themselves closer to Indigenous-based constructions of Mexicanness (Lewis 2000), although there is some evidence for their increasing identification as *negro* (Telles and PERLA 2014).

Recognizing that meanings and labels attributed to Blackness in Mexico are highly contextual, I was careful not to impose U.S. racial categorizations during interviews and avoided generalizations. In efforts to avoid conflating American Blackness with local Mexican understandings of Blackness, I tried to be as specific as possible with the descriptors I used, such as "Negros Norte Americanos" to refer to "Black North Americans"; "Afro-Americano" as a direct translation for "African American"; "Afro-Latino" or "Latino Americano de Afro-decendencia" to refer to "Latin Americans of African descent"; "inmigrantes Africanos" when referring to "African immigrants" from African nations; as well as "Mexicanos Afro-decendientes" to refer to Mexicans of African descent. Although I recognize that meanings of Blackness are constantly negotiated and that people racialized as Black display a wide range of articulations of Blackness (Thomas and Clarke 2006; Clerge 2019) throughout this book, I broadly define "Black Americans" as African descendants who are born and raised in the U.S., including second- and third-generation Black immigrants. I use the terms "African American" and "Black American" interchangeably, unless otherwise noted.

In a similar vein, what constitutes "White" and the boundaries of Whiteness are contextual and can vary between Mexico and the U.S. In the Mexican context, for example, a light-skinned Mexican might be referred to as "Blanca," referring to "White," or "Guera," which translates to "White (skin)" or "light-skinned." When applied to Mexicans, this color label does not typically indicate a person's perceived race (a light-skinned or "White" Mexican would likely be perceived as racially Mexican as opposed to Anglo or of the White race). To describe racially White persons or Anglos, particularly White Americans, Mexicans tend to use terms like "Americano/a," "Gringo/a," "Anglosajón," the demeaning terms "Gabacho" or even "Yankee," as well as the more neutral descriptors "Blanco/a" and "Guero/a."

Racial terms and classifications are, much like race, social constructs with no real biological value. As such, I use these terms contextually, with an understanding that they are ever-evolving. Nonetheless, Mexican respondents were conscious of racial and color differences, demonstrating that race—and the terms used to talk about it—continue to be crucial in sociological interaction because they can have powerful real-world consequences.

Organization of the Book

Chapter 1 takes the reader "back to Mexico" by reviewing the historical origins of racial thinking in Mexico. Drawing on interviews with migrants and non-migrants, I show that on-the-ground understandings of race, ethnicity, and discrimination in central-western Mexico reflect dominant nationalist ideologies of mestizaje that praise White European elements, marginalize the Indigenous, and situate Blackness as foreign to the nation. I argue that this nationalist ideology of race shapes the way ordinary Mexicans make sense of social inequality and racial and ethnic discrimination in their origin society—and that it is distinct from how they imagine race in the U.S. Ultimately, this chapter establishes a fuller understanding of the racial "lens" through which Mexicans view race in their origin country, thereby laying the foundation for understanding how migration to the U.S. reconfigures individuals' racial understandings.

Chapter 2 details the imagined picture of "American race relations" from the perspective of individuals who have never migrated themselves but whose lives are affected by the migration of friends and family. This chapter shows how global U.S. media and social ties with immigrants in the U.S. play a central role in exposing would-be migrants in Mexico to distinctly American racial narratives about discrimination, White-on-Black racism, and the precariousness of illegality and anti-immigrant hostility more broadly. By highlighting how a combination of racial ideologies and practices originating in Mexico and the U.S. shapes Mexicans' preconceptions about U.S. racial dynamics, Chapters 1 and 2 challenge the notion that racial ideas are bound by national boundaries, and argue that Mexicans' preconceptions of racial life in *el norte* are crucial to understanding broader subsequent experiences of migration and incorporation into U.S. society. Thus, any consideration of how transnational lives impact immigrant incorporation into the U.S. must take these racial remittances seriously.

Chapter 3 describes the racial landscape of Los Angeles through the eyes of an immigrant newcomer. I argue that crossing the border into U.S. territory marks the end of mestizo privilege and the beginning of a distinctly American racial journey—one rife with hard lessons about living as a marginalized racial minority with precarious legal status in an anti-immigrant White supremacist society. I highlight the crucial role of established immigrants who engage in race brokering—the "schooling" of newcomers about the rules of race in the U.S.—in shaping newcomers' racial attitudes and, in some cases, helping to reinforce the anti-Black racial baggage they bring from Mexico. These early observations and encounters with the U.S. racial system set the tone for how immigrants navigate subsequent interactions with racial "others," including newly adopted strategies of avoidance and silence to assuage racial tension, ultimately shaping how newcomers come to view their own place in broader U.S. society.

Chapter 4 takes a deeper look at the racialization experiences of more seasoned immigrants and unveils how over time these experiences can cement perceptions of their group's position on the bottom rungs of the U.S. socioracial hierarchy. When viewed through a transnational lens, it is clear that the racialization of the "illegal" immigrant is a distinctly U.S. brand of racialization that, although nonexistent in understandings of inequality in the sending society, features prominently in the transnational racial journey of immigrants—even those who have lived in the U.S. for decades. I argue that this profoundly affects how Mexican immigrants view their status vis-à-vis other groups, particularly U.S.-born Latinos and Black Americans, who come to be viewed as comparably privileged due to their birthright American citizenship.

In the conclusion, I revisit my theoretical contributions and main findings, arguing that immigrants are not clean slates when they arrive in the U.S. Rather, they travel with racial baggage that has implications for how they come to see their racial position in the host society. I further explore the theoretical implications of this study for the possibility of racial alliances between Mexican immigrants (and Latinos more generally) and African Americans. Lastly, I revisit the merits of a transnational approach to race for theorizing how different immigrant groups of color will navigate their unique racialized position in an increasingly diverse America, and what this means for how global migration is reconfiguring race in contemporary U.S. society.

Race in Mexico

Mestizo Privilege

NATIONALIST IDEOLOGIES of race in Mexico, like in many other Latin American nations, reflect what scholars FitzGerald and Cook-Martín (2014) call "one of the great paradoxes" of race relations and inequality. Even as the Mexican government has overtly discriminated against certain ethnoracial groups and altogether erased Blackness from the image of the nation, it has promoted the racially inclusive idea of *mestizaje*, the racial mixture of various groups, and claimed the Mexican nation is free of racism.[1] This "racist anti-racism" contradiction emerged in the postrevolutionary period of the 1920s from a particular brand of nation-state-building that was aimed at cultivating patriotism and loyalty to the nation and positioning Mexico as an equal political player on the world stage. Indeed, what we recognize today as the quintessential Mexican figure—the Brown-skinned mestizo—is based on an image produced by a carefully curated racial project that Mexican elites enacted as part of nation-building.

Such nation-building, of course, reflects asymmetrical relations with Mexico's powerful neighbor to the north, a nation defined by chattel slavery, racial lynching, Jim Crow segregation, and race riots (Sue 2013; Hooker 2017). Thus, Mexican intellectuals and government officials promoted Mexicanness as directly contrasting with the Anglocentric United States. While the idea of Mexico as a mestizo utopia is a fiction, for the millions of Mexicans who have embarked or will embark on the journey north, arrival to the United States marks the first time they must reckon with the racial dynamics of one of the few countries (along with South Africa) with a history of such strict legal enforcement of the Black-and-White color line (Telles 2004). The U.S. racial landscape, then, is one that Mexicans crossing the Mexico-U.S. border anticipate and fear and for which they cannot fully prepare.

In contrast to the U.S. racial paradigm, which is historically defined by its long-standing Black-White color line, the main social distinction in Mexico is that between the majority mestizo population and the Indigenous (Villarreal 2010). This also makes Mexico distinct from other Latin American countries, such as Cuba and Brazil, where Blackness is more central to the racial image of the nation. Although Latin America and the United States share a common history of colonization, slavery, Whitening practices, and mestizaje, distinct social and economic structures, demographics, and nationalist ideologies have differentially shaped racial thinking in each country. In Mexico, the ideology and social practice of mestizaje has so effectively homogenized the Mexican population into a single "race" that, until recently, race and ethnic relations had received little attention from social scientists. As sociologist Christina Sue (2013) lays bare in her study of race mixture in Mexico, the foundation of the nation's contemporary racial thinking comprises three key ideologies: mestizaje, non-racism, and non-Blackness. What it means to be Mexican is thus defined by (1) the glorification of race mixture, particularly the mestizo, along with the ideas that (2) Mexico is a non-racist country and (3) being Mexican means not being Black because, presumably, Afro descendants have been

Christina Sue (handwritten signature)

fully absorbed into the larger mestizo population through extensive race mixture (Sue 2013, 17). Taken together, these "ideological pillars" not only uphold dominant discourses and practices that the state reproduces, but they powerfully shape the way everyday Mexicans think and talk about race.

This chapter analyzes the origins of contemporary racial thinking in Mexico and explores the paradox of how the racially mixed mestizo came to represent the quintessential Mexican, even as everyday understandings of race and discrimination continue to reflect Mexico's colonial legacy of anti-Indigeneity and anti-Blackness. As Oboler and Dzidzienyo (2005, 16) note, "The stigma of being Black or indigenous is similar throughout the Americas, [but] the *experience* of blackness and indigeneity is unique everywhere." The first part of the chapter examines the colonial roots of Mexican racial thinking and the notable turn toward mestizaje ideology in the early twentieth century. To highlight the key logics of the Mexican racial system for readers less familiar with Mexico, I use comparisons to the United States when appropriate.[2]

In the second part of the chapter, I detail the ways in which nationalist ideologies of race inform contemporary Mexican racial attitudes, with references to interviews I conducted in Mexico. I highlight the "everyday talk" of ordinary Mexican mestizos about race relations in Guadalajara and Mexico more broadly. My interviews reveal that the dominant discourse of Mexicanness as synonymous with mestizaje is central to how mestizos make sense of social and racial inequality in Mexico and their own place in the local ethnoracial hierarchy. These racial conceptions are distinct from how Mexicans imagine U.S. racial dynamics, where the Black-White divide takes center stage. Ultimately, this chapter establishes a fuller understanding of the racial baggage potential migrants carry with them into the U.S., thereby laying the foundation for understanding how immigrant newcomers reconfigure racial conceptions, learning and incorporating—for the first time—Anglo-American cultural and racial norms, values, and behaviors.

The Roots of Mexican Racism

Spanish colonial rule in Mexico began in 1521 with the fall of Tenochtitlán and lasted over two hundred years, establishing a complex system of social stratification that continues to impact how Mexicans live today.[3] Race, color, class, and status determined social standing throughout the colonial period but in ways that shifted over time (Chasteen 2001). Initially, White people born in Spain or Europe—*peninsulares*—were the elite class who benefited from a system of economic development that relied on the labor of enslaved Africans. Whereas in many Latin American countries enslaved people outnumbered the free population (Andrews 2004), this was not the case in Mexico. One estimate of Mexico City in 1612 reported a population of 50,000 "Black and *mulato*" residents, 15,000 "Spaniards," and 80,000 "Indians" (Palmer 1976). It is estimated that in the same period, the number of total enslaved Africans in the country was around 2 percent of the population, but many were concentrated along the coastal regions of Veracruz, Oaxaca, and Guerrero, where slave ships docked (Palmer 1976).[4] The Mexican populace was, therefore, largely Indigenous, Black, or mulato, or a result of mixture between these groups and European descendants.

This racial mixture complicated the social hierarchy, creating several new ethnoracial categories that ultimately changed the way society classified and positioned individuals, by placing an emphasis on ancestry (Chasteen 2001). Scholars have referred to Mexican society as a pigmentocracy, a social system in which skin color determines individuals' social and economic standing (Telles and PERLA 2014). Mexico, like other Latin American countries, never adopted the one-drop rule, which legally relegated the offspring of White slave-owner and enslaved African into the Black category. Rather, it institutionalized a *sistema de castas*, defined as "a cognitive and legal system of hierarchically arranged socioracial statuses created by Spanish law and the colonial elite in response to the growth of the miscegenated population in the colonies" (Chance and Taylor, quoted in Katzew 2004, 43). This system allowed Mexico to accommodate various intermediary categories such as mulato, mestizo, and *castizo*, but they were positioned below "pureblooded" Mexicans with Spanish ancestry, who occupied the top position in the hierarchy. Although *casta* was a term used to refer to the various races, it also indicated the specific socioeconomic status of each race. The infamous casta paintings, a series of artwork popularized in eighteenth-century Mexico, were used to not only classify and showcase the various racial mixtures but also demonstrate their rightful place in the socioeconomic hierarchy. These paintings served as a quite literal illustration of colonial authorities' efforts to police ethnoracial boundaries by sorting individuals into fixed categories in order to exert social control over the increasingly mixed population (Katzew 2004). Mulatos of half-Black and half-Spanish parentage in colonial Mexico held a privileged status relative to "pure" Black Mexicans, just as half-Indigenous and half-Spanish mestizos were positioned above "pure" Indigenous persons. While the caste system reflected the idea of human "pedigree," similar to modern conceptions of race, it also relied on social and physical characteristics to determine social and racial positioning. In addition to phenotype, these included a person's clothing, education, place of residence, and wealth. The fact that these characteristics are malleable created an opening to negotiate up the socioracial hierarchy in ways unimaginable in the U.S.[5]

Mexico's racial classification system simplified after independence from Spain, in the early nineteenth century, although Mexicans of Spanish descent maintained their privileged position. A bipolar model comprising Indigenous and White individuals, with an intermediate class of mestizos, emerged (Lomnitz-Adler 1992). In this system, skin color became a key signifier allowing those on the lighter end of the spectrum, including Indigenous individuals who could pass as mestizo, to achieve upward mobility. Ironically, during this period, Mexico's second president, Vicente Guerrero (April 1, 1829–December 17, 1829), abolished slavery (as Guerrero was mulato, it seems reasonable to assume he did so out of genuine conviction, but it was also a tactic to prevent slaveholding Anglo settlers from occupying Texas territory in their quest to expand U.S. slavery). Black people began to flee the United States to northern Mexico—many from Texas, after it became a U.S. state in 1845. Mexico became a safe haven for those escaping slavery, as it refused U.S. demands to return them, proclaiming all enslaved people free when they set foot on Mexican soil (Baumgartner 2020). However, their descendants, the Mascogos, currently face social and economic disadvantages, as their dark skin and Afro phenotype is stigmatized and their livelihood in village farms is impacted by severe droughts.

The first half of the twentieth century brought the most significant transformation in Mexico's evolving racial paradigm and race relations: a new generation of Mexican elites promoted a nationalist ideology that hailed Mexico as a mestizo nation. Manuel Gamio, an influential anthropologist and disciple of Franz Boas, and José Vasconcelos, the minister of education (1921–1924) and author of the highly influential 1925 text *La raza cósmica* (*The Cosmic Race*), were the leading intellectual and political figures in this new mestizo nationalist project. Vasconcelos spent part of his childhood on the Mexico-U.S. border attending schools in Eagle Pass, Texas, where he grew increasingly critical of American culture. He argued that Mexicans should avoid imitating America's materialistic ideals and instead forge a new "cosmic race," the race of the future, with all the strengths of "the virtues of Indians and Europeans" alike (Vasconcelos 1925). He used his capacity as minister of education to promote his ideology, producing curricula and textbooks for the public education system and sponsoring public murals by some of Mexico's greatest modern artists like Diego Rivera and José Clemente Orozco.

In a period of political upheaval, officials like Vasconcelos advanced mestizaje as the answer to national cohesion and thus synonymous with progress and modernization. Elites purported they would position Mexico as a global player on par with Europe and North America through a vision of Mexicanness that directly challenged racist, Eurocentric ideologies of North America. If the U.S. had positioned itself as a modern and "superior" Anglo nation, Mexico would promote itself as a great mestizo nation built by a Spanish-Iberian and Aztec amalgamation. Mexican elites wanted to establish national pride in Mexico by positioning it as a mixed-raced nation free of racism, in contrast to the United States (Sue 2013). The figure of the mestizo became the physical embodiment of the nation and was hailed as superior to the "arrogant, shallow, aggressive, and lacking in spirituality" Anglo to the north (Lomnitz 2001, 54).

Mestizaje ideology was solidified in 1917, when the Mexican constitution officially recognized the nation's "multicultural composition." A few years later, government officials decided to eliminate

the race question from the Mexican census. This key political transformation helped give rise to the popular belief that racism does
not exist in Mexico (Knight 1990), further positioning the country
in direct contrast to the racist and morally corrupt United States.
Reflecting this tradition, the Mexicans I interviewed who claimed
that Mexico is not racist often justified it by looking to bigoted attitudes and practices in the U.S., such as racial segregation, as a foil.
The racially mixed mestizo was now treated as normative and synonymous with *Mexican*, while racial purity and White supremacy
became associated with Anglo arrogance. For more than a century,
then, to be Mexican has been equated with being mestizo.

Anyone deemed not fully mestizo was cast outside the national
imaginary. This included darker-skinned elites who had fought
against Spain for Mexican independence, including Vicente Guerrero, Mexico's second president. Guerrero is the rough equivalent
of George Washington in Mexico's national imagination, and yet
his image was reconfigured in order to fit the Eurocentric vision
of the modern Mexican nation-state. The unabashed Whitening of
Guerrero's Blackness reflects the overall eradication of Blackness
from the national imaginary. Still, in yet another ironic twist emblematic of Mexico's racist anti-racism, in 1922 the Mexican government funded a research project on Afro-descendant communities aimed at "recovering" the nation's *raza olvidada* (forgotten
race) that resulted in one of the first studies of Afro-Mexicans.

While Mexican elites engaged in Black erasure, the "Indian
problem" simultaneously preoccupied them. A unique feature of
Mexico's vast geographic landscape is that regional differences are
highly racialized and often determine who is perceived as Indigenous. The intersection of race and region can be traced back to
the Spanish conquest and colonial social stratification systems.
Despite strong evidence that Indigenous people have, through the

centuries, often migrated into urban sectors for economic reasons, there is a belief that Mexico's Indigenous are not as mixed with the Spanish race because they were tucked away in remote areas where conquistadores rarely ventured. Mexican cultural institutions tout the nation's Indigenous people as the "real soul" of Mexico, "living proof of Mexico's noble pre-Hispanic heritage" (Friedlander, *Being Indian*, p. xvii, quoted in Knight 1990, 101).

At the same time, Indigenous people are subject to systemic oppression and discrimination. In addition to geography, this can revolve around language and accent. Like most countries in the Americas, Mexico does not have an official language, but Spanish is dominant. The country's various Indigenous groups speak several hundred different languages, of which the state recognizes just over sixty and for which it provides some protections, such as bilingual education (Casas et al. 2014). Still, discourse around Mexicanness is embedded in ideas about Spanish cultural influence, which furthers the stigmatization of Indigenous people, who are seen as not speaking "proper" Spanish. As historian Alan Knight (1990, 100) puts it, "Anti-Indian prejudice ... is rooted in the subsoil of Mexican culture. . . . A whole range of prejudices and discriminations therefore exists, but exists in defiance of official ideology. Indian languages are officially endorsed, but unofficially frowned upon." If sharing a common Spanish language binds the nation together, Indigenous groups not fluent in Spanish or who acquired it as a second language are by definition excluded from Mexicanness.

Indigenous people are highly stigmatized. *Indio, india,* and the diminutive *indito* are derogatory terms for Indigenous people, and *pinche india,* meaning "fucking Indian," is a common epithet used to degrade Indigenous and non-Indigenous Mexicans alike. Indigenous identity is constructed in direct relation to mestizos, the product of Spanish colonizers and an Indigenous "past."

By this logic, any "remaining" Indigenous peoples of today are by default regarded as a "pure race" (essentially unmixed) and relegated to the lowest rungs of the ethnoracial hierarchy. The Indigenous in Mexico are racialized as the embodiment of uncivilized backwardness, intellectual inferiority, cultural deficiency, and all that is counter to enlightenment and modernization. In Mexico, the worst thing you can be is indio.

Thus mestizaje ideology produces a paradoxical form of national belonging for marginalized groups like Indigenous people and peasants, who are positioned as the essence of *Mexicanidad* and called upon to preserve the traditionalism of Mexican society yet are considered central barriers to the realization of progress in the country. The outright social and political exclusion of Indigenous peoples showcases the paradox inherent in casting the vast majority of the population as outside the nation while simultaneously a central part of it (Vaughn 2013).

Yet, when I discussed issues of ethnic and racial inequality with Mexican respondents, many claimed that racism, a system rooted in racial difference, either does not exist or does not affect them personally. Reflecting on this, I wondered how ordinary Mexican mestizos make sense of ethnoracial "otherness" and the rampant social inequality intricately linked to it. More broadly, as a central question of this book, I further asked how Mexicans' racial understandings shift, if at all, when they migrate to the vilified "racist" north.

Mestizaje and the Denial of Racism

Latin American governments have exhibited three different types of denials of racial discrimination: interpretive denial (what is happening is actually something else), justificatory denial (what is happening is justified), and literal denial (nothing has happened). For instance, a Mexican representative to the United Nations Committee on the Elimination of Racial Discrimination exemplified literal denial in 1994, saying that racial discrimination simply did "not exist in Mexico" (Muñoz 2009). Indeed, many Latin American nations have concealed, twisted, and outright denied racism and racial discrimination in their countries (Dulitzky 2005). Ordinary people, like the Mexicans in my study, can also deny the existence of racism using different interpretations, such as when respondents interpret discrimination against the Indigenous and other racialized groups as a symptom of class, not race (Muñoz 2009).

While some may vehemently deny that the mestizo nation is racist, scholars maintain that mestizaje is the root of racist thinking and practices in Mexico today (Treviño Rangel 2008; Vaughn 2013; FitzGerald and Martín-Cook 2014). Mexican sociologist Javier Treviño Rangel (2008, 672) categorizes Mexico as a racist state based on its dominant role in the development and reproduction of hegemonic racial ideologies that determine the social inclusion and exclusion of non-mestizo populations. Mestizaje, then, is emblematic of eugenicist "Whitening" projects carried over from Europe and adapted throughout the Americas that sought to eliminate those deemed racially inferior and homogenize a citizenry into a single "master" race (Stepan 1991; Wade 1993). Cementing the notion of a superior mestizo "race" effectively masks racial difference in Mexico and exacerbates the national exclusion of Black and Indigenous groups (Vaughn 2013).

To this day, talking about racism is taboo in Mexico. In her discussions with mixed-race Veracruzanos, Sue (2013) found that Mexicans commonly silenced discussions of racism, or outright denied its existence, and very rarely challenged mestizaje ideology. For them, calling Mexico a racist nation would contradict the essence of Mexicanness and, therefore, their sense of self. Unfortunately,

Mexicans' hesitance to openly talk about racism or assert its role in sustaining the country's inequitable social relations only reinforces the status quo (Sue 2013).

In contrast to the politicization of Black identity in the United States, the erasure of Blackness and active denial of racism in Mexico has hindered a similar mobilization of Black identity there (Hoffmann 2006; Sue 2013). Whereas Brazil has seen the emergence of a powerful national Black movement equivalent to Black Lives Matter, Mexico has no such equivalent. The systematic erasure of Blackness has led to the prevailing view that Black people do not exist in Mexico the way they do in other countries. Even though Afro-descendant Mexicans are beginning to embrace their Blackness as a source of cultural pride and resistance, many distance themselves from the stigmas associated with Black identity (Vaughn 2013) or remain unaware of their Black ancestry (Lewis 2000).

Even Brazil, which touts itself as a racial paradise—though it is far from it—collects race data in the national census that allows for careful analysis of discrimination; however, Mexico has hidden its racial discrimination in plain sight. The Mexican government funded the establishment of a program in the 1980s called *Nuestra Tercera Raiz* (Our Third Root) to support research on the then-current state of African-descended peoples. While these research efforts have helped promote Afro-Mexican heritage, the real push came from the grassroots sector. *Mexico Negro*, or Black Mexico, an activist group founded in the 1990s in the state of Guerrero, has been at the forefront of the fight for official state recognition of Afro descendants in the Mexican census. Mexico Negro continued demanding recognition without much government response for nearly two decades. Indeed, the active denial of racial discrimination in Mexico has created a vicious cycle where denial leads to a dearth of data and evidence necessary to prove its existence in the first place (Casas et al. 2014).

In 2015, the Mexican government finally included a question about Black ancestry on a national survey for the first time in over two centuries. CONAPRED, the National Council for Preventing Discrimination, implemented the official count of Black Mexicans and followed up with a 2017 national survey on discrimination. The 2020 Mexican census was the first official count of the Afro-Mexican population, and experts expect the total to be around 2 million (up from 1.3 million in 2015—still, a relatively low figure for a country with over 126 million people). Their small numbers give credence to claims that Afro-Mexicans have nearly disappeared as the result of racial mixture with the larger mestizo population. Grassroots activists, however, point out that this number could be higher if Black identity were celebrated rather than stigmatized. While these and other efforts to promote awareness and policy reform that would benefit some of Mexico's most neglected populations are underway, there is still a long way to go toward full acknowledgment of the contributions that Afro descendants have made—and continue to make—in the formation of the Mexican nation.

Denial of racism may be particularly common in Jalisco, the hometown of many of my migrant respondents and the base of my research in Mexico. Jalisco, particularly the highlands, is regarded as a bastion of ranch culture, or *cultura ranchera*, famed for its particular brand of Mexicanness best defined by *vaqueros* (cowboys) and *charrería* (rodeos). Rancheros in the highlands are of predominantly European descent and have relatively low rates of racial mixing (Farr 2006). Beauty pageant contestants from Jalisco— many of whom have very pale skin; tall, slender bodies; and light-colored eyes—are lauded and admired as gendered and racialized representations of Mexico's beauty. Los Altos Jalisco, a rural town in the highlands, epitomizes this beauty standard: hailed as the "cradle of ranchero society" and glorified as a region with some of the most "beautiful" people in the country—largely tall, thin, blond Mexicans with blue or green eyes. Afro descendants are rare. "White" and mestizo identity in Jalisco is thus formed primarily in relation to the Huicholes, a local Indigenous group living in the mountain range in the highlands known as *la Sierra Madre Occidental* or, more informally, *la sierra*.

During my fieldwork in Guadalajara, I came across Mexicans with phenotypes that ranged from very light skin with blond hair and other European features to brown skin with Indigenous features or features of African origin.[6] Still, an overwhelming majority of Mexicans in this region of Jalisco, and in this study, identify as mestizo (Casas et al. 2014).

Mestizos' "Everyday Talk" of Mexican Race Relations

How do Mexican mestizos think and talk about race relations and social inequality in their home country? To answer this question, I present interview data from Mexican respondents living in Guadalajara. I focus on the meaning that respondents give to the social and racial inequality they see around them—and sometimes experience—in their daily lives. Because Mexican racial sensibilities are undergirded by a belief that being Mexican signifies living in a country free of racism and thus not engaging in racism (Sue 2013), discussions of prejudice and discrimination emphasize themes of class and color distinctions. With a few exceptions, mestizos tend to downplay racism because it continues to be generally understood as emblematic of the American racial system. These interviews further help us see how Indigenous *marginalization*—not racism per se—becomes a way to talk about how social inequality plays out in the Mexican context.

In terms of mestizos' racial attitudes, I demonstrate how they discursively situate Indigenous people as simultaneously central to Mexican (mestizo) identity and othered as a distinct racial group on the margins of Mexicanness. Afro-Mexicans, on the other hand, far from occupying a central place in national constructions of the Mexican race, are invisibilized and situated outside the nation. To echo historian Alan Knight (1990), being able to grasp Mexican race relations is of critical importance if we are to understand the nuances of Mexican racism. As I argue throughout this book, it is particularly important to comprehend how mestizos make meaning of the racial hierarchy and their place within it because their views arguably reflect those of the "Mexican mainstream"—that is, Mexicans who are neither Black nor Indigenous and who embody racial privilege in the Mexican context.

Perceptions of Social Inequality: Class, Color, or Both?
It was rare for respondents in Mexico to use the term *racism* unprompted. Knowing that it is a social taboo, I used the term selectively in the interviews. I often began by asking the respondents whether they believed that Mexicans were treated differently due to their appearance or other characteristics. This yielded plenty of discussion of class disparities as the root of Mexican social problems. For some, they viewed discrimination as based solely on class, not race or skin color. Others, however, shared lifelong observations and, in some cases, personal experiences with intersecting inequalities rooted in class and color differences, revealing the ongoing significance of skin color, ethnicity, and race in Mexico's social stratification system (Flores and Telles 2012).

Estela, a thirty-year-old administrative assistant, is emblematic of the "class, not race" perspective in Mexico and much of Latin America. Perhaps conscious that I live in the United States and eager to explain the Mexican context, she assured me that any differences in the treatment of Mexicans "isn't necessarily discrimination against someone's race, like in the United States. You see, we [Mexicans] have the misfortune of being the type who discriminate based on someone's appearance, in the economic [sense], and in the way one talks." Like Estela, many respondents made direct comparisons to the "racist" United States to make the point that although Mexico might have real social problems, race is not per se one of them. Note, however, that some of the characteristics Estela describes as forming the basis of discrimination—appearance and language or accent—are in fact highly racialized characteristics that can prompt racism.

Erika, a twenty-eight-year-old receptionist at an insurance company, similarly emphasizes "economic" differences and denies the existence of racism in Mexico. "More than anything, there are people who like to discriminate against others who are not at their level," she explained. I asked her what she meant by *level*. "Economic," she replied, and continued, "For me, there is more racism here in Mexico based on economics than people discriminating against you based on [skin] color." While Erika may have some understanding that racism by definition implies unequal treatment, she ironically (and incorrectly) uses the term to downplay discrimination based on phenotype and to assert that Mexican mistreatment stems primarily from individuals' sense of upper-class superiority.

While most Mexicans see class discrimination as a major social problem in their country, it became particularly clear when they talked about the mistreatment of Indigenous Mexicans and Mexicans with dark skin or Afro phenotype. Virtually all respondents recognized that disparities in class status are linked to skin color and that dark skin was viewed as synonymous with low socioeconomic status and, conversely, Whiteness with higher status and wealth. When I explicitly asked respondents to describe a scenario they might consider racist, they often described lifelong observations of preferential treatment being given to upper-class, typically light-skinned Mexicans and the stark contrast in the treatment of Mexicans with "fewer opportunities," a euphemism for poorer and darker persons.

For example, Carmen acknowledged the common association of dark-skinned Mexicans with lower class status. "Almost the majority of Mexicans—or I think everyone—has that opinion that just because you see someone as *prieto* or very *moreno* [dark], you believe he is inferior to you. And sometimes they have more money than you!" Carmen herself, a homemaker in her late thirties, has darker brown skin, yet she referred to prietos as "they" as a way to distance herself from that identity, and suggesting that she does not see herself as someone who faces the stigma of dark skin.

On the other hand, Marcos, an electrician in his forties, believes that his medium-brown skin and working-class status shapes his unequal relations with "White" Mexicans on the job. Marcos is a maintenance worker for a luxury condominium located in a trendy, upscale part of town. Over the years, he has had many encounters with tenants, whom he described as "upper-class White Mexicans." When I asked Marcos if he had ever experienced discrimination, he recalled several instances in which he felt that upper-class Mexicans treated him in a demeaning way because of his dark skin and lower-class status. Instead of making polite requests for maintenance, some tenants rudely ordered him around, demanding that their service requests be completed immediately. Part of Marcos's job entails entering tenants' apartments to do maintenance work like fixing a leaking faucet. He prefers to do his work while tenants are out, but sometimes they are home. Occasionally, some of the friendlier tenants offer him something to eat, but he has never been invited to sit at the table. Instead, he is expected to take the food back to his work area or eat in the kitchen standing up. Marcos recounted several similar experiences leading to demeaning interactions with upper-class Mexicans, who are almost always also "White." For Marcos and a majority of the Mexicans I spoke with, these social interactions constitute discrimination based on a combination of social class and skin color, not race. This view was reflected in respondents' reluctance or ambiguity in labeling something as racism, even when asked directly and even when the treatment they described would be widely recognized as racist, such as restaurant policies prohibiting domestic workers and drivers, many of whom are Indigenous, from dining in with their employers (DePalma 1995).

A few respondents, like Samuel, a twenty-nine-year-old assistant director of a small manufacturing business, suggested that racism does exist in Mexico. They noted its connection to color and class hierarchies:

> Well, I think [racism] functions in terms of difference based on color. You get labeled or they marginalize you. Like I just said about money, Mexicans will put you in a certain socio-economic status based on your [skin] color. I've seen instances where they don't let *morenos* in certain restaurants or businesses.

For Samuel, color prejudice is the root of discrimination in Mexico because others rely on skin color to make stereotypical assumptions about a person's social class status. The association of light skin with status, money, and education often results in the privileged treatment of "White" Mexicans, sometimes even by dark-skinned Mexicans who internalize the association of "White" Mexicans with high-class status.

Indeed, Mexicans with darker skin tones told me that they have been targets of discrimination by fellow Mexicans who assume they are working-class or poor. Samuel, who has medium-brown skin, recounted a time he went out to dinner in a trendy part of the city with associates from his manufacturing business. The men were dressed in nice jeans, polo shirts, and loafers. They walked up to the hostess, a young woman he described as "White," and asked for a table. "We were asked to wait, and as we stood there a group of *blancos* [White Mexicans] came right in and were seated before us." Samuel believed that he and his friends were overlooked in favor of "White Mexicans" because "the waiters assumed they have more money and think they will spend more or tip better," he explained. Interestingly, rather than challenge the implicit association of Whiteness with wealth, he seemed insulted by the idea that his relatively dark skin would relegate him to a lower place on the social hierarchy. "I know I'm not White . . . but I'm not totally Black [either]," he qualified. That White Mexicans get preferential treatment is sometimes taken for granted, as if it were a fact of life. Here, Samuel seems to suggest that he should not have been overlooked by the hostess—but not because it is simply wrong, rather because he is not "totally" dark-skinned.

While I sometimes found it difficult to disentangle Mexicans' thoughts on color- versus class-based discrimination versus

racism, it is clear that in a pigmentocracy such as Mexico that cov-
ets White skin and light eyes and hair, those with Indigenous and
Afro features experience not only the greatest barriers to economic
mobility but also social stigma attached to their phenotype. Skin-
color prejudice, and its resulting negative emotional and psycho-
logical effects, permeates nearly all aspects of life and can be observed in the most intimate of settings, including those of family,
marriage, and friendship (Sue 2013).

Take, for example, Mario, a forty-six-year-old construction
worker in Guadalajara who described his skin color as moreno
(dark brown). I interviewed him at work, in the courtyard of a luxury condominium where he was repairing the swimming pool.
When I asked if he ever felt that he was treated differently due to
his skin color, he sighed deeply and began recounting a painful
childhood experience. "When I was eight years old, I auditioned
for the chorus group in school, and the winner was going to go on
and represent our state in a national competition held at the nation's capital. I was the best vocalist out of the four who were recruited [to audition]," he said proudly. But the teacher ended up se-
lecting one of his classmates instead. "I cried. And when I asked my
teacher why I wasn't chosen, she said, 'It's because that boy—well,
he's *güerito* [fair-skinned].' It was because of my color," he said. "It
hurt me in my soul. It left a mark on my life that I've carried for
many years." Unfortunately, the childhood memory of being ostra-
cized for having dark skin was not unique to Mario; several respondents recalled painful or embarrassing moments in their past when
they attempted to lighten themselves with face cream or "scrub
off" their dark skin while bathing, for instance.

Dark-skinned respondents were more likely, even in childhood, to be the objects of racial jokes as well. José, a fitness trainer

in his midtwenties, described being called *pinche tepocate* ("You damn tadpole") by other kids in his neighborhood. "I don't even know what that is," he said, "but I think it's a really dark animal. I think they make the comparisons because it is something really black and ugly. It's like, 'You are just as black as that thing.'"

Racialized nicknames are very common in Mexico, and according to José, they may even be terms of endearment. As Sue (2013, 151) illustrates in her work, this type of humor is derogatory and demeaning toward the recipient, who often goes along with the joke so as not to breach the social etiquette of challenging racial humor. Terms like *negro* and *Memín* are commonly used to refer to Mexicans with dark skin or Afro phenotype, while *India Maria* is a popular term used jokingly and derogatorily to refer to women with Indigenous features or in Indigenous dress, or, most problematic, possessing stereotypes associated with Indigenous people, like the speaking of nonstandard Spanish, a lack of cultural capital, presumed intellectual inferiority, and exaggerated humility or modesty.

Color prejudice can also take the form of dating preferences or family (dis)approval of romantic and marriage partners. Carolina's husband is from San Miguel el Alto, which has a similar reputation to Los Altos Jalisco in terms of the "Whiteness" of its inhabitants. Although Carolina looks mestiza and does not identify as Indigenous, she has dark brown skin, and long, straight black hair, features associated with Indigenous Mexicans. She said:

> When I got married, my father-in-law didn't like me because they're White. Tall. In San Miguel el Alto, over there near Tepatitlán, there are a lot of *gente güera* [White people], and since I'm *morena* and everyone there is White, they didn't like me because I'm supposedly *india* [Indigenous].... He would

always say [about his son's marrying me], "*Pinche india* that he went and found himself," and he told me that himself. . . . But many years later, once we got to know each other, well, he changed and stopped calling me *pinche india.*

Carolina's father-in-law's disapproval of her as a suitable wife for his son stems from Mexico's colonial legacy of *blanqueamiento* and, later, eugenicist ideologies in which "White" Mexicans are regarded as racially superior and are thus expected to marry other light-skinned Mexicans in order to maintain their place at the top of the socioracial hierarchy. By this logic, someone from "*los altos*" marrying an Indigenous person is not only taboo, it is considered a step backwards, racially speaking.

Although there is widespread acknowledgment by Mexicans that those with dark skin have fewer opportunities for upward mobility (Flores and Telles 2012), it is noteworthy that among those who recounted personal experiences with color prejudice, all had darker brown skin. Several lighter-skinned Mexicans also readily acknowledged that skin-color prejudice is common but admitted that it occurred mainly against those with dark skin—not themselves. When asked if she believed she had ever been discriminated against due to her appearance, Jackie responded, "No. Up until this point, no." She explained, "Maybe it's because I am a bit Whiter. If I were morena—well, I'd be saying something different, right? I'm a bit more White. I don't appear to have sunburnt, very dark skin, that's why. If not, I'm certain I would be answering that differently." Jackie's nuanced views on skin-color discrimination demonstrate that a person does not need to directly experience skin-color prejudice to be aware of it, in line with findings from other studies conducted in Mexico (Telles and PERLA 2014).[7]

The Paradox of Glorification and Marginalization of Indigeneity
In certain regions of Mexico, Indigenous people make up a large
share of the local population. In Guadalajara, however, the Mexicans I interviewed reported having very limited interactions
with Indigenous people in their daily lives. Still, it was difficult
for them to deny the reality of anti-Indigenous sentiment in Mexico. Ricardo, a thirty-year-old musician who described himself as
moreno, explained how pervasive the derogatory remark *pinche indio* is throughout the country. "Look, you see it even in the lower
middle class. They insult others with 'pinche indio.' And that's
what you see here in Mexico." Ricardo alludes to how common it
is for people—including those with darker skin—to hurl the racial
epithet to make fun of or insult just about anyone for acting in ways
that are associated with anti-Indigenous stereotypes, such as being
"uncivilized," being simpleminded, or even showing extreme def-
erence or shyness. Recall also the story of Carolina, presented earlier in this chapter, whose father-in-law voiced disapproval of his
son's marriage to her by repeatedly referring to her as *pinche india*
rather than giving her the dignity of calling her by her name.

Almost none of my respondents believed they had any Indigenous neighbors or coworkers. "They don't really live in Guadalajara. They come down from *la sierra* [the mountains] to sell hand-
made crafts and food items in the city's main plazas," explained
Eva, a retail worker in her mid-thirties. Perhaps unbeknownst
to Eva, her description of local Indigenous persons reflects the
widespread association of Indigenous communities with remote
mountainous or rural locations—thus, quite literally outside the
boundaries of Mexicanness. This stands in sharp contrast to the
urban life of most respondents. In a comment typical among respondents, Eva said that she had never had a conversation with an

Indigenous person, only that she had bought things from Indigenous street vendors. "It's delicious, their traditional food," she said.

In fact, many respondents commented on the prevalence of Indigenous street vendors, and not all the comments were positive. Karina, a hairdresser in her late twenties, refuses to buy food from Indigenous vendors because she feels that the food stands are dirty and unhygienic. She explained, with an equal measure of disgust and pity, "They're sleeping in the streets. They work so hard selling their potato chips, but no thanks. Sometimes people don't buy from them because they look dirty. Poor things." Her remarks reveal a difference of opinion with Eva about where such vendors live, but both similarly engage in the "othering" of local Indigenous people.

Alicia, a thirty-eight-year-old homemaker, disagreed with the many respondents who acknowledged that Indigenous groups face discrimination in Mexico. She said, "They live here and have the same services, the same opportunities to frequent the same stores, to walk the same streets." Alicia's understanding of racial discrimination seems to be rooted in images of U.S. Jim Crow segregation, in which Black people were prohibited from entering "Whites-only" establishments or expected to step off the sidewalk or move to the street side when White people were approaching. She also saw the cultural fetishization of Indigenous people in a positive light: "I see there is respect for their way of dressing, because it is very different." Her comments are based on a definition of racism that is limited to the systematic, legal, and institutional realm and ignores individual acts of prejudice and discrimination in hiring or housing.

Reflecting the erroneous view that geography, rather than individual and structural discrimination, has led to a lack of racial mixing between Indigenous and other Mexicans, Carmen, the homemaker in her late thirties who has dark brown skin, said,

"Indigenous peoples in Mexico have suffered a lot because they [Mexican society] don't give them their place as true Mexicans. It shouldn't be the case that one is [considered] Whiter or darker. We're all Mexican. Just because here [in Guadalajara] people carry the Spanish race? Well, they [Spaniards] conquered more over here. And for [the Indigenous] in the *pueblos* farther away, it's just more difficult for them [to racially mix with the Spanish race]."

Similar to other respondents who glorify Indigenous people as the true soul of Mexico, Carmen alludes to mainstream society's marginalization of Indigenous groups, even going so far as to suggest that skin-color hierarchies shouldn't exist because "we're all Mexican." At the same time, her quote reflects an understanding that Indigenous people are othered because they are presumed to have little to no Spanish ancestry and are therefore not recognized as full members of the "Mexican mainstream" as defined by mestizaje.

When discussing social interactions with Indigenous people in the city, I'd ask respondents to clarify how they knew that a Mexican was Indigenous. Some people mentioned phenotypic differences. For example, Martin told me that he occasionally interacts with an Indigenous neighbor. When I asked him how he knew that his neighbor was Indigenous, he answered, "I say they're Indigenous because, I don't know, their skin is a bit different from ours [mestizos]. You can see it even in the hair and from the face; their phenotype is different from mine." Another respondent, Pablo, similarly referenced physical attributes as well as language as highly visible markers of difference. "You know the vendors? I figure they are Indigenous because—well, I am short. But the characteristics of an Indigenous person are moreno, short, and—what do I know—the way they talk, because they have a certain accent if they have a distinct language, right? You can tell right away."

Although respondents rarely admitted to holding prejudicial views toward Indigenous people, most agreed that "Mexican society" holds such views. Samuel said, of Indigenous people in Mexico:

> I believe they are a forgotten race. They are a group of people who are completely forgotten by the government, and I don't get too involved in government issues . . . but I'm sure that they are completely abandoned and persons who I've seen in many pueblos that are *Tarascos,* and their homes are made of adobe with the roof made of cardboard and laminate. I've gone to some of the stores where they don't speak Spanish. It could be my point of view that the government has forgotten them because they are a marginalized people because they are very poor. And it shouldn't have to be that way.

When I asked if Indigenous people face discrimination, Samuel said:

> I think so. There is a lot of discrimination. We are a society that speaks Spanish, and there are the Indigenous who speak their language. There is a very marked separation between those of us [mestizos] who speak Spanish and those who speak their Indigenous language.

In suggesting that the government has abandoned Indigenous communities, Samuel seems to hint at the larger structural forces shaping the lives of Indigenous people. He nonetheless frames their marginalization as rooted in ethnic rather than racial difference (e.g., "They don't speak Spanish"). Similarly, early on in my interview with Carmen, she denied that racism existed in Mexico, saying she had never seen it or experienced it. Yet later in the interview, she acknowledged that Indigenous people face prejudice. "I think it's unfair when Indigenous women street vendors set up the things they're selling only to be harassed by authority figures for not carrying permits," she stated. This seeming contradiction suggests there are different interpretations of race-based discrimination in the Mexican context; Carmen sees discrimination against the Indigenous as an issue of ethnic prejudice rather than a manifestation of systemic racism by police. It also underscores how discourse on racism remains largely taboo in Mexico.

Blackness in Mexico: The Paradox of Visibility and Invisibility
What it means to be black in Mexico is inextricably linked with what it means to be indigenous and, likewise, with what it means to be mestizo.

BOBBY VAUGHN (2005, 119)

If Mexico's Indigenous people are the "true soul of the nation," then its Afro descendants are invisible and foreign to the national imaginary. During my fieldwork in Guadalajara, I spent many late afternoons in the main plaza observing pedestrians and taking in the scenic views of its signature cathedral. On one of these days, the city government was sponsoring a large outdoor arts and crafts festival that featured a special performance in celebration of Mexico's "multiethnic" diversity. The dances were beautiful and intricate, and the dancers wore traditional costumes from various regions of the vast country. But not a single one of the performances represented Afro-Mexican culture. Knowing the systematic and historical erasure of Blackness in the construction of the modern Mexican nation-state, my just being in the audience made me feel complicit in this erasure.

A majority of interviewees reported having very little exposure to Black people in their neighborhoods and workplaces. Many had never set eyes on a Black person before, much less thought about issues affecting the group. Respondents who recalled meeting a Black person tended to remember it as a onetime encounter, such as a few words exchanged with a Black tourist. In a few cases, relatives who immigrated to the United States returned for a visit to Guadalajara with a Black American husband or wife. However, my own observations of social life in Guadalajara suggested that Black people are virtually invisible.[8]

Because they see Blackness and Mexicanness as mutually exclusive, respondents often assume Black people are Cuban, from the Caribbean, or African. They do not realize that Mexico has a Black population because they do not typically come across Afro-Mexicans in their hometowns. This point of view also reflects mestizaje ideology, which suggests that racial mixing has essentially absorbed Afro-Mexicans into the larger Mexican populace.

I even referenced the widely popular Mexican soccer star Giovani dos Santos, who looks phenotypically Black, in interviews. Eva's comment was typical: "Black? [Dos Santos] isn't. He has [Black] features. If you see him, he does have those features, but he isn't Black." Respondents often suggested that "true" Black people come from the U.S. or Africa; a Mexican who may display African ancestry is not "really" Black. This racial logic falls in line with mestizaje ideology, and although it challenges the Indigenous-Spaniard exclusivity of Mexicanness by recognizing the African element, it nonetheless situates Afro-Mexicans closer to mestizaje by identifying them as mixed—not Black—individuals.

When I asked respondents about their views of Black people, or "*personas negras*," without specifying Black *Americans* or Afro-descendant *Mexicans*, in hopes of learning about their racial attitudes toward Black people generally, their first thought was that I was referring to mestizo Mexicans with very dark skin. Diego stated, "Well, I notice sometimes that personas negritas are treated as less than." I asked Diego to clarify what he meant by *personas negritas*, and he replied, "Mexicans," demonstrating the more common use of *negro/a* to refer to mestizos with darker skin.

Indeed, it was not until I specifically asked about Afro-descendant Mexicans that respondents realized I was referring not to dark-skinned Mexicans but rather to Mexicans who have Black ancestry. Meanings of Blackness are locally constructed, such that in Guadalajara, Black people as a *racial* group are not a primary reference group for Mexicans looking to make sense of their own identity. As detailed in subsequent chapters, however, migration to the U.S. changes the meaning that Mexicans attribute to Blackness, from relatively little salience in Mexico to one of the main groups immigrants reference when interpreting their own racial status in the U.S.

In the few cases when respondents acknowledged that some Mexicans might have African ancestry by virtue of their hair type or skin color, they described them as *morenos*. Blackness, when acknowledged in Mexico, therefore, was described using a skin-color metaphor for racial ancestry and was contrasted with "pure" Blackness from the United States or Africa. These boundary-making discursive strategies make sense in a nation that promotes mestizaje, as they illustrate how everyday understandings of Mexican Blackness reflect dominant racial paradigms of Mexicanness as synonymous with race mixture.

Whereas a Mexican with Afro phenotype is described as not "really" Black, Black Americans and Africans were almost always described as phenotypically much darker and therefore more authentically Black. Take Marcia, who explained:

Blacks from over there, the United States, are very Black. Their skin is very Black, and the ones from over here are not. They are a combination; their skin is Black, but it is a little bit lighter, that of the [Afro] Mexicans. Their skin is more coffee-colored, and over there it is more like chocolate, very deep.

The distinction that Marcia made between "coffee-colored" Mexicans and those with a "deep" skin color reflects common conceptualizations of Afro-Mexicans as racially mixed. Black Americans, on the other hand, are thought of as racially pure, reflecting a version of Blackness rooted in the rigid one-drop rule of the U.S.

Despite Black people being a rare sight in Guadalajara, anti-Black images and discourse are pervasive in Mexican culture. A popular cultural icon that came up in interviews is the beloved comic book character Memín Pinguín. This comic, created by Alberto Cabrera in 1943, has arguably done more to introduce tropes of Blackness into the Mexican psyche than personal encounters with Afro-Mexicans have. Memín is a poor and mischievous boy with dark skin, kinky hair, and exaggerated thick lips. He lives in Mexico City, does poorly in school, and has jobs shining shoes and selling newspapers.[9] Memín became the subject of controversy in 2005, after the Mexican government issued a postage stamp with his image as part of its "History of Mexican Comics" series. African American civil rights leaders, including Jesse Jackson, disapproved of the stamp, pointing out the similarity between Memín's image and racist Black caricatures made popular in minstrel shows of the 1800s and 1900s. In fact, Memín's character followed the tradition of nineteenth-century Cuban minstrel shows known as *bufos Cubanos*, which featured stereotypical enactments of Afro-Cubans (Gonzalez 2010). These wildly popular forms of entertainment in various Latin American countries (as well as the U.S.)

gave rise to the negrito Memín as an important part of Mexicans' cultural repository (Gonzalez 2010). Despite the controversy surrounding Memín's postage stamp, it sold out in two days.

I asked respondents about their thoughts on Memín, feeling it would reveal nuances of local interpretations of Blackness and race more generally. In line with the understanding that Blackness is foreign to Mexico, they agreed that Memín was Mexican, but they hesitated to identify him as Black (Lewis 2000; Hernández Cuevas 2004; Sue 2013; Telles and PERLA 2014). A handful of respondents, however, did identify Memín as a Black boy, and when asked to describe him, they noted the character's large, exaggerated lips and resemblance to a monkey. Even so, they denied that the comic books were racist, citing Memín's charming character as evidence that he is adored in Mexico.

Local understandings of Blackness are further shaped by national and global media representations of Black identity. Gaby, a homemaker in her early fifties, referenced the classic 1948 Mexican film *Angelitos Negros* (the film stars Pedro Infante, one of the biggest Mexican actors of his day). *Angelitos Negros* centers on a wealthy "White" Mexican woman named Ana Luisa who gives birth to a daughter named Belen and is horrified when the child turns out to be a dark-skinned *mulata*. Ana Luisa refuses her daughter and blames her mestizo husband for tainting the family with his African ancestry, only to realize later that the woman she believed all her life to be her Black nanny was actually her own mother. For Gaby, this classic film is proof that Mexicans harbor deep-seated anti-Black prejudice.

Even today, images abound throughout Mexico depicting Black people in highly problematic ways. In 2010, a nationally broadcast Mexican television sports show portrayed South Africa, which was then hosting the World Cup, and its people as primitive.

Light-skinned Mexican sportscasters donned blackface, Afro wigs, animal skins, and spears in a racist parody of South Africans. It is not uncommon to see anti-Black stereotypes on television, in advertisements, and even on food packaging. For decades, Mexico's leading chocolate snack cake, similar to Little Debbie Swiss rolls in the U.S., was named *El Negrito* ("Little Blackie") and depicted a caricature of a Black boy. The company ceded to pressure by social justice advocates in 2013; the cakes have been renamed *Nitos*, but the wrapper still features an arguably caricatural image of a boy with a giant Afro.[10]

These century-old stereotypes of Mexico's Black inhabitants are also evident throughout Latin America and are a contrast to hegemonic images of Black Americans as inherently urban, "ghetto," and prone to drug use and crime (Oliver 2003). One study, for example, found that Brazilians of all colors perceived Black people in Brazil to be "friendlier" in contrast to "racist" and "self-segregating" Black people in the U.S. (Joseph 2015). While these discursive distinctions suggest that racialization looks different across national contexts, they also reflect the global nature of anti-Black ideologies.

Conclusion

No amount of glorification of mestizaje or denial of racism can hide the devastating reality that a majority of Indigenous and Afro-descendant Mexicans remain impoverished, marginalized, and geographically isolated. Although the national ideology of mestizaje officially disregarded White identities in favor of the unifying mestizo category (Casas et al. 2014), Mexico is a pigmentocracy in which the Whitest-looking citizens reap the greatest social and economic advantages. On the other end of the spectrum, Mexicans with the darkest skin tones—the Indigenous, Afro-Mexicans, and some mestizos—are greatly disadvantaged; they remain among the poorest and are severely underrepresented in higher occupational and educational levels (Villarreal 2010; Flores and Telles 2012, 486; Sue 2013; Telles and PERLA 2014). Still, respondents had generally assimilated the belief that racism is a U.S. problem, not a Mexican one.

The tides of racial thinking in Mexico are slowly turning, but cross-border ties may help speed them up. Recent waves of Afro-Mexican migration to the U.S. have influenced Afro-descendant Mexicans' understandings of their socioracial location in both nations (Jerry 2014). Mexico's anti-racist advocates are also looking to U.S. racial justice movements for framing strategies and inspiration. Thanks to these efforts, the Mexican government is taking the initiative to recognize the country's diversity, and national campaigns are working to raise public awareness about the social harm of discrimination across different social axes, including gender expression and age. In 2001, Mexico amended a constitutional article to proclaim the right of Indigenous peoples to their own culture and their own language, and, for the first time, to officially penalize any form of discrimination based on ethnicity, language, gender, or race (Telles and PERLA 2014). Although Mexico officially recognized the existence of racial discrimination, state efforts to promote national diversity continue to be framed as *multicultural* celebrations—mostly of Indigenous traditions—rather than multiracial. Some argue that these advances are not enough, citing the relative absence of Black social movements, which are still seen as a challenge to national identity because they contradict the essence of what it means to be Mexican (Casas et al. 2014).

My interviews with Mexican non-migrants revealed that Mexican racial thought is riddled with contradictions, and ordinary Mexicans must negotiate this daily. On one hand, Mexican nationalism was built on the seemingly progressive idea that Mexico, and all of Latin America, was home to a new and morally superior "cosmic race" comprising the best elements of the various races. Embracing and promoting racial mixture posed a direct challenge to North American White supremacy. On the other hand, what was perhaps a promising ideal of a racial paradise devoid of conflict turned out to be yet another racial project that benefits individuals who fall on the lighter end of the racial and color spectrum. Still, mestizo respondents enjoyed a privileged position in the local (and national) ethnoracial hierarchy in relation to Indigenous and Afro-Mexicans, one that helps to anchor their sense of belonging to the nation.

Traditionally, studies of race and ethnicity in Mexico have focused on regional and national characteristics, or comparisons with other Latin American nations with similarly large mestizo populations. Yet as I discussed in this chapter, the transnational exchange of racial ideologies and discourses with the U.S. has long influenced Mexican elites and intellectuals, who have both challenged and emulated American racial ideals. In the next chapter, I expand the scope of these transnational racial exchanges to look at how ordinary migrants who move across borders also enact the power to create global culture at the local level, exposing nonmigrants to distinctly U.S. racial conceptions. As I further demonstrate in Chapters 3 and 4, the racial baggage that Mexicans carry into the U.S. informs how they come to see race there and subsequently navigate "new" racial hierarchies in Los Angeles.

CHAPTER 2

Racial Border Crossings

I GREW UP TRAVELING to Mexico every few years to visit family. I distinctly remember watching television with my sister there one evening and tuning in to an episode of one of my favorite shows, *The Fresh Prince of Bel-Air*. In Mexico the show's title translated to *"El principe de rap"* (*The Prince of Rap*). We laughed in amusement when we heard the dubbed Spanish voice of Will, the African American main character. Having been born and raised in inner-city Los Angeles, we were both quite familiar with the characters of the show and its distinctly (Black) American cultural references, even with the less-than-perfect dubbed Spanish. But I couldn't help but wonder how much of the characters' essence was lost in translation on those who didn't have U.S. social and racial sensibilities, let alone those who had never even met a Black American.

Years later, on a sunny weekend afternoon, as I strolled through central Guadalajara during my fieldwork for this book, I came upon a *tianguis*, an open-air street market. These flea markets typically set up shop one day a week in towns all across Mexico. The tianguis was located in a large open space adjacent to a small cathedral. Locals and tourists alike had come to shop. As I walked through the maze of stands selling household items ranging from fresh produce to socks and undergarments to children's toys and kitchenware, I noticed a large stand displaying hundreds of low-priced pirated DVDs of American films. Men, women, and children stood around, perusing movie titles that they would later enjoy in the comfort of their own homes. Hollywood blockbusters dubbed in Spanish also appear regularly on Megacable, a popular cable service based in Guadalajara that broadcasts in over twenty-five different states. With the availability of pirated DVDs and television delivery services like satellite and dish TV, one could easily consume American films just about every night in Mexico.

Arguably, the traveling of racial ideas across geopolitical boundaries is as old as the history of conquest and colonization throughout the world. Even in modern history, there is a well-established tradition of racial ideas from Europe making their way into U.S. and Latin American politics. U.S. military occupation and government intervention in various Latin American countries has also resulted in the imposition of distinctly U.S. racial projects. For example, the United States implemented racially segregationist policies in Cuba's armed forces over the course of its occupation of Cuba during the Spanish-American War (De la Fuente 2000). Similarly, after the U.S. acquired Puerto Rico in 1898, the American government began conducting a census of the island's population using the United States' own rigid Black-White racial taxonomy, even though this was at odds with the racial classification system used by native Puerto Ricans (Duany 2005). These studies reveal that racial ideas are not bound by national borders—and that some borders, like the California-Mexico one, which spans 140 miles, can be particularly porous.

Yet sociological studies of immigrants' transnational lives that focus, as many do, on economic remittances and political involvement in hometown associations (see, for example, Waldinger 2013 and Duquette-Rury 2019) do not examine the impact of racial ideas as they cross borders. But in fact the same social relationships that facilitate economic remittances and participation in local elections back home facilitate racial remittances—the transmission of U.S. racial ideologies, schemas, discourses, stereotypes, and practices to the immigrant sending community (Levitt 2001). These racial remittances, in combination with preexisting racial ideas born in the sending region, shape the racial baggage that migrants bring with them when they come to the United States. This baggage, then, affects how new arrivals to the U.S. negotiate social relations with different groups, including Black Americans and U.S.-born Latinos and Asians.

Sociologist Peggy Levitt's (2001) concept of social remittances— the ideas, behaviors, and practices that immigrants learn in the host society and transmit back to sending communities—is useful for understanding not only the richly transnational lives of migrants but also how migration affects the people they leave behind. In her groundbreaking study of the transnational lives of Dominican migrants to New York, Levitt (2001) found that Dominican migrant women shared their newly acquired views about U.S. gender norms, such as men's obligation to help with household chores, with relatives back home. These social remittances on gender then transformed the views of women in the Dominican Republic, who began to adopt Americanized ideals of gender egalitarianism into their own lives (Levitt 2001).

In relaying newfound racial knowledge back to loved ones who remain in the homeland, ordinary migrants are enacting the power to "create global culture at the local level," much like state institutions and global media (Levitt 2001, 11). In light of this, scholars have called for a "transnationalism from below," which pays attention to how the social worlds and everyday behavior of individuals help to create transnational social spaces while considering how these social interactions are embedded into larger structures such as federal immigration laws and economic policies (Mau 2010). Transnational racialization "from below" draws attention to how racist ideas and practices can be sustained not only by ordinary individuals who migrate to a new society but also by those in the origin country who maintain ties to migrants, or who were once themselves migrants and returned to the homeland, whether voluntarily or as a result of being deported. In other words, whether one engages in transnational racial exchanges directly or symbolically, it is nearly impossible to escape their influence (Itzigsohn et al. 1999).

My interviews in Mexico revealed that Mexicans were quite savvy about U.S. racial dynamics. I argue that racial remittances are an important mechanism framing Mexican non-migrants' racial perceptions, and whether one engages in these social interactions directly or not, few individuals are left untouched by their influence. Even those with no plans to leave their country had heard stories about life in the U.S. and watched enough American television to form their own opinion of how race in Mexico plays out differently in comparison to *el norte*. Transnational social ties and global media thus play a central role in exposing would-be migrants in Mexico to a uniquely American brand of racialization, including anti-Blackness, the Black-White racial divide, racial discrimination, and nativist xenophobia. Immigrant racial remittances overwhelmingly cast African Americans as aggressive and dangerous, while portraying White Americans on a spectrum from benevolent employers to anti-immigrant racists. By highlighting how a combination of racial ideologies originating in Mexico and the U.S. molds Mexicans' understandings about race in the U.S., this chapter disrupts the notion that racial ideas are bound by national

74

borders and paints a more nuanced picture of the "racial baggage" that travels with Mexican migrants.

Racial remittances and global media exports to Mexico not only affect racial formation processes there (e.g., the development and maintenance of racial attitudes, identities, categorizations, and policies), they also impact how Mexicans might navigate U.S. racial boundaries in the event that they migrate north. (For a more thorough discussion of the impact on new arrivals to the U.S., see Chapter 3.) Thus, racial remittances sent to the immigrant home country are critical for understanding the effect of U.S. immigration beyond national boundaries in influencing the views and attitudes of those abroad who may one day migrate to America (Zamora 2016). Any consideration of how transnational migration impacts the way would-be and newly arriving immigrants make sense of their own place in the U.S. racial and status hierarchy must take this racial baggage seriously.

Transnationalism from Above: Global Media
Hollywood (Racism) Goes to Mexico
Given the global pervasiveness of U.S. media (Rodriguez 2018), it was not surprising that when I asked respondents in Mexico how they imagine race relations in the United States, a society they have never lived in, many referenced television and movies to describe a racial landscape very different from their own country. Elizabeth noted:

> I would see in movies that *los Americanos* [White Americans] were always in big, beautiful homes, with more privileges than Blacks. Blacks were put in ugly ghettos with lots of drugs, alcohol, prostitution, all of that. Movies always show Whites in the upper classes, and Blacks are always in the lowest class.

American television represented a powerful tool that fed the collective imaginations of non-migrants in Mexico. These programs brought not just entertainment value to Mexican audiences; they also brought faraway people, places, and even bygone eras into the consciousness of respondents. For example, influential films like South Central L.A.–based *Boyz n the Hood* provided a window into the world of Black urban America in the early 1990s, when the crack epidemic was ravaging poor Black and Brown communities nationwide. Maricela found the film fascinating. She said, "I found out how it really is over there [in the U.S.] from watching lots of movies [like *Boyz n the Hood*], even though you haven't lived it in the flesh. But there isn't much left to the imagination. . . . You start watching films, and you begin to see how it is out there."

Historically, the American film industry has been a major exporter of anti-Black tropes worldwide, and Mexico has received many of these exports. In fact, the majority of respondents were quite familiar with racist stereotypes of Black Americans as prone to crime, poverty, and drug addiction, and not one respondent described a film where Black Americans occupied a higher social status than White Americans. Given the pervasiveness of anti-Black stereotypes in U.S. film and television, I had expected this. But I wanted to learn more about where these distinctly American ideologies were coming from and perhaps whether and how these racial remittances impacted non-migrants' conception of the U.S. How might their visions of an America divided along Black and White racial lines, with White people having the privileges of wealth and "the good life," affect their view of U.S. society?

Guadalajara locals have virtually no social contact with Black persons. Thus, they had little personal experience to draw on. As I mentioned in Chapter 1, this racial context stands in stark contrast to other Latin American countries, namely Brazil, where Afro descendants make up the majority of the population.[1] There, it is common for non-Black Brazilians to form friendships with and have coworkers who are Black or *mulato* (Telles 2004). Irma acknowledged this when I asked her if she has had any interactions with Black people: *Irma*

> I never really dealt with them. Just from what I see in the news or TV shows. But, like, deal with them? No. Usually they are Black, the ones fighting for the drugs. I tell my husband, "Oh, that one looks like he'd be a murderer, like he's a bad person," because there are some Black people who seem friendly and Black girls who are very attractive, very pretty and all. But there are some that you can tell they are killers, drug addicts.

Similarly, when Eduardo mentioned Black Americans, I asked his opinion of them. He said, "I figure that they're very explosive, that they don't really think twice about things that they do. Looking at the situation, they seem like a dangerous race." I asked about the basis of his opinion, and he said: "The movies they show on television. I mean, it's like anything else: there are Blacks and Whites who are thieves, but the majority that I've seen are Black people. I think it's because of how they live. [Black people] want everything in life to be easy. They don't want to work, and it seems easy to just 'Let's steal this.' That's what I imagine."

Mass media and popular culture do not merely reflect the dominant racial ideology of the time; they also shape that ideology to begin with. For example, the American television show *Cops*, in which camera crews follow U.S. police during patrols and narcotic stings, is a staple of Mexico television under the title *Polecias*. During our discussion of the popular show, Samuel enthusiastically performed the show's signature theme song, *"Chicos malos"*

("Bad Boys"), which has been translated into Spanish. "I remember watching *Polecias*, where White cops would beat up Black people even after handcuffing them, so at that point the beatings are excessive," he remarked. The racist slant of *Cops* and its warped reflection of law enforcement has been well documented (Deggans 2020). Not only does the show position police as a positive force combating lawlessness and "cleaning up the streets" of dangerous criminals—most of whom are Black and Brown—but one report analyzing hundreds of *Cops* episodes found that it depicts "roughly four times the amount of crime than there is in real life, three times as many drug crimes, and ten times the amount of prostitution" (Garfield 2019). Although *Polecias* effectively transmits anti-Black stereotypes of criminality and lawlessness to respondents in Guadalajara, it can also serve as evidence of the excessive use of force by police in Black communities.

Samuel described Hollywood's slanted portrayals of Black Americans without suggesting they matched reality:

I'm not sure why, but in American movies they always show Blacks as the bad guys, thieves, murderers, gang members, drug addicts. They show lots of conflict within families: even amongst themselves, they fight and kill. I'd say if they have those problems within their own families and communities, then imagine with someone who isn't part of their community? . . . They even come out killing cops. I mean, they're against law.

Samuel acknowledged the possibility that these portrayals were not based in reality—though, in any case, he felt that they would affect the behavior of Mexican immigrants to the United States:

So, I don't know if—in reality, if you go to the United States and go into a Black neighborhood, if it's really like that. I'm not sure if it just happens to be the movies that I've watched or if that's really what life is like for Black people in the United States. . . . Still, I imagine that a Mexican [immigrant] over there, when they see a Black person, they'll walk faster to flee from him.

In other words, Samuel would consider a Black person a potential risk, even though he acknowledges that Hollywood portrayals may be inaccurate. It is worth noting, however, that even though Samuel and others might suspect that these portrayals of Black Americans are exaggerated, in the event that Samuel migrates to the U.S. and lives side by side with Black people, carrying the racial baggage of fear and suspicion could have an even higher cost for both himself and his Black neighbors.

Some Mexicans had received a different message from these films. When Raquel and I spoke about racial discrimination in the U.S., she asked me innocently whether I believed Black people face discrimination in the United States. Instead of answering, I asked her what she thought. She paused and pondered, then said, "I'd say they are, right? I don't know, but in movies you see that . . . [White people] don't like them because of their [skin] color." For Raquel, Hollywood films provided a small window into the United States' long history of White-on-Black racism and cast White Americans in a negative light.

Media, like popular culture, has the potential to both reproduce and challenge aspects of dominant racial discourse. Micaela specifically had a positive impression of Black people because of film. When asked about her views of Black Americans, Micaela perked up, exclaiming: "I love the way they sing! I've always seen in movies that they're in their churches and their choirs. I love listening to their music. I view the Black race as a people with lots of strength, lots of fight in them. Very hardworking. They have gone through so much, but they're always able to keep pushing forward." She mentioned in particular one film that had shaped her impressions: *Sister Act*, a wildly popular 1992 comedy starring Whoopi Goldberg as the director of a struggling convent choir.

Of course, non-migrants were not merely receptacles of global flows of Black American culture in film and television. Some respondents, including Manuel, a non-migrant in his twenties who regularly watches American movies, went further, directly questioning the portrayals they see. Manuel said that he had noticed that Black people (in film) "live in poor neighborhoods and there is a lot of crime and shooting." However, when I asked him if he thought the portrayals were accurate, he said, "Well, no, I don't. Because movies just exaggerate things." On the other hand, he retreated a little bit, admitting that he lacks the real-life experience to solidify his skepticism: "I've never seen [Black people] in person, so I really can't say that that is how they are." Although a few non-migrants, like Manuel, questioned the reliability of Hollywood films, stating that movies often exaggerate their storylines, by and large non-migrants had swallowed the dominant, racist message of American film and television.

U.S. Breaking News in Mexico: Structural Racism on Display
During my fieldwork in Guadalajara, President Barack Obama was campaigning for a second term in the White House. President Obama's election in 2008 as the nation's first Black president was a watershed moment in U.S. racial politics, and Mexicans in Guadalajara watched in awe. They then eagerly hoped for his second

term. Some Mexicans took Obama's presidency as a sign of U.S. racial progress, while others concluded that America is, and has always been, rife with anti-Black and anti-immigrant racial violence.

Victor recalled watching news coverage of the night Obama won the election: "I noticed on TV when it was announced that [Obama] had won, that the majority of Black people were really happy. And you could see that White people seemed mad that he won." Non-migrants who narrated their reactions to the historic election night seemed to imply an understanding of American-style racism in which support, and disdain, for a presidential candidate is divided along racial lines. Francisco, who was also pleasantly surprised Obama had won, echoed Victor's comment: "It seems that Whites don't want someone who isn't White to be their president, but I think it's a good thing [Obama] won."

Raul, a non-migrant in his late twenties who told me he watched television news that covered the presidential campaign, also correctly perceived a sharp racial divide in American politics:

> White people give a lot of support to their own race. You see with President Obama how they criticized him, and you wondered, "How was it possible that a Black man would become president?" Because Whites mainly support their own people. You see that Whites criticize Blacks, but when Whites do something worthy of criticism, nobody ever tells them anything. White Americans criticize [Black Americans] even though they're from the same country, just because that person is Black. And it's because [Whites are] racists.

Enrique is among a handful of respondents who watch news with regularity. Like the others, he demonstrated a clear-eyed view of structural racism in the U.S.:

It has cost African Americans a lot of work to achieve a common lifestyle like everyone else in the U.S. They still haven't succeeded, to be honest. There are many who have [said], "Just look at Obama as president." But we're talking about someone very notable, right? But there are so many [Black people] who continue suffering.

For Enrique, a Black American rising to the presidency is the exception, not the norm, and this accomplishment certainly does not signal the end of anti-Black racism. "I've always been on the side of those who are most vulnerable," he said, adding, "And on the news, I've seen lots of videos of cops badly beating African Americans, and all the cops are White."

In fact, the more recent proliferation of "viral" video recordings of violent police altercations and tragic killings of unarmed Black people has not escaped the notice of Mexicans. Several respondents even recalled the 1992 Rodney King beating that took place in Los Angeles, as it was heavily televised around the world. Referencing the five days of unrest that followed the acquittal of King's attackers, Julieta reflected a nuanced view of U.S. protests against police brutality:

I'm not sure how it is now, but as you know, there was a war between Black and White people, and they [Whites] don't like Black people. I think Black people have suffered a lot, and they've fought hard to be equal to Whites. . . . I've seen on the news here in Mexico that Blacks fight and burn cars . . . because problems arise from the killings of Black people. [Police will] kill a Mexican or a Black person, and everyone unites and they attack police cars, right? But in reality it's *los Americanos* who take advantage.

Julieta was twenty-one years old when the L.A. unrest took place, and it left a lasting impression on her view of the U.S. racial divide. Her references to the events of 1992 further highlight Mexican news-watching respondents' awareness of the long history of Black racial oppression in America. While perhaps swallowing a racist narrative that most protests of police brutality are violent, she notes that White Americans benefit from the prevailing system.

Racial Violence on the Mexico-U.S. Border

For Eduardo and others in Mexico, there is also a clear understanding that "hunting" down Mexican and Central American immigrants at the Mexico-U.S. border is part and parcel of American racism—and an extension of White-on-Black racism.

> I've seen on the news . . . that Texans are the worst ones, that they hunt immigrants down as if they were animals. It's not just Mexicans, necessarily, 'cause it could be a *Salvadoreño*, an *Hondureño*, who knows what—just, migrants in general have been found dead. Have you heard about some kids that were crossing the Rio Bravo and the border patrol shot one of them? I think that's just wrong. I say that's racism. And what I've heard, that the United States is sending more military or marines to the border area—well, that's just very dangerous.

Raquel, a divorced mother of two living in Zapópan, echoed a similar sentiment when I asked her what she thought about White Americans' general treatment of Mexican immigrants. "Well, from the news, I know they treat them very badly, right? There are places where they don't like Mexicans, right? Especially in Texas. They are in opposition to Mexicans and reject them." Referring to the Min-utemen and other border vigilantes known to violently "patrol" the Mexico-U.S. border in the name of national security, she exclaimed, "If you're [an American] patriot, then you'll kill a Mexican! That's what it must be like over there."

Respondents in Mexico were attuned to the ways in which the Mexico-U.S. border becomes a site of racialization whereupon migrants are effectively ascribed an inferior racial and legal status. As discussed in Chapter 1, this is a clear departure from the prevailing belief in Mexico that racism does not exist. In this case, Mexicans who have never left the mestizo nation are nonetheless articulating racial knowledge of a distinctly U.S. version of (anti-Mexican) racialized illegality. Global media and other forms of racial remittances thus facilitate a shift in how Mexicans make sense of not only the racial status of White and Black Americans but also the relative positioning of Mexican immigrants in the U.S. racial hierarchy, a topic I turn to in Chapter 4.

Occasionally, the racial violence at the border is so abhorrent that it makes international news and reaches much wider audiences throughout Mexico. A few months prior to my interviews in Guadalajara, U.S. Border Patrol Agent Jesus Mesa Jr. fired into a crowd of young boys near the Mexico-U.S. border, killing fifteen-year-old Sergio Adrián Hernández Güereca as he stood in the street on the Mexican side of the border (Mesa fired his weapon because the boy was allegedly throwing rocks at agents over the border fence). The boy's parents filed a civil lawsuit, but it was thrown out on the grounds that because their son was killed in Mexico, the U.S. Constitution did not apply. In the end, the U.S. Justice Department announced that it would not press charges against Mesa, even though the boy was unarmed and eyewitnesses said he was just a bystander.

Although few respondents watched the news with regularity, incidents like the Güereca shooting easily become the talk of the town. In fact, many of the non-migrants I spoke to, including those who said they rarely watch the news, mentioned the shooting as evidence that "Americans don't like Mexicans and even kill them at the border." Victor commented:

> Well, I've heard [on the news] about racism against Mexicans, that they are treated as less than [human] [in the United States]. . . . I've even seen that sometimes [Americans] kill people when they are crossing the border. I think it's the government, the police, and sometimes the people who kick Mexicans out because they're not from the United States, because they don't have papers. Recently, I heard on the news that a Mexican boy got too close to the border and was shot. I can't believe the [Border Patrol] was willing to do that. It's so wrong because they don't do anything to deserve that. Even if he was a rebel kid, it doesn't matter! We're all just trying to get by.

The idea that a Mexican can become a target simply because they are perceived to be an immigrant threat reinforces the notion that Mexicans are viewed and treated as inferior and criminal in American society. Some non-migrants even referenced the violence at the border as a reason why they would not choose to migrate to the U.S., saying that they felt bad for those who risk their lives doing so.

It is important to note that of those who reported watching the news regularly, all but one were men. This could be a result of women doing the bulk of the childcare during evening hours, when one might otherwise tune in to the evening news. Still, it was evident that Mexican television network coverage of U.S. politics powerfully shaped non-migrants' perceptions of the American racial system—particularly the ways White racism and police violence affect the safety of African Americans and the most vulnerable migrants at the border.

Transnationalism from Below:
Immigrant and Non-Migrant Social Ties

Racial baggage can vary and circulate across borders in different ways, depending on whether it is diffused on a broad scale, such as mass media and political and economic institutions, or through one-on-one interactions between immigrants and their social networks in Mexico. Sociologists refer to social interactions as "micro-level cultural diffusion" because, in this case, ideas about race are communicated directly via visits, phone calls, letters, text messages, and video chats between immigrants and loved ones back home, as opposed to macro-level exchanges, which make up the "faceless, mass-produced nature of global cultural diffusion" (Levitt 2001, 64). Although racial remittances are distinct from other forms of global cultural exchanges, they often reinforce and are reinforced by one another. When similar racist messages are transmitted from both micro and macro levels, their impact can be particularly powerful.

As Nadia Kim (2008) and Wendy Roth's (2012) studies of Korean, Dominican, and Puerto Rican transnational migration demonstrate, cross-border social ties are a key mechanism for the diffusion of hegemonic U.S. racial ideologies to non-migrant communities. Kim (2008) found that immigrant social ties—along with global media and the U.S. military presence in South Korea—transmitted U.S. racist ideologies of White superiority, White masculinity, and anti-Blackness that influenced non-migrants' understanding of the U.S. racial hierarchy long before they arrived in the U.S. Roth (2012, 125) similarly found that "people who remain in [the Dominican Republic and Puerto Rico] not only learn about the physical environment and daily activities of their migrant ties, but they also learn about . . . [U.S.] systems of classifying race and ethnicity." My interviews with Mexicans on both sides of the border point to similar racial remittance exchanges, highlighting how cross-border ties create a transnational social field in which the daily occurrences of immigrants in the U.S. transcend national boundaries to become a reference point for those who remain in the homeland.

Racializing Black Americans in Mexico
During my interviews in Mexico, I was astonished at how easily non-migrants' imagination forayed into U.S. racist ideologies of African American aggression, criminality, and welfare dependence. For instance, the ease with which Mario, a construction worker in his forties, recited a common trope of Black welfare reliance speaks directly to how pervasive this U.S. ideology is abroad: "Well, I can't confirm it. I'm just saying I've heard in conversation [with family in the U.S.] that Blacks, since they're American, that the government helps them; even when they aren't working, the government provides for them. Like a pension, so to speak. So, in reality, I don't think Blacks are treated really badly. I'm not sure in what aspect they can be treated badly because I haven't seen it."

Racial remittances further confirmed for some in Mexico the imagery of the "angry Black man/woman" they had already been exposed to through global media. For instance, Carmen, a homemaker in her thirties, drew on Hollywood film depictions when describing her views of Black Americans as "more impulsive, more furious than Whites," whom she described as "more pacified." It was not until her brothers shared the experiences they'd had with their Black neighbors in Texas that her sentiments about Black Americans were "proven":

First, I would see it in movies—well, one thinks that they're like that, right? But it was proven to me that they do have strong personalities because I would see in the movies that they'd scream at each other and were very impulsive and would throw things and fight, and from what my brother tells me about how they fight over there . . . [it] proved to me that what I was seeing on TV was also reality.

For Carmen, media depictions blended with racial remittances to affirm a convincing reality of Black depravity.

It should be noted that a majority of stories about violence or aggression remitted to non-migrants derived from secondhand narratives circulating within the immigrant community rather than direct encounters with Black Americans. Karla, a forty-year-old homemaker, illustrated this point well: "But the people would say we need to be very careful with Blacks because they're dangerous and like to fight and everything! Did [my relatives] tell me [Blacks] did something to them? No, nothing. But among them [immigrants], it was said to 'be careful with them.' It was a warning, perhaps." Karla's family, despite never having personally experienced such incidents, regularly shared stories with her and other relatives in Mexico that portrayed African Americans as dangerous.

Martin, an administrative assistant in his late twenties, provided one of the only personal examples of a non-migrant, or a close contact of a non-migrant, having a violent personal encounter with a Black person. Juan, Martin's best friend, had migrated to Sacramento several years earlier. Martin had recently lost touch with Juan, but they had managed to stay in contact for several years, often calling each other on the phone. As we started discussing race relations in the U.S., Martin quickly referenced a conversation he had had with Juan regarding Juan's first experience with Black people. "He told me, 'I ran into a little group of Black guys when I was walking down the street, and they beat me.'" Martin pointed out that this happened to Juan almost immediately after his friend had arrived in the U.S., remarking sarcastically, "They gave him a nice welcome." He told me Juan had previously mentioned having frequent conflict with his Black neighbors:

> One day the neighbors even broke into [Juan's] place to rob them, and that's why they had to move location. . . . I had that conversation with him, and he told me that it was too many problems living with Black people because they look at you as if they don't like you.

Although Martin, like the other non-migrants I interviewed, had never visited the U.S., he was able to draw extensively from these transnational exchanges to paint a portrait of what it is like living among Black Americans. These personal exchanges also exposed Martin to stereotypes about Black people as conflict-ridden and aggressive toward immigrant newcomers. Given that this was the first example Martin shared as we entered a discussion of U.S. race relations, it is clear that Juan's racial encounter in Sacramento had deeply affected him.

Interviews with immigrants indicated that some non-migrants eagerly sought racial remittances. Julia, who migrated to Los Angeles over thirteen years ago, calls her family in Mexico several times a week. "Some [family members] have asked, 'Is it true that there are a lot of Black people over there?'" she told me. When I asked Julia what she has told her family about Black Americans, she replied, "That we [Mexican immigrants] have to be very careful with [Black people] and make the least possible contact with them."

Alejandro, a young factory worker in Guadalajara who talks regularly with his male cousins in Atlanta, offered a different perspective of the racial remittances recounted to him:

> From what my cousins told me . . . an African American gets along better with a Latino than with a gringo American. Because they told me that, I think, before, there was more slavery of Blacks by Whites, and I think that's why they are resentful or angry with the gringos. . . . African Americans don't have anything against Mexicans, they just want to be treated fairly by the gringos, so they have problems with them.

Like many non-migrants, Alejandro had been exposed to negative transnational stories about Black Americans as "angry" and aggressive. However, his cousins' interpretation of why African Americans might get along better with Latinos than Whites dispels the essentialist view that Black people are inherently aggressive. Instead, Alejandro's cousins give a more nuanced view of U.S. race relations in which they attempt to explain African Americans' so-called aggressive behavior as an outcome of the historical legacy of White enslavement of Black people, not as some innate quality.

Marvin described a United States not only deeply divided along Black and White lines but also one in which Americans kill due to race. He told me about a friend who had lived in California and later returned to Mexico, emphasizing "the conflict between Whites and Blacks" that prevailed in the United States. "My friend told me that [Americans] kill because 'You're Black and I'm White,' and they fight and even kill due to someone's skin color." Lacking the historical context to make sense of White racial terror against Black people in the U.S., Marvin got the impression that racial prejudice was meted out evenly by White people against Black people and vice versa, saying, "I think that [in the U.S.] if you're Black, [Black people] see you positively, and if you're not Black, they see you negatively." Despite his limited understanding of U.S. race relations, Marvin was clear about one thing: "I'm not sure if it's discrimination, but there is conflict between Blacks and Whites."

Julieta's description of the racial remittances she received complicate the picture provided by her earlier comments about police brutality and the responsibility of White power structures for Black-White tensions. On the one hand, her mother had recently migrated to Wisconsin and settled in the predominantly Black neighborhood where her brother lives. When her mom told Julieta that she had a lot of Black neighbors, Julieta responded, "That's cool." According to Julieta, her mother agreed: "My mom says they greet each other, that they're very friendly, charming, talkative." However, Julieta went on to say, "I'm glad because I've also heard that they steal. They stole from my brother, Francisco. He used to live in Texas. They never caught them. He didn't want to report it 'cause, you know, [the thieves] might try to get revenge or, what do I know, burn houses down." Notably, Julieta did not explain how she knew that Black people had stolen from her brother when the thieves were never caught, and she accepted without question the racist assumptions her brother made about the possibility of escalating violence. On the other hand, she did not believe that Black people "act like racist types toward Mexicans," asserting, "On the contrary: they do what's possible to live better. It's cost them a lot of struggle to be put on the same level as the other Americans, right?"

Selena also presented some contradictions. She shared the many positive things her niece, who was born in the U.S., had told her about her African American boss. "Her boss is Black, and she says he's a really nice person, that he treats her really well." Likewise, her brothers have had Black neighbors, and Selena said that they had "good luck and haven't had any problems—[Black people] are very affectionate and likeable and very sociable." Selena demonstrated recognition that stereotypes probably do not describe all Black Americans: "Imagine that, more than anything, there are Blacks who commit crimes, and, sadly, everyone assumes that they're all alike. But that's not how life works, see. There are Black Americans who are very loving, good people." Like Selena and Julieta, some non-migrants were exposed to positive stories communicated by immigrants who came into contact with Black people at work and in the neighborhood.

Other non-migrants, like Antonio, a maintenance worker in his mid-forties, expressed both credulity and skepticism about racial remittances. He returns to his hometown in Zacatecas when family members who live in Texas visit, a common practice, to see his relatives and partake of the parties and dances that are held. He said:

> [W]e get to talking, and that's where you really learn what it's like over there [in the U.S.]. I'd be lying if I told you that I've lived that situation in the U.S., 'cause I don't really know the reality of it. I'm commenting on the things I've heard and what they've told me, but I really haven't lived through it in the U.S. Truthfully, I'd like to see how they live, to know for sure, to believe what they're telling me.

The ambivalence of various respondents notwithstanding, the general consensus among Mexicans was that they would want to avoid Black people if possible. As racial schema theory holds, even when immigrants experience friendly relations with Black people, they more readily adopt negative views because anti-Black schemas so powerfully override the positive ones. The emphasis on negative stereotypes is often subconscious and reflects larger sociocultural understandings of race and difference. Although some immigrants relayed racial remittances to non-migrants about pleasant encounters with Black men and women, these experiences were either dismissed or overlooked in favor of overgeneralized stereotypes that confirmed preexisting anti-Black discourse. This explains why immigrants remitted "bad experiences" most often, exposing non-migrants to racist American ideas and thus reinforcing the transnational racialization of Blackness in the U.S.

Racializing White Americans in Mexico
Although scholars have recently shown a growing interest in studying Mexican racial attitudes (Telles et al. 2014), research on Mexican perceptions of White Americans remains limited. However, Mexicans have long and complicated relations with White Americans not only as immigrants navigating the U.S. racial system but also in social interactions with White Americans who travel to Mexico. Research on racial attitudes has primarily focused on social contact theories suggesting that greater contact with the out-group can foster one of two outcomes: a sense of familiarity and trust or tension and conflict (Oliver and Wong 2003). In a recent study of Latino immigration to the U.S. South, immigrants expressed an openness to forming friendships with both White and Black locals (Ocampo and Flippen 2021). However, those who reported social contact with the groups said they found interactions with White Americans alienating, while contact with Black Americans led to more favorable views of the group. Put differently, the more contact immigrants had with White Americans, the more likely they were to express negative perceptions of them, presumably because they felt that White people were unwelcoming (Ocampo and Flippen

2021). Given that very few of the non-migrants I interviewed had regular and meaningful interactions with White Americans, this survey might suggest I would find favorable views of Whites. But in fact, my interviews show that non-migrants in Mexico had even more ambivalent feelings toward White Americans than the research finds for U.S. immigrants. Although non-migrants generally described White Americans as kind and benevolent, they also viewed them as arrogant and self-serving. Others described White people as openly hostile, violent, and racist toward immigrants and African Americans alike.

Racial remittances do not fully explain Mexican non-migrants' ambivalence toward White Americans, as they generally felt far more positive about White people than about Black Americans. Whereas non-migrants seemed to rely primarily on media stereotypes when speaking about Black Americans, media portrayals did not seem to play an important role in their impressions of White people. Instead, non-migrants zeroed in on one type of story among immigrants' racial remittances. When I asked non-migrants to share what they knew about how White Americans and Mexican immigrants get along, they almost always responded with anecdotes based on immigrants' experiences with White bosses at work.

Work life is an important part of the Mexican immigrant experience in the U.S., and immigrants often share stories about matters at work, including relationships with White employers or co-workers. "White Americans like Mexicans as workers but not as friends," explained Gaby, a homemaker in her fifties whose brother migrated to the U.S. five years ago. "My brother knew an American lady, and he would tell us that there is everything. There's [White] Americans who are good and others who are tough . . . they don't want to have races from other parts of the world." She concluded,

"All I know is that they do like Mexicans, but they also don't. They like Mexicans to work for them over there in the U.S. but not to interact with them. Because if they did like Mexicans, they would give them more support, more opportunities to do well." Gaby's comment reflects an understanding about the ways White people's "benevolence" toward immigrants can sometimes uphold the unequal and exploitative power dynamic between the groups.

There were non-migrants who openly praised White Americans, typically in reference to immigrants' experiences with a boss they described as great, nice, helpful, supportive, and all-around benevolent. Selena had heard from her brother in the U.S. that "gringo" bosses are great. She said, "Some Whites treat people very well. I've heard from my brothers who have worked with gringos, and they've been treated great, they've never been done wrong, never treated badly. I mean, my brothers have worked with good people over there; they're American, and they're good people. I can't say anything bad because what I've heard . . . that [immigrants] who have worked with gringo bosses, that they're really nice people." Similarly, Sophia's sister-in-law, Eugenia, once told Sophia that her boss, a White woman, is very supportive because she has allowed her to live in her home rent-free for nearly fifteen years. Sophia admitted to me that Eugenia would have been worse off if it hadn't been for her boss's help but noted that her sister-in-law was also very vulnerable as an undocumented worker and never felt as if she could voice her opinions. In another example, Irma told me her aunt had a White neighbor whom she described as "one of the few who help out the illegal ones, especially by hiding them during immigration raids so they don't get taken away."

In sharp contrast to the "benevolent American" narrative, some non-migrants perceived White Americans as openly racist and hostile. Indeed, the same Hollywood stereotypes that exposed non-migrants to anti-Black images and discourses also exposed respondents to the atrocities of slavery, Jim Crow segregation, and other forms of White racial violence. Some respondents told me they had watched American movies about slavery or the Civil Rights Movement that hearkened back to the era of the lynching of young Black men, such as Emmett Till, who in 1955 was terrorized and killed after a White woman accused the teenager of flirting with her in a grocery store. For Estela, a thirty-year-old administrative assistant, these racial remittances influenced her perceptions of White Americans as racist and threatening: "I know that Blacks used to be slaves and treated badly. . . . I know that . . . Whites [more than other groups] will do something to you just because you're Black. It has always seemed that way to me. I think it's because Whites feel like they're better than Blacks and can get away with anything."

American Tourists and Retirees in Mexico

Another way that U.S. racial ideas cross the border into Mexico is via American tourists and retirees. As the second-largest city in Mexico, Guadalajara is a major tourist destination for North Americans. Indeed, it is common to see leisure activities in which most people taking part are White Americans, including retirees living in Chapala, a large lake located on the outskirts of Guadalajara. However, non-migrants generally did not have personal encounters with them.

Irma is an exception. She works in a hotel restaurant that caters to foreign tourists, and she said: "I always felt that gringos are conceited, that they feel they are superior to a Mexican or a Black or Chinese or Japanese person." Anna-Maria and others based their perceptions of White Americans not on personal encounters but rather from observing them in tourist areas. "I think that, just by looking at them, I feel like they're racist. Because they look at you as if you're beneath them. That's how I feel. I mean, I may be wrong, but that's how I see it," Anna-Maria said.

Indeed, the apparent wealth of White American tourists, who stay in the best luxury resorts and hotels, aligns with popular depictions of White wealth and status in Hollywood films. Similar to Anna-Maria, Victor formed his opinion of White Americans from the tourists he sees in Guadalajara. "I hear that the United States is one of the most powerful countries, right? And Whites—well, all you see on TV is that the people in power are all White. . . . I see the tourists who come to *el centro* [downtown], and they stay in the most expensive hotels, and I think they have money and live well," he said. Eduardo echoed Victor's opinion, seeing White American tourists as proof that the United States subsidizes White people's lifestyle: "Americans are capitalistic people who like to be the boss but not do the work. . . . I think they receive a lot of government benefits. The proof is in their vacations [to Mexico]. They come to enjoy themselves with all the benefits they have."

Mario's experiences of American tourists were likewise negative:

When American tourists come here [to Mexico], you can see how they sometimes try to humiliate us Mexicans and the Mexicans over there [in the U.S.] too. I've heard tourists say things like "Mexico is dirty . . ." They want to humiliate us.

Another factor affecting Mario's impressions of White Americans was his experiences with the American consulate. As he explained:

It's the same with the American Consulate: they don't wanna give visas for us to go to their country. They denied me a visa because they saw my wife was pregnant and thought we

97

wanted to have our baby over there to get American citizenship, but it wasn't like that. I have my own house [here in Guadalajara] and everything. They think just 'cause we're Mexican we don't have money. They discriminate. They're hard on people from other races, aren't they?

Mario's experiences reveal that the racial subordination that Mexicans are subjected to in the U.S. can sometimes replicate itself in the Mexican context and powerfully shape how non-migrants perceive—and perhaps interact with—White Americans.

Antonio, who returns to Zacatecas periodically to see visiting relatives from Texas, described his impressions of an African American who visited from the U.S. along with his immigrant friend. He said: "I met a Black guy who came to my barrio. He was my buddy's friend, and they came to hang out with us and drink some tequila and stuff. My buddy was translating for us, and I asked [the Black man] if he liked the Beatles, and he said, 'I like how they play, but they're White, so fuck them!' And then he says, 'Us Black people in the U.S., we're better than Whites. Our music is better.'" I asked Antonio what he made of this, and he replied: "I was like, 'Oh, shit!' I realized quickly that the United States doesn't have good race relations."

Julieta came to see White Americans in a positive light after meeting her sister's boss, who visited Guadalajara from Wisconsin. Mari, Julieta's sister, worked in Milwaukee as a personal chef to two White American sisters. Mari had always described the sisters as easygoing. One of the sisters had a destination wedding in Guadalajara, and she paid for Mari to accompany her, to attend the wedding as a guest. Mari then invited the White American sisters to visit her family in town, where they were introduced to Julieta. "You wouldn't believe it!" exclaimed Julieta. "[Mari's boss] wanted to take my father back home with her! She was very charming, very easygoing." She added: "I've also seen Americans in Chapala, and a lot of them smile and wave at the children."

The Lasting Influence of Racial Remittances

Transnationalism is a mechanism for the extension of U.S. racial—and racist—ideologies into Mexican society. Some scholars have argued that Mexican, and Latin American immigrants more broadly, arrive in the U.S. with anti-Black racial baggage and that this baggage is simply carried over from Spanish colonialism (Hernandez 2007; McClain et al. 2006). While it is true that racial ideas indeed travel with migrants to their new places of settlement, this chapter illuminates that this racial baggage is not confined to the racial logics of the sending society. My interviews in Mexico reveal that Mexicans are savvy about U.S. racial dynamics long before they set foot in the U.S. Immigrant racial narratives, which often reflect dominant U.S. discourse on Blackness, circulate within a transnational social field to become a point of reference about Black (and White) Americans that individuals in Mexico draw on to make sense of new racial encounters at home and abroad.

In her study of Brazilian return migrants, Joseph (2015) found that Brazilians who spent time living in the U.S. largely rejected Brazilian anti-Black stereotypes in favor of more positive views of Black Americans. They saw respected African American actors, athletes, and community leaders as signals of their equal status to White Americans and generally regarded Black Americans as attractive, well-dressed, put together, and upwardly mobile—opinions that they did not share of Black people in Brazil. Lack of familiarity and contact with Black Mexicans, however, renders racial remittances particularly effective in shaping my respondents' negative perceptions of Black Americans. In our globalized world, racial ideologies flow ever more freely across geopolitical borders; this is especially the case with Mexico, a neighboring country to the U.S. that shares hundreds of miles of physical border.

The sociological literature on Latino immigration, however, has focused primarily on the consequences of migration for individuals *after they arrive* at their new destination. When I set out to explore how people in Mexico perceive U.S. race relations, I did not initially focus on the role of racial remittances. My fieldwork in Mexico, however, yields new evidence that racial remittances via global media and the stories conveyed by immigrants are a powerful force in shaping Mexicans' racial views of U.S. race relations, including White racial violence enacted toward Black Americans and undesirable immigrants at the border. There is further evidence to suggest that the global transmission of U.S. racial ideologies is transforming how Mexicans abroad—who largely uphold the notion that Mexico is free of racism—articulate anti-Mexican and anti-Black racism, albeit in the U.S. context. This is important because it suggests that U.S. immigrants arrive in the U.S. with more-nuanced interpretations of the American racial system than the existing literature suggests.

Take, for example, non-migrant Santiago, who has never traveled to the U.S. but is clearly trying to make sense of the plight of undocumented migrants by piecing together the stories he has heard from an immigrant friend.

> That guy I told you about who was out there [in the U.S.] for a good while, he told me he only worked nights at this restaurant because in the daytime *la migra* [ICE] would come by and snatch them out of there! But his boss really liked him because he's a hard worker, so he'd help him out economically. But I also think to myself, "If I had a worker—I don't

know U.S. laws, I'd be lying if I said I did—but if I had a good employee from another country, I'd make a real effort to help him fix his papers because he's working for me." I feel bad because if you're telling me your boss really liked you, why didn't he help you get legalized? Or maybe they're not allowed to do that? I'm not really sure how things work there. I'm not too familiar with that country, but I do know some things.

Here, we see how Santiago is both privy to the circumstances of his immigrant friend yet struggling to make sense of why his employer would hesitate to help his friend get legalized. Racial remittances, thus, form the basis of immigrants' racial meaning-making when they arrive in places like Los Angeles, where they are no longer mestizos who enjoy the privileges associated with Mexican citizenship and instead encounter a U.S. racial system that positions them on the lower rungs of the socioracial hierarchy.

Given the pervasiveness of anti-Black stereotypes in mass media and popular culture, it is perhaps unsurprising that Mexicans in this study cited films, television shows, and news when describing how they imagined African Americans as a group. Specifically, the media fueled non-migrants' portrayals of Black Americans as living in ghettos, prone to crime and drug use, and aggressive in nature. In contrast, far fewer non-migrants relied on media portrayals when sharing their opinions of White Americans; they relied more heavily on racial remittance exchanges of White Americans as "friends" and "benevolent" bosses to immigrants. This aligns with broader patterns of White racial privilege, in which White people are more commonly treated as individuals, and rarely are stereotypical portrayals—even atrocious acts, like school shootings—taken as representative of the group as a whole.

Racial baggage does not travel in only one direction; it is always in circulation, influencing how non-migrants view race in the U.S. prior to migration, how new immigrants interpret race in their new society and then re-remit racialized ideas back home—all the while transforming them in the process (Levitt and Nieves 2011). The next chapter reveals that the racial baggage immigrants carry over into the U.S. is not simply a reflection of Spanish colonialism in Mexico, nor are these racial ideas merely "made in the USA" in the process of adaptation to their new society. Rather, I show that these two processes interact with each other and that they are facilitated by the deeply embedded transnational lives of Mexicans on both sides of the border. Those who ultimately migrate may find themselves in a country different from what they had imagined. Far from being outsiders in a society defined by a Black-and-White color line, they encounter one of the most diverse cities in the world—which also happens to have a majority Latino population.

First Encounters with Race in *El Norte*

Patricia still remembers the day she arrived in Los Angeles, after an arduous journey from Mexico. It was after dark, and she was tired and hungry. "It was so difficult, crossing the border. We walked for hours and hours. My entire body was sore and aching for days," she said. Her cousin Lorena had picked her up near San Diego and driven her two hours back to Long Beach, where Lorena would be letting Patricia stay with her, but first they stopped at a fast food restaurant to get hamburgers. As they pulled up to the drive-through window, they noticed several young Black men brawling in the parking lot. Then suddenly they heard gunshots.

Patricia recalls, "We got scared, and Lorena said, 'Oh, God! No, no, no! Let's get out of here and just go home. We're not going anywhere tonight!'" Patricia told me she will never forget the fear she felt that night, and she acknowledged that she had avoided going out at night since that evening. "I had never seen a shooting!" As she recounted, she asked Lorena why she had brought her "to this area with all these *negros* [Black people]."

"Shut up! Don't say 'negros'! Say '*morenos*,' because here 'negros' is a bad word. They don't like it," warned Lorena.

In Mexico, the terms "negro" and "*negra*" do not always carry the same negative connotations as the terms do in the U.S. The words often refer to darker skin, and people use them to describe their own family members, sometimes even endearingly. Patricia realized that Lorena had acquired a new kind of racial knowledge from her time in Los Angeles. From that moment on, she would have to depend on Lorena's know-how in order to navigate an entirely new racial context. "I would just stay quiet and listen to everything Lorena would say," she said. Beyond instructing her on which terms were appropriate to use to discuss race in the United States, Lorena taught Patricia several lessons about life as a Mexican immigrant newcomer in multiracial urban America.

Like Patricia, many newcomers mentioned that they had never been in close proximity to Black Americans until arriving in L.A. Yet, as detailed in Chapter 2, the transnational flow of racial remittances predisposed Mexicans to hold anti-Black prejudices long before entering the U.S. When newcomers arrive to Los Angeles, they must reconcile their racial baggage with their new racial reality, thus embarking on a uniquely transnational racial journey. Immigrants' personal experiences navigating U.S. racial encounters varied. In some cases, like Patricia's, the anti-Black racial baggage they carry is triggered by traumatizing encounters in places like South L.A. involving mainly young Black men. Although a few immigrants who internalized anti-Black stereotypes closed themselves off from potentially befriending Black Americans who could defy these stereotypes, many expressed feelings of respect and a sense of commonality with Black Angelenos. Others formed budding friendships with Black neighbors. Gradually, immigrants adopted complex and nuanced understandings of how race, nationality, citizenship and class shape the U.S. racial hierarchy, a topic discussed more extensively in Chapter 4.

New arrivals who are still very much in the throes of making sense of a new and distinctly American racialized system relied on guidance from more-established immigrants to "school" them on race, a process I refer to as race brokering. Although sociological studies of immigrant incorporation have long underscored the importance of context of reception in influencing how immigrants will fare in their new society, we know less about the role of race in the initial stages of incorporation. If a central aspect of newcomers' adaptation to U.S. society is acclimating to "American" values, norms, and beliefs, then how migrants incorporate the values, norms, and beliefs around race and race relations is crucial to the immigrant experience (Nteta 2006).

This chapter illustrates how immigrants' first racial encounters, along with race brokering by more established immigrants and observations of America's hostile treatment of Mexican immigrants more broadly, impact the way new arrivals come to understand race and inequality in the U.S. I further illustrate how language barriers presented new challenges in navigating racial encounters that immigrant newcomers simply did not contend with prior to migration, and how neighborhood context and gender produce variations among newcomers in understandings of local racial hierarchies. For example, the absence of White residents in immigrant neighborhoods partially explains why the lessons imparted by race brokers featured Black Americans most prominently. Newcomers generally trusted the racial advice they received from established immigrants, regarding them as relatively knowledgeable about their adopted country's racial norms. Ultimately for Mexican immigrants, crossing the border into U.S. territory marks the end of mestizo privilege and the beginning of a distinctly American racial journey—one rife with hard lessons about living as a marginalized racial minority in an Anglo supremacist society.

These early observations of and encounters with the U.S. racial hierarchy set the tone for how immigrants navigate subsequent interactions with different racial groups and ultimately come to view their place in broader American society.

First Impressions of Race in the U.S.

America has long been associated with Whiteness, and when immigrant newcomers recall their first impressions of the U.S. racial hierarchy, they allude to the age-old system of racial segregation. Many newcomers were quick to notice that White Americans lived in much nicer neighborhoods than their Black counterparts. Elizabeth observed this glaring pattern and believes it has to do with the unequal treatment of Black people in the U.S. "It makes you think, 'Well, it's their [Black people's] country too, so they should have the same opportunities as Whites.' You wonder, 'Why do Whites [have opportunities], and why don't Blacks? I mean, what's the difference, if they're from the same country?'" Elizabeth had also noticed right away that White people were nearly nonexistent in South East L.A., where she lived after she first migrated.

Pablo is a musician who arrived in the U.S. almost twenty years ago. Prior to migrating from Mexico, Pablo had envisioned the country as a primarily "Anglo nation, yet with a sizable Black population." Traveling throughout Los Angeles with his band soon after arriving in America, Pablo quickly noticed that different neighborhoods were characterized by their racial and ethnic groups. He recalls,

> I noticed that each race had its own neighborhood.... I would ask my bandmates, "Where do all the Mexicans live?" and everyone would say, "In East Los Angeles." And "Where do Blacks live?" South Los Angeles. And "Where do the Chinese

live?" North of the city. It was then that I realized all the races live in their own areas.

Pablo had imagined he would draw racially mixed audiences to his concerts. As he said, "I thought it was going to be like Carlos Santana's concerts, where he played for all races. I quickly learned I was wrong . . . there were nothing but Latinos, my own people. . . ." Pablo's observation was a striking one. Mexican neighborhoods, known as *colonias*, are typically segregated by socioeconomic status, with elite Mexicans of various skin tones living in wealthy residential enclaves far removed from poor and working-class co-ethnics. Newcomers were shocked that American neighborhoods, in stark contrast to those of their home country, were defined by their predominant racial and ethnic groups. Pablo was especially surprised to find that Latinos in Los Angeles seemed to be among the most segregated, living mainly among other Latinos.

Indeed, newcomers quickly noticed that White people were largely absent from the places Mexican immigrants frequent. Much of this has to do with the demographic shifts in recent years in California, particularly in L.A., where Latinos have outnumbered all other racial and ethnic groups. Logan and Turner's (2013) study of Latinos in gateway cities across the United States found that those in the L.A. region are more residentially segregated than their counterparts in other cities. It did not take long for new arrivals to make note of it, saying things like, "[Whites] like to live with their own kind." They attributed this preference to White Americans' racism and general dislike of non-White people.

Immigrants to L.A. find that they are unlikely to form meaningful and intimate relationships with White Americans. Carlos articulated this in describing how he responded to a query by his mother, who still lives in Mexico: "'So what happened? Aren't you going to find a *gabachota* [White girlfriend]?' I had to explain 'No, Mom. You think that's how it is out here? If it weren't for the big buildings and the dollar, you'd feel like you were in Mexico! . . . The majority of the people here, after Whites and Blacks, well, it's us Latinos. But mostly Mexicans.'" Carlos's mother assumed that his main options for a girlfriend would be White; however, as Carlos pointed out, there were plenty of Mexicans he might date.

Joanna shared that when she migrated she expected White people to be "good-looking people, and nice." This characterization was based on her family's opinions of White Americans, much of which she had heard prior to migrating and in her early days in L.A. When I asked what opinion she had formed about White people in the three years since she arrived, she said, "There are some sweet White people, and there are also sour ones. . . . More than anything, Mexicans and Whites don't relate with one another." Race, many learned, largely determined where individuals live in the United States, and it appeared to them that White people show a strong preference for keeping to themselves.

Race in Public Places
Where migrants live and spend most of their leisure time influences how they come to see the U.S. racial hierarchy and their place within it. Los Angeles, a premier destination for immigrants from Mexico, has one of the largest concentrations of Mexicans in the nation. New arrivals tend to settle in places where earlier immigrants have already settled, creating ethnic enclaves and tapping into existing social networks (Portes and Rumbaut 2006). The presence of large and historic ethnic communities in Los Angeles facilitates migrants' transition to the host society by providing a variety of resources for and valuable information on housing and job opportunities.

Time and place, particularly the neighborhoods where immigrants land, play an important role in shaping newcomers' racial encounters (Hondagneu-Sotelo and Pastor 2021). Immigrants who arrived in South L.A. in the 1980s and 1990s faced a community that was reeling from joblessness, poverty, and a crack cocaine crisis and were thus more prone to "shut in and shut out" than their peers in majority-Latino neighborhoods (Hondagneu-Sotelo and Pastor 2021). Even in situations when social isolation is the norm, newcomers encounter people from different racial and ethnic backgrounds while doing mundane tasks such as going for a walk to the market, taking the kids to the park, or riding the bus to work.

For example, newcomers tend to rely on public transportation since many do not own a car or have a California driver's license. In fact, the vast majority of bus riders in L.A. are low-income Black and Latino residents who do not either own a car or have regular access to one (Nelson 2019). In line with others' research, I found that respondents who entered the U.S. without authorization were keenly aware of the risks associated with driving while undocumented (Gonzalez 2016; Prieto 2018). Although riding local bus routes can take twice as long as driving a car, immigrants use them to avoid being targeted by police, who might demand a driver's license, impound their vehicle, and even report them to ICE (Prieto 2018).

Carol was one of many immigrants who would regularly ride the bus from her first home in South L.A. to her job at a local manufacturing plant. After several months of taking the same route to and from work, she grew acquainted with a Black man with whom she occasionally engaged in small talk. When I asked about her initial encounters with African Americans, she recalled the man's romantic attentions:

I was single back then, and there was a Black man that liked me. He was American but spoke Spanish very well. He said he had previous girlfriends who were Latina. Every time I'd ride the bus home, I'd see him. He used to try to sit next to me and asked me out, but I didn't want to go out with him. . . . [W]hen I arrived in this country, I used to watch the news, and I'd always see Blacks being violent, so no. I was afraid to get to know him, so I didn't want to go out with a Black man.

Only a handful of immigrants told me they had personally experienced a traumatizing event involving an African American. The majority of respondents who expressed anti-Black sentiment were primarily influenced by media stereotypes, immigrant narratives of Black aggression and violence, and personal observations. Take Elizabeth, for example. The visibility of transient Angelenos on L.A. streets, at bus stops, and near storefronts reinforced the pervasive stereotype of the downtrodden urban drug addict:

I see that Blacks are the only ones in this country that don't contribute anything. The majority that I've seen are vagrants in the streets drinking beer or drugging themselves, asking the government for money. It's rare that I go to a store and see a Black person working there—it's very rare. They should do something for their country. They have the opportunity to do good, but no. They shouldn't be out in the streets.

Although narratives like those of Elizabeth's were pervasive within the Mexican immigrant community, it is important to acknowledge that these prejudicial sentiments are based on deeply embedded and long-standing stereotypes of the Black "welfare queen" and "druggie" that have been shaped within a broader social and economic context of deindustrialization, joblessness, incarceration, criminalization, and resulting poverty (Rendón 2019; Hondagneu-Sotelo and Pastor 2021).

Racial stereotypes had a powerful way of staying with immigrants, however, and often limited their social interactions with Black neighbors. Patricia has had many pleasant encounters with her Black neighbors in South L.A., but two years after the shoot-out in the parking lot of the drive-through, she remains fearful whenever she leaves her house. She explained, "I live in the middle of the block, and there are Black neighbors on both sides. Every Saturday the lady next door has a yard sale, and when she sees me she'll say, 'Come and look, I have lots of clothes.' I try to smile at her and make small talk so that I don't show them my fear. I would move out of here if I could, but I don't have any money." Immigrant newcomers' social isolation, limited English-language skills, and experiences of violence from both gangs and police have created situations in which minimal contact with African Americans appear to be the norm, even on the neighborhood block (Hondagneu-Sotelo and Pastor 2021).

An undocumented immigrant who migrated to the U.S. over twenty years ago, Elena lived in what was then majority-Black Watts for ten years before moving to a Mexican neighborhood in Southeast L.A. Indeed, most migrants could not afford White neighborhoods and instead settled in more-affordable Black and Latino communities in South L.A. or adjacent Latino enclaves. Like the majority of respondents, Elena also claims she had never seen a Black person before migrating to the U.S. She recalled that when she lived in Mexico, she rarely gave much thought to Black people, "as if they didn't exist." Elena told me she mostly kept to herself when she lived in Watts. She worked babysitting the neighbor's kids at home and would venture out only when necessary, although, lacking a washer and dryer at home, she regularly had to walk two blocks to the nearest laundromat. One summer evening, she noticed two Black women arguing in the laundromat. She did not understand English and could not make out what they were saying. "All of the sudden they started fighting [physically]," she remembered. Frightened, she ran outside, even though she had not finished her laundry. "When I first encountered Black people, they left a very bad impression on me. I tell you, Black people are very violent . . . and I don't like that. I keep my distance from them," she said. This experience occurred nearly twenty years ago, but her opinions are unchanged.

Elena's vivid memory reflects the fact that particularly negative racial encounters that uphold dominant stereotypes and resonate with preexisting racial perceptions tend to leave a strong impression (Roth 2012). Many respondents brought anti-Black ideologies from Mexico. The acts Elena and Patricia witnessed soon after moving to the United States became emblematic of Black life in urban America and powerfully shaped their desire to maintain distance from Black people even as they continued to embed themselves socially into other spheres of life in the U.S. Respondents living in South L.A. or, like Elena, who had once lived there, had more daily contact with Black people than those living in SELA, and many of them recounted similar anecdotes.

Samuel, a twenty-nine-year-old sub-director of a small manufacturing company in Guadalajara, was one of two non-migrants who had traveled to the U.S. During his three-week visit with his cousin in Sacramento, he had a racial encounter that greatly affected his impression of U.S. racial dynamics and reflects the anti-Black narratives that make their way back to Mexico:

It was five days after I got there. My cousin had told me, "Don't go out because there are lots of Blacks in the area," but I was out of cigarettes and he was at work, so I said, "Let me go to the supermarket." And as I was crossing the street, three Black guys were coming toward me and kept looking at me. . . . When I turned back, I saw they had turned around and were following me. . . . They looked like they were going to beat me up. Later, my cousin got upset with me for leaving the house, but I told him, "Well, that's part of what you have to live through in another country."

Samuel likely viewed this racial encounter through the lens of preexisting anti-Black prejudice formed prior to migrating and reinforced by his cousin's warnings to stay indoors. While it is not apparent whether the Black men he saw "following" him were in fact approaching him, let alone had hostile intent, Samuel's sentiment that the three guys "looked like they were going to beat [him] up" echoes socially entrenched, racist tropes of Black men on the street as dangerous thugs. Moreover, it merits noting that Samuel viewed these types of racial encounters as an inevitable aspect of the immigrant experience, likely as a result of prior exposure to racial remittances. Indeed, Samuel had a fiancée and other family in Guadalajara, to whom he relayed these experiences upon his return to Mexico.

Others had prior experience navigating racialized encounters back in Mexico that worked to dispel rigid stereotypes in L.A. Jacobo, who grew up in Mexico City and rode the bus regularly, remarked with pride: "Look, I'm always on the bus [in Los Angeles]. I'm the type of person who likes to communicate. I'm very sociable, and I will talk to everybody, young or old." He recalled a time a Black man on the bus asked him for money—something that might have reinforced others' anti-Black prejudices—and expressed a neutral point of view. Matter-of-factly, he said, "Those are minor, everyday things that take place in any country, not just the

United States." His premigration experience of relying on public transportation in one of the world's largest cities likely helped him interpret an interracial encounter in a neutral way. This suggests that the demographic context in the sending region is important in shaping the racial baggage of newcomers; like Jacobo, those from diverse cities may navigate racial encounters in the U.S. differently than migrants from rural regions of Mexico, where these encounters are more unlikely.

Race at Work

Some respondents' first real foray into the American race and class structure took place in the workplace or while searching for work. Although most relied on family and friends in L.A. to gain access to employment opportunities, some learned, to their surprise, of the broad cultural and ethnic diversity of the U.S. while on the job. "There are people from all over the world!" said Sergio. Commenting on his many years working in the restaurant industry in a diverse neighborhood in Pasadena, he said: "I'm gonna be very honest. I used to think that all Asian people were the same. Like, I didn't know there were Koreans, Chinese, Filipinos, Taiwanese. You think, 'OK, well, this person is Filipino, and this person is that, and this person is that.' I didn't know. But we learn when we come here [to the United States]."

Manuel is a mechanic who has lived in America for over ten years. Recalling his first years in the U.S. working at his cousin's auto shop, he said this: "Well, sometimes you're among Whites and Blacks at work, and you do get scared, worried. [People tell you things like] 'Well, *los gabachos* [Whites] are racists and *los morenos* [Blacks] are gonna rob you' or something. And you're not familiar when you first arrive."

Although his English was limited, he came into frequent contact with a variety of customers at the shop. The only things he could rely on, at least initially, were the alarming stories he had heard from other migrants about racial conflict in America. After several years living in the city, he no longer feels scared like he did in those early days.

Another thing migrants learned on the job was the relative positioning of different racial and ethnic groups along a hierarchy of wages and status. Most respondents observed that relative to other groups, Mexican immigrants held the lowest-paying and most dangerous jobs. A stay-at-home mom in Huntington Park, Chela said, "At my first job I worked in a company that made ceramic pots, but the majority of the people [working there] were Mexican men and women. . . . The only ones who weren't Mexican were Chinese, and they were the owners. There weren't any Chinese, White, or Black workers there because it was very heavy work. Dirty work." Much as sociologist Carolyn Pinedo-Turnovsky (2019) described in her ethnography of day laborers on a New York City street corner, employers racialized workers and sorted them into a labor-market hierarchy in which Mexican migrants were at the top and considered desirable because they were believed to be undocumented, desperate, and thus "hardworking" and "obedient." African American men, on the other hand, were stigmatized as "troublemakers," "lazy," and "bad workers" by employers and Mexican workers alike, who preferred to physically distance themselves from Black workers by positioning themselves on a different corner. My interviews with newcomers navigating U.S. labor-market hierarchies for the first time revealed that they, too, quickly learned that their workplaces strongly preferred hiring Mexican immigrants because employers regard them as fast and cheap labor. Newcomers also formed opinions about which racial and ethnic groups made "good" employers and which to avoid.

For example, Josue's impressions of Black people were formed after he had negative experiences working for them. He took only a few days to settle into his new life in Los Angeles before going out to look for work, and over time he came to feel that Black employers were untrustworthy. His brother told him about a known day laborer site, where he waited with other migrant workers for a paying job. One afternoon, he and another man were hired by a Black man to install new tile flooring in his Compton home. "He picked us up and took us to do the tile floor. We spent a whole week doing that work, and when we were done he didn't want to pay us." Seeing that they were not going to get their wages, he and his partner took tools and other items from the man's house as a form of compensation. Another Black employer underpaid him: "We spent four hours doing garden work for a Black man in Wilmington, and he only gave us ten dollars!" The *L.A. Times* reported that although California labor laws protect all workers against wage theft regardless of immigration status, many undocumented immigrants experience such exploitation, and those few who sue for back pay almost never recover what they are owed (Kirkham and Hsu 2015).

Josue claimed he did not have any negative opinions about African Americans prior to those experiences. He said that when he first encountered Black people in L.A. he was in awe. "It wasn't discrimination; it was curiosity about seeing someone with hair so tightly curled. You think, 'Wow, there are so many different kinds of human beings in this world.'" But after those two professional experiences, he said he no longer likes to work for Black people. Asian employers, he said, "also don't pay much, but they keep their word. What they say they're gonna pay you is what you get." He once found temporary work in a restaurant owned by a Chinese man, whom he described as strict and mean. "He would get angry if I didn't do things right, and I just didn't know how. I eventually learned [how to do the work], but now that I understand a little bit of English, I can tell you that he used to curse at me." Josue references a popular saying in Mexico—*"Me puse las pilas"* ("I got with the program")—to explain how the experience helped him adapt and feel less afraid of navigating tense racial dynamics at work.

If Josue claims to not have racial baggage, Santos makes no such claims. One of his first jobs in L.A. was in the construction business, where he worked alongside a few African American men. He came to the U.S. having heard his cousins, who lived in Los Angeles, call African Americans *"los mayates,"* a Spanish term meaning "dung beetle" and a racial slur. Santos said he did not strongly consider U.S. racial dynamics before migrating because he thought America was majority White and assumed he would not often come into contact with Black Americans. Like Josue, he was curious when he saw Black people for the first time, after he got to L.A. "I kept looking at them; it was very interesting to me [to see Black people]," he said. Perhaps noticing him staring curiously, Santos's cousin told him to stop. He should not look at Black people directly or say "mayate" because "it bothers them, and they'll get angry and insult you." Santos listened and avoided any negative interactions; however, he says, the advice "stayed with [him]" for a long time and kept him from making any real attempts to befriend Black coworkers. Santos's cousin, who is nicknamed Flaco, was acting as a race broker.

Established Immigrants and Race Brokering

Santos's cousin Flaco, like Patricia's cousin Lorena, was a seasoned immigrant with years of accumulated knowledge about the U.S. racial hierarchy. These more-established immigrants were often the first ones to welcome respondents to Los Angeles and played a pivotal role in migrants' first stages of racial incorporation. Those who weren't direct relations of the new migrants generally came from the same town in Mexico. Thus, they served as a direct link between migrants' old and new worlds. As Massey et al. note, the "social capital, emotional and cultural support, and entry into various settings that facilitate the circulation of additional information and assistance" may be even more important than providing a safe place to sleep and information about job hunting (Massey et al. 1987, cited in Hagan 1998). Migration researchers generally find that social networks have positive long-term benefits for migrants.[1] However, the racial lessons imparted by established immigrants worked to keep migrants' existing anti-Black views intact. My interviews reveal that information included significant race brokering. New arrivals were repeatedly schooled—and warned— to keep their heads down, focus on work, and avoid certain neighborhoods, street intersections, or businesses frequented by Black people and cholos (Latino gang members).

Linguists' analysis of language brokering offers a useful conceptualization of the race brokering I found. Language brokering takes place when more-experienced immigrants or their U.S.-born children translate the English language for monolingual family members who are less acculturated to the U.S. (Jones and Trickett 2005). Often, young children of immigrants fill this role when they help interpret during parents' doctor's visits or translate important documents. Language brokers may assist new arrivals in navigating the social and political system as well (Jones and Trickett 2005; Guan, Nash, and Orellana 2016; Baran 2017). Like race brokering, translating the English language—and in particular American slang—necessitates prior experience with U.S. culture.

Race brokering in the early stages of immigrant settlement involves mediating and interpreting, not merely transmitting, racial knowledge for new arrivals (Tse 1996). Established immigrants were found to shape important decisions about which places or people newcomers should avoid, and which were deemed safe to approach. For example, based on anti-Black notions that African Americans are prone to aggression and disruptive behavior, race brokers urged newcomers to keep their distance from Black people in order to avoid causing trouble that could lead to police involvement, warning that it carries the risk of detainment and deportation. However, none of the study participants referenced the potential dangers involved in getting into trouble in exclusively White neighborhoods or on the job with White employers—even though White employers have been known to report undocumented persons to immigration officials (Griffith and Gleeson 2019). There were virtually no White people living in South L.A. or South East L.A. when I interviewed Mexican immigrants for this study; therefore, they remained relatively absent from stories of neighborhood racial encounters, especially negative ones. The inability to speak fluent English and engage in meaningful conversation with monolingual English speakers also shapes newcomers' early experiences with the U.S. racial hierarchy.

Nearly all of the recent migrants I spoke with had little or no proficiency in English. They were aware that their inability to do things like read signs in English, carry on entire conversations with English speakers, or decipher the nuances of American slang profoundly shaped their experiences as new immigrants. New immigrants are constantly engaged in an ongoing process of boundary work, and language barriers help shape the perceptions of different groups, including U.S.-born Latinos. Social boundaries involve creating conceptual distinctions that can reinforce feelings of similarity and group membership or heighten a sense of difference between groups (Lamont and Molnár 2002). Social boundaries tend to differ across national contexts; thus, part of the new immigrant experiences involves contending daily with the distinctly American contours of racial and linguistic boundaries.

For example, the language barrier has often worked to solidify the social boundary between immigrants and U.S.-born groups. In some instances, it exacerbated the social distance that already existed between immigrants and African American coworkers or neighbors. Lorena's race brokering for Patricia involved this barrier. As Patricia reported, Lorena said to her, "Listen carefully: don't be talking to [Black people] because they don't speak Spanish, so be careful." The assumption that Black Americans do not speak Spanish was perhaps a racially coded justification for established immigrants to caution newcomers to avoid interacting with Black Americans. While language barriers can certainly lead to miscommunication, the warnings imparted by race brokers only added to immigrants' desire to keep their distance from Black people.

At times, migrants went to great lengths in their efforts to get by, communicating via signs, gestures, or other nonverbal cues like smiling. Other times, however, newcomers' unfamiliarity with the nuances of English meant that they were unable to recognize racial slurs when they became targets of it (Joseph 2015). Andres, a recent migrant living in Watts, recalled an incident where he felt attacked for being a Spanish-speaking immigrant. "They had free giveaways at a community center up the street, and we were making a line. There was a moreno. He was the first Black person I met who was against us [immigrants]. Everything bothered him. He spoke only English, but he would say things like 'What's up, *paisas*! Fuck paisas! Go back to Mexico!' in front of us. He would yell at us when he'd hear us speak Spanish to each other. He didn't want us to speak Spanish." Andres learned that in the U.S. "paisa" is a slang term, short for *"paisano,"* referring to Mexican immigrants from the country, akin to the offensive phrase "country bumpkin." Andres told me he felt frustrated that he could not ease the tension, both because he did not speak English and because he feared things would escalate to a physical altercation. Experiences like this one reinforced the social boundary line that immigrants drew between themselves and their Black American neighbors.

Much to the surprise of migrants, however, many Black residents of South L.A. know basic conversational Spanish and make efforts to get to know their immigrant neighbors. The constant replenishment of Latino immigrants in L.A. means that longtime Black residents have been significantly exposed to the Spanish language. Some newcomers like Erika, who does not speak any English, engaged in neighborly etiquette with Black neighbors who "speak a little bit of Spanish." She explained, "In the mornings when we see each other on the way to work, we don't speak English; it's more like 'Buenos dias!' 'Hi!' or 'Hola.' I mean, to coexist these days, I think it's easier for Blacks, Chinese, and Whites to learn Spanish than for Mexicans to learn English." I asked her how she feels about her neighbors making an effort to greet her in Spanish. "Well, I'll tell you what. When they greet me or say something in their language [English], I understand, but I just can't respond to them the way I'd like to. It makes me feel bad." The longer a respondent has lived in the U.S., the more likely it is that they have picked up some remedial English language skills, at least enough to understand what others are saying, even if they cannot respond effectively.

Still, other newcomers were pleasantly surprised to learn that they could get by just fine, relatively speaking, with Spanish only.

Prior to migrating to L.A., Isabel used to worry that her biggest challenge getting by in *el norte* would be her inability to speak English:

> If I'm going to live in the United States and if I don't speak English, what am I gonna do in order to communicate with others? I'm scared to go to school. I thought I would feel really strange because I imagined that there wouldn't be anybody who speaks Spanish. But it's the total opposite! I mean, there are so many of us Latinos from different nationalities, but you're able to communicate because there are lots of Latinos here.

Settling in an ethnic enclave has documented benefits that migrants described, such as an easier time communicating in Spanish and a sense of familiarity brought on by a plethora of ethnic grocery stores and restaurants. In Isabel's case, she realized her fear of not speaking English was quickly washed away by the dominance of Spanish-speaking Latinos in her neighborhood.

Although newcomers believed that living in majority-Latino neighborhoods brought with it many benefits, some found to their surprise that other Latinos, namely the U.S.-born children of immigrants, would look down on them—or, worse, target them as vulnerable immigrants. These interactions informed newcomers' sense of their subordinate position in the U.S. social and racial hierarchy.

Research on intra-Latino relations in Los Angeles neighborhoods has shown that immigrants can experience social distancing from more-established Latino Americans (Bedolla 2005; Huante 2021; Ochoa 2004). Alfredo Huante's (2021) study of the rapidly gentrifying barrio Boyle Heights reveals that social boundary lines in the majority-Latino community are drawn between foreign- and native-born residents. Huante contends that highly educated middle-class Mexican Americans were aligned more closely with an "honorary White" status that fostered social distancing from poor and working-class immigrants who were relegated to the bottom rungs of the local racial hierarchy. In another study of a mixed-income Latino neighborhood, Ochoa (2004) finds a continuum of conflict and solidarity among the Mexican-origin population, ranging from immigrants facing pressure from the U.S.-born to assimilate, to being viewed as co-ethnics sharing a similar culture and history of struggle against broader anti-Mexican discrimination.

Irma, whom I interviewed in Guadalajara but who had been a migrant once, remembers her time in San Diego unfavorably. Although she found a good job soon after arriving in 1989, she felt unsafe and rarely went out except to go to work. She recalls noticing almost immediately that Mexicans were looked down upon, even by those she considered fellow Mexicans. As she said, "There's people who would see you below them because you were Mexican." She had an aunt in California but lived with relatives of that aunt's because they were closer to her job. She felt that her hosts' children, who were Mexican American, treated her with disrespect. She said:

> The children felt like they were gringos, and there was discrimination [against immigrants]. They wouldn't tell you directly, but it was their comments, that they spoke English a lot. And I would tell my aunt, "Why do they talk in English if we are Mexican? We are all the same; why do they talk in English?"

Irma describes her hosts' children as "gringos" because of their clear preference for speaking English, even around a recent immigrant arrival like herself who did not understand the language. Some immigrants take this as disrespect and a sign of the inevitable Americanization of the second generation. Indeed, in her study of Latino political dynamics in the Mexican neighborhood of East L.A., Bedolla (2005) explains that some Mexican Americans stigmatize immigrants because they themselves want to avoid the stigma of illegality associated with Mexican newcomers.

On the other hand, some immigrants associated young Mexican American men with gangs and drew social boundaries between themselves and U.S. Latinos. Those living in South East L.A. told me they did not feel quite safe in their neighborhood because of local Latino gangs. Los Angeles has been labeled the "Gang Capital of America" due to its large gang population and prevalence of gang-related crimes (Harris 2007).[2] Commenting on the largely Mexican presence in South Gate, where she lived, Isabel said, "Well, I see more Mexicans than anything. And truthfully, I didn't like it when I first moved here. It's not because of the people. I don't know. I just felt like there were too many cholos, and I didn't feel safe, especially the first year." Isabel first moved to South Gate because she wanted to be closer to her mom, who lived there and had convinced Isabel to rent nearby after Isabel's husband lost his job. "I didn't really like it here, but the house was comfortable. I also didn't think it was right for the kids to keep changing schools," she offered as an explanation of why she decided to stay.

Regional context played a significant role in the type of racialized warnings migrants received about the "good" and "bad" parts of Los Angeles—which relied on stereotypes about the racial groups predominating in these spaces. In majority-Latino neighborhoods, for example, racialized warnings extended beyond Black men on street corners to other groups deemed potentially dangerous to unsuspecting newcomers, such as cholos. In fact, several recent migrants felt that cholos in their neighborhoods see them as easy targets. And indeed, members of Mexican gangs are generally U.S. citizens, while studies have shown that crime rates among undocumented immigrants are low compared with native-born groups (Light, He, and Robey 2020). As Martin put it, "They're born here, and sometimes instead of helping us out, we're against each other. When I first got here [from Mexico], I saw how they'd look at you a certain way and bother you or want to beat you up."

Lalo had been in the U.S. for less than a year when I interviewed him. He did not have family who could take him in, but other migrants involved in Victory Outreach, a Christian ministry located in downtown L.A., channeled him to a local church that runs a shelter.[3] "The church leaders explained to me, 'You know what? Don't be out late at night. Because here in East L.A., this is the barrio. The gangsters shoot at each other,'" he recalled.

In predominantly Latino immigrant neighborhoods where Black people, White people, and Asians were largely absent, cholos came to represent the dangers of inner-city life in L.A. This parallels the findings of a study by Jessica Vasquez-Tokos (2020)[4] that examines how region, including local demographics, shapes Latino racial identity. She found that Latinos from Los Angeles regions with a large and "visible Latino underclass and gang segment of the population" tended to engage in social distancing strategies from fellow Latinos whom they associated with gangs and poverty, illustrating how social distancing can be an *intra-racial* relations strategy for distinguishing oneself from stigmatized groups as much as it is an *interracial* strategy.

Interviews with Mexican newcomers revealed that local demographics was an important factor in shaping social distancing strategies among respondents. In South East L.A., where Latinos are the vast majority, newcomers made sense of the racial landscape in direct relation to other Latinos, specifically Latino gang members or those perceived as such, and others they deemed "different" from themselves.

Latino regional dominance also shaped race brokering for migrants living in SELA. When Martin arrived in Los Angeles, he stayed with his uncle, who was a long-time resident of Lynwood. "He would say, 'Be careful with the neighbors.' My uncle would point out, 'Look, that's so-and-so's son' to let me know they were the children of Mexican parents. Over there in that neighborhood, there were lots of cholos. He'd say, 'Try your best not to get on their bad side,' and I'd ask him, 'But why, *tio*? They're Mexican just like us.'" Martin's seemingly naive response to his uncle implies betrayal and even confusion at the idea of a child of Mexican immigrants posing a threat; it also implies that Martin's uncle thinks non-Mexicans *could* be a threat.

In addition to cholos, boundary lines were drawn around those of other nationalities, particularly Central Americans. I asked Sandra if she remembered her first experience with someone of a different race in the U.S. and was surprised when she described an incident involving a Guatemalan immigrant. As she said:

> The first time I had an experience meeting someone of a different race was, I think, with a Guatemalan lady. It was when I heard her talk. She started asking me questions, and honestly I couldn't understand anything she was saying. I was understanding her words, but I understood them differently because they use certain words that we use too, but with different meaning. So that was my first experience: a miscommunication.

Central Americans, mainly from El Salvador and Guatemala, make up the second-largest Latino group in L.A., rendering it highly likely that Mexican immigrants will encounter these groups in their neighborhoods and workplaces (Census 2020). For most respondents, migration to the U.S. marked the first time they engaged in lengthy interactions with people from different Latin American countries. Those living in majority-Latino neighborhoods, like Sandra, drew social boundary lines around differences based on country of origin and even accent—characteristics that are often situated differentially within a social hierarchy.

Nonetheless, new arrivals who landed in majority-Latino communities like Southeast L.A. felt more confident venturing out than those in historically Black South L.A. The presence of ethnic grocery stores and restaurants, as well as store signs in Spanish, goes a long way in making newcomers feel at home in what can be a strange new country. Something as seemingly simple as taking a walk down the main streets and encountering co-ethnics who speak the same language could provide a tremendous sense of comfort for a recent arrival who might not speak English.

New migrants face many challenges as they navigate ethnoracial dynamics between themselves; Mexican Americans; Latinos of different nationalities; and White, Black, and Asian Americans. Of course, although their understandings of race were almost always shaped in direct relation to regional context because this determined the main reference group shaping these understandings, these racial lessons were not exclusive to neighborhood settings. The racial encounters migrants experience beyond their immediate neighborhoods also determine their understanding of their status position within the U.S. racial hierarchy.

Although immigrant newcomers were typically preoccupied with surviving the daily grind of earning a living and putting food on the table, when time or money permitted, they also found respite from the hard work of acclimating to a new world by slowly branching out and expanding their social networks. Gender played a significant role in migrants' networks, such that migrant men appeared to gain more-nuanced understandings of the U.S. racial hierarchy because they ventured out more than female migrants, who tended to heed the advice of established immigrants and regularly stayed home. In some cases, venturing out beyond the influence of race brokers served to call into question and even directly challenge dominant narratives circulated by peers and the media.

For example, Walter, who has lived in a predominantly Mexican immigrant neighborhood for two years, likes to release stress after work by playing soccer in the evenings with friends at a park in South L.A. He told me most of his friends are Mexican and Central American but that participating in a soccer league has expanded his social world to include people from different racial and ethnic backgrounds. "Sometimes I interact with Black people when we're playing soccer, and we always get along well. They're nice," he said. He said he has never had a Black person discriminate against him and maintained that, in fact, both groups suffer injustices brought on by negligent politicians. Of Black Americans, he said, "They're good people, and just because four or five people are one way, it doesn't mean we should generalize to the whole group. Not all Black people are the same."

Lorenzo, who relies on an old bike to get around, heard from his race brokers that being out after ten o'clock in L.A. is to risk one's life because it could get you killed. One evening, while he was at a friend's house, he lost track of time and suddenly realized it was nearly midnight. He didn't live far, only a few blocks away, so he decided to take the short trip home, which brought him through a busy intersection. "I realized that it [what they had told me] wasn't complete lies, but there were certain things that just weren't true

. . . that you're risking your life past ten o'clock. I don't believe it anymore." Prior to this experience, Lorenzo admitted, he had been nervous about leaving the house after sundown.

Martin's resistance to the racist narrative was based on direct experience, although he had migrated to L.A. less than a year ago and never graduated high school. He said, "Well, look. When I started to socialize with Afro-Americans, they're a very educated people too, and they're good people just like us Mexicans, and that's the total opposite of what people say about them—that they're bad people." He lived briefly in a Black neighborhood, and he said, "I liked it because they're very sociable and polite. Very joyful. Every time I'd see a Black person, I would chat with them, even though I speak really bad English, but they understand a few things I say, and they greet me and I greet them."

A majority of the people who had reversed their views of Black Angelenos were men, and others' research suggests this may reflect a broader pattern. In her study of undocumented Mayan migrants in Houston, Texas, sociologist Jacqueline Hagan (1998) shows that social relations in workplaces and neighborhoods create different network structures for newly arriving men and women. She points out that this leads to different opportunities, such as the ability to find good jobs and attain legal status. Ultimately, gendered network structures differentially affect the incorporation experiences of migrant men and women. Hagan (1998) explains:

> Newcomer men often have access to more extensive and well-established male networks in the neighborhood and workplaces that create more opportunities to forge links with non-ethnic neighbors and coworkers and are exposed to more wide ranging information from the weak ties they generate through their more extensive networks.

The majority of the men I interviewed appeared to engage in more-varied networks and information flows through their involvement in gendered recreational activities like soccer leagues and a night out at the cantina. Men tend to be socialized to face their fears and explore their surroundings, all of which might help explain their greater willingness to go against some of the warnings by established immigrants to avoid being out late at night or crossing into certain neighborhoods. On the other hand, immigrant women appeared to be more protected by their families. These gendered protections included clear expectations that women be home before dark, as well as explicit warnings to stay clear of Black male suitors, perceived to be a sexual threat, making the women I spoke to less likely to seek out cross-racial interactions, at least initially.

Conflict-Minimizing Strategies

Migrants acquired new strategies for defusing potential racial conflict that were unique to the U.S. context. Isabel likes to go shopping in an affordable fashion district located in downtown L.A. known as *"Los Callejones"* for the alleyways that run through the various districts in the area. In many ways, Los Callejones is a microcosm of multiethnic America. Immigrant merchants hail from many different parts of the world, including Armenia, Korea, China, India, Latin America, and Iran. Customers tend to be working-class Latino immigrants, but Isabel regularly saw people from other groups. As she said,

> I've been to areas like downtown L.A., and I'm not afraid. I don't feel like Black people are gonna do something unless you disrespect them or something. But I do notice sometimes

that they can be aggressive. For example, if you keep looking at them, they're gonna think you're criticizing them. That's when I feel like they wanna fight you. But if you laugh and say hi, then they won't feel so uncomfortable that a Latina like me was looking at them, right? If I was in a place with lots of Blacks, I'd try to make them feel good and make myself feel fine too so they could gain my trust, and then maybe we could start to communicate with one another. If I see Black people, I smile so they know I'm cool with them, but I wouldn't be afraid. . . . I would actually do that with anybody I don't know, to start a friendship. If I see something I don't like or they bother me, well, then I just stay quiet. *Calladita te ves mas bonita* ["You are prettier when quiet"].

Mateo expressed similar feelings. He lives in Watts. However, he recalled:

One day we were making a line because they were giving away free things, a razor and stuff like that. It was me and my friend, and he said, "Go get in front of the line." There was a Black guy standing in line, and he said, "Hey, what is up with you?" He told me that those things were only for them. "Only Black people" and shit like that. 'Cause the majority were Black. But I kind of ignored him. Why get involved in the controversy? I was better off staying silent.

Several participants described staying silent and projecting a cheerful demeanor to elicit positive interactions as strategies to navigate unfamiliar racial territory. And in fact participants generally felt, in line with others' qualitative research, that cross-racial and ethnic interactions are characterized by civility and that their strategies to minimize tension and conflict were effective (Rios and Martinez 2014; Rosas 2019).

However, I did not find that close proximity to Black Americans generally established cross-racial familiarity or trust among the newest arrivals. Research on racial attitudes among Latino immigrants has been mixed, showing that social contact in neighborhoods or at worksites can either improve racial attitudes toward Black people (Oliver and Wong 2003; Roth and Kim 2013) or lead to perceptions of competition (Jones-Correa 2013; Ribas 2016). Immigrants' attitudes toward White Americans are also shaped by the extent of social contact, such that having White neighbors and friends has been associated with greater feelings of closeness to White people than Black people (Britton 2014; Marrow 2009) or, conversely, with more negative views of the group (Ocampo and Flippen 2021). In the largely segregated suburbs of Los Angeles, however, White people are socially, economically, and residentially removed from the central areas where migrant newcomers coexist and form community. In light of the apparent social boundary with White Americans, and migrants' closer residential proximity to Black Americans, we might expect Mexicans to express warmer feelings toward the latter than the former. But this was not the case.

A number of factors influenced respondents' views that interactions with Black Americans are more rife with tension and conflict than with White Americans. Many newcomers carried over anti-Black racial baggage from Mexico. Their preexisting views were then reinforced by the racial brokering they received from trusted networks upon arrival to the U.S. In addition to preconceived notions rooted in global anti-Black ideologies, personal observations and experiences leading to tense racial encounters, especially in the earliest stages of settlement, reinforced migrants' racial attitudes. To get by, many quickly adapted to a range of conflict-minimizing strategies—primarily to avoid potential conflict with Black Americans. At the same time, the absence of social contact with White neighbors and friends kept premigration attitudes about White Americans (as either benevolent or hostile toward immigrants) largely intact.

In terms of gender, findings reveal a general pattern of anti-Black sentiment held by male and female immigrants alike. Although past research indicates that immigrant *women* hold more negative attitudes toward African Americans than immigrant men do (Mindiola, Niemann, and Rodríguez 2002), anti-Black narratives were quite pervasive among male and female respondents living in different neighborhoods. Notably, immigrants made no real distinction between men and women in what they described as Black aggression or boisterous behavior. This points to the power of U.S. hegemonic racist ideology and imagery of Black Americans that inculcates widespread phobia and disdain of Blackness.

Adapting to a New Racial System

Upon setting foot on U.S. soil, immigrants encounter a distinct North American racial system that is markedly different from the Mexican racial context. The Mexicans featured in this chapter journeyed north with little money and big dreams of earning their rightful place in the land of opportunity. The cost of economic opportunity, however, includes a harsh incorporation process for certain groups. When arriving in Los Angeles, my respondents found that their Mexicanness instantly cast them as outsiders relegated to the bottom rungs of the racial hierarchy, imposing on them a newly subordinated status they did not contend with in Mexico. There, class status and skin color—not race, language, and legal status—are the most visible markers of marginality. Immigrants see Indigenous people as being on the bottom rungs of Mexican society, and now they undergo a racialized transition that situates them as alien and inferior. As the stories in this chapter reveal, the racial encounters new migrants face in the U.S. represent a clear and profound departure from how they experience race in Mexico.

Life for Mexican newcomers in Los Angeles is rife with challenges, and those who live in the most densely populated and impoverished parts of the city face more. While most respondents maintained civility with neighbors across race and ethnic lines, racial and intra-ethnic encounters in these immigrant neighborhoods could be unpredictable. At worst, navigating racial boundaries involves social interactions that are fraught with tension and conflict due to language barriers and other miscommunications. At best, it means ordinary and pleasant cross-racial and ethnic interactions, and perhaps a budding neighborly relationship, all of which are also structured by local regional dynamics and gender.

Race brokering by more seasoned immigrants who "school" newcomers on race, however, hinders the potential for forming friendly relations with Black neighbors and coworkers, and fosters social distancing from U.S.-born Latinos taken for cholos. This highlights a dimension past research has not addressed, even as it underscores that migration is a network-driven process in which those who migrated previously play a crucial role in guiding new arrivals. As we can see from respondents' stories, race brokers powerfully influence how newcomers make sense of their local environment in the early stages of adaptation to U.S. society. Recent arrivals quickly learn to dispel the myth of America as the land of opportunity as they encounter pervasive anti-immigrant prejudice from Americans of all racial and ethnic backgrounds, including U.S.-born Latinos.

Mostly, however, encountering a new racial system involves learning and engaging in strategies to avoid unwanted attention that could cause trouble—such as keeping to oneself, remaining quiet, or expressing superficial niceties. Other factors that differentially shape how migrants learn about race has to do with their personal experiences with racialization, geographic region and neighborhood context, including local demographics, the structural conditions in the places they settle, and, as I argue in the next chapter, the common association of Mexicans with illegality.

By considering the experiences of the newest arrivals from Mexico, we can see that how new immigrants view the role of race in the process of becoming "American" involves much more than social interactions with racialized "others." Indeed, immigrants' experiences with race in America are intricately linked to the racialization of their presumed illegality (Golash-Boza and Hondagneu-Sotelo 2013). The social, political, and economic effects of legal status—and the stigma surrounding it—are most pronounced for poor and working-class men and women like those in my study (Golash-Boza and Hondagneu-Sotelo 2013). As discussed in the next chapter, recent migrants quite literally become racialized as "illegal" overnight. The threat of having *la migra* (ICE) called on you is unfortunately central to newcomers' integration into the U.S. racial system. I argue, then, that this uniquely American brand of anti-immigrant racism powerfully shapes how Mexican immigrants come to see their place in the U.S. socioracial hierarchy, even after decades of experience living in the U.S.

CHAPTER 4

Settling In

Illegality and the U.S. Color Line

CARLA AND I MET in her home. At the time of the interview, she was in her late fifties and had been living in the Watts neighborhood of South L.A. for twenty-two years. Her husband, Juan, had been an aspiring musician when he migrated to the U.S. He lived in California for several years and bought their home before sending for her and their three kids in Mexico City. Watts was what they could afford, but violent crime was a common occurrence when they first came, at the height of the crack epidemic. Carla recalled:

> There used to be lots of shootings, and we always had to get down on the floor. If you came home at 8:00 or 9:00 p.m., you had to make sure your car headlights were off so you wouldn't shine a light on anyone who might be hiding [from enemy gangs]. Sometimes they'd point a gun at you and tell you to turn off your porch light. It was very dangerous, very dangerous in those times.

The family of five was one of two Latino families on an all-Black street at that time. They had not experienced such violence in Mexico.

Carla's story is reminiscent of those María Rendón (2019) documents in her study of immigrant incorporation in Los Angeles's inner-city communities. Violence and fear in L.A. during the 1980s and 1990s reinforced negative stereotypes of Black communities as hotbeds of drug use and violence carried over from Mexico.

Carla said things have changed:

> What you see now is nothing compared to before. Some people are scared to even walk down the street, but thank God I'm not afraid. Sometimes you see crowds of, like, fifty Blacks out front, but I like it because they know that I live here and they watch out for me. If someone they don't recognize comes by, they let me know right away. They call me "mama." I've lived on this block since I got here [from Mexico], and I have my little store [in a back room of the house] where I sell candy and everything [to neighborhood kids]. They have a lot of affection for me, and I do too because I've known them since they were kids. So I'm not afraid, but most of the new [Latinos on the block] are really scared of them.

Carla sees herself as a proud Watts resident who has earned her status as an old-timer on the block. She has built long-lasting relationships with her Black neighbors and was the first person from the Latino community to join her local neighborhood watch.

Carla's greatest source of unhappiness seems to be her concerns about her eldest daughter's legal status. Carla and Juan have naturalized, and their two younger children have as well. But for reasons Carla did not explain, their daughter Cindy has been unable to, and not for lack of trying. Carla said sadly:

> [Cindy] has been here over twenty years, and they haven't given her papers. . . . I feel bad for her, poor thing. She studied

[in the United States] and did everything here. She won a [college] scholarship, but they didn't give it to her because she doesn't have papers. She's suffering, putting up with a bad job with low pay. It's horrible, just horrible. She's been at that job for eighteen years and does the same work as when she first started. We all have papers except her. That's what brings me sadness, my poor daughter.

The stories presented in this chapter reflect the experiences of established immigrants, such as Carla, who have lived in the U.S. for ten or more years. In contrast to the recent arrivals featured in the previous chapter, who held precarious employment or were in search of work and still in the throes of the initial shock of settling into urban America, many established immigrants I interviewed had relatively stable housing, income, and social networks, including adult children who were U.S. citizens. Some arrived in the 1970s and 1980s and, unlike recent arrivals, have witnessed significant U.S. social, political, and economic transformation, including the 1994 L.A. unrest and significant racial turnover in their communities. Although none of the established immigrants had a college education, several, like Carla, were homeowners because they or their spouses had arrived in Los Angeles prior to the 1980s, at a time when stable union jobs were plentiful.

Carla's daughter Cindy is experiencing what scholars have identified as the "legal liminality" that immigrants experience when they migrate to a new country, which includes but is not limited to living with an undocumented status (Gonzalez 2016, 9). The liminal stage follows a period of separation from their previous way of life and precedes full incorporation, which typically comes through citizenship and financial stability. It is an in-between legal state, and my interviews suggest that Carla's daughter is not unusual in remaining stuck in the second liminal stage, even after a long period in the United States. A number of Mexicans I interviewed in L.A. continue to experience uncertainty and instability in employment, housing, and general well-being—whether personally or due to a family member's status.

Despite their lengthy residence in the U.S. (sometimes three or four decades), nearly half of the established immigrants I interviewed remained undocumented. Sixteen out of thirty respondents were legally authorized to be in the U.S. They ranged in status from permanent residency to naturalized citizenship; the other fourteen were undocumented. Of the respondents with legal status, some were beneficiaries of the 1986 Immigration Reform and Control Act (IRCA), which granted amnesty to millions of undocumented immigrants. Others gained legal status through a family member or spouse. Overall, as might be expected, established immigrants had significantly more experience navigating U.S. institutions and workplaces than their newer counterparts, and they had gained noticeable familiarity with, and in some cases greater ease with, U.S. social customs and racial norms.

Utilizing a transnational lens to examine how Mexican immigrants are adapting to the U.S. racial hierarchy as first-time racial minorities, this chapter uncovers the ways in which established immigrants come to make sense of the U.S. racialized stratification system, one shaped by White-Anglo supremacist ideology and draconian immigration laws that positions Mexicans as racially and legally inferior. Specifically, I use a relational formation of race framework to examine how this racialization affects how established immigrants position themselves in the U.S. socioracial hierarchy in relation to other subordinated groups like African

Americans and U.S.-born Latinos. A relational framework treats racialization as a dynamic and interactive process whereby "group-based racial constructions are formed in relation not only to whiteness but also to other devalued and marginalized groups" (Molina, HoSang, and Gutierrez 2019, 2). Whereas past research has examined how subordinated groups relate to White people, exploring relationships between subordinated groups provides new insights into how immigrant newcomers navigate multiracial and ethnic spaces and view the role of race in the process of becoming "American."

My interviews reveal that illegality—both as a political status and racializing discourse—remains central to immigrants' understanding of the American opportunity structure and racial hierarchy, even for immigrants who have gained citizenship and upward economic mobility. I show that the main social boundary informing where Mexican immigrants position themselves relative to American-born groups is rooted in a foreigner-citizen demarcation that positions citizens as ideally situated to make claims for rights and resources that are increasingly out of immigrants' reach. Whether citizen advantage really accrues to people considered non-White or not, perceptions of such advantage powerfully shape where immigrants position themselves in the U.S. socioracial hierarchy.

Whereas some scholars argue that Latino immigrants construct symbolic boundaries with Black Americans—namely by identifying as "White"—in efforts to disassociate from a "stigmatized minority status and as protection against the type of discrimination faced by Blacks in the U.S." (Frank, Akresh, and Lu 2010), others suggest that they will align themselves with African Americans and ultimately reject Whiteness (Jones 2019). Yet, few have examined how social exclusion and illegality—regardless of actual legal status—is shaping how Mexican immigrants view their position in the U.S. socioracial hierarchy relative to other racialized groups.

My transnational study offers evidence that prior to coming to the U.S., Mexican mestizos give little thought to issues of illegality and citizenship in their own lives. In much the same way that Latino pan-ethnic identity is a U.S. social construction (Mora 2014; Suárez-Orozco and Páez 2002), so too is Mexican illegality "made in the USA." Crossing the Mexico-U.S. border into the U.S., then, marks the pivotal moment in which Mexicans become seen and treated as "illegal" inferiors. While Afro-Mexicans, Indigenous people, and other racialized groups are treated as second-class citizens relegated to the margins of Mexicanness, mestizos in Mexico enjoy the privilege of citizenship and a strong sense of national belonging. This relative privilege, however, is stripped away after they set foot in the U.S.

As sociologist Roberto Gonzalez (2016, 179) observes, the stigmatizing mark of illegality is the most consequential feature of immigrants' lives in the U.S. For undocumented immigrants in particular, illegality is a *master status* that dominates all other statuses. Gonzalez (2016, 15) cites sociologist Everett Hughes, who observed in the United States in 1945 that certain labels or traits, such as lacking documentation, carry stigma and thus "play a key role in ranking social position and shaping access." The literature on immigrant incorporation in the U.S. addresses how immigrants experience illegality in their day-to-day lives and, to a lesser extent, how race shapes this process. When viewed through a transnational lens, it is clear the racialization of the "illegal" immigrant is a distinctly U.S. brand of racialization that, although nonexistent in understandings of inequality in the sending society, features prominently in the transnational racial journey of immigrants—even those who have lived in the U.S. for several decades.

Experiences with Discrimination

I conducted my interviews in 2012, during Obama's presidency. While never as vocally anti-immigrant as the administration that followed it, the Obama administration had for five years been deporting unprecedented numbers of undocumented immigrants. Of the more than two million people deported between 2007 and 2012, over 90 percent were of Latino descent.[1]

Much like newer immigrant arrivals, the established immigrants I spoke with highlighted varied experiences with discrimination, ranging from differential treatment based on linguistic differences and anti-immigrant harassment by authorities to anti-Mexican racism, including a general sense that "Americans" dislike Mexicans. Some contrasted U.S. racism with glorified depictions of greater racial equality in Mexico. For instance, Judith, a thirty-four-year-old immigrant with fourteen years in the U.S., said:

> There was no discrimination [in Mexico] of the kind you see here. The majority of people [in Mexico] are the same race, so there is no racism. . . . In this country, you do see discrimination against the Mexican immigrant. I have seen that racism here. . . . In this country, a majority of the time you see more racism from *gabachos* [White Americans]. . . . It's why *el moreno* [a Black person] is also very discriminated against in this country.

Marcos, a sixty-five-year-old naturalized citizen living in Watts, had been quite surprised by U.S. racism when he migrated two decades earlier. Prior to immigration, he had imagined the U.S. as a beautiful country where "everyone is equal. . . . Then you come here and realize that there is racism. They didn't like us. They still don't like us," he said. I asked him who "they" were. "*Los Americanos*. Not all of them, but the majority," he replied. Later in the interview, I asked him directly about his opinion of White Americans. He alluded to Joe Arpaio, the Maricopa County sheriff and White Republican infamous for his unlawful and discriminatory police misconduct against Mexican immigrants.[2] "That's pure racism, what's going on in Arizona. Mexicans come to work wherever they can find [jobs]. But when they're apprehended, it's a [White] American deputy every time, right? So that's where you see the racism," explained Marcos.

Immigrants like Marcos were acutely attuned to the fact that America values them for their labor yet devalues their rights and claim to belonging.

Similarly, Olga, who has been in the U.S. for twenty-eight years and is undocumented, summarized her experiences of a hostile U.S. reception: "Well, I come here and this isn't my country, so they look at you like 'What are you doing here? Go back to your country because you're just another mouth to feed, you've come to take what's ours.' That's how I see it. . . . It comes from people who have more money than you, or citizenship—people who are from here." Like Olga, several established immigrants had accrued numerous reminders over the years of their outsider and subordinate racial and legal status. Sometimes it was an overtly xenophobic slur like "wetback" or "illegal" being hurled at them by White and Black Americans alike. Others described more subtle yet unmistakable racist incidents, like being stopped and questioned by police for looking "out of place" in a rich White residential area after dark.

Although most immigrants acknowledged discrimination and racism more broadly, some either told me they have never personally been discriminated against or played down the significance of personal experiences that some may consider discriminatory.

The literature on Latino experiences with discrimination suggests that those with more experience navigating White spaces, such as middle-class professionals in white-collar jobs, report more discrimination than Latinos who enter these spaces less regularly (Feagin 2013). Immigrants with more time in the U.S. and greater English fluency may similarly have more opportunity for cross-racial experiences and therefore report more discrimination than newer arrivals (Roth 2012; Dowling 2014). However, even long-term immigrants who live in segregated communities and spend their time mostly among other Latinos may report less discrimination simply because they have few interactions with other groups. This may help explain why some Mexican immigrants, for example, report more discrimination from other Mexicans than from White or Black Americans. At the same time, immigrants may operate with a cognitive framing of America as a merit-based society—where discrimination does not impede social mobility—because it helps justify the unspeakable sacrifices immigrants endure in search of a better life in the U.S. Another reason Mexican immigrants might not report discrimination is that, as discussed in Chapter 2, they arrive with some knowledge of U.S. racist practices (Zamora 2016). In this case, immigrants might have low expectations of how "Americans" will treat them; therefore, they do not readily identify discrimination when they experience it (Dowling 2014, 87)—although this might be changing.

Among respondents who did report some form of discrimination, the workplace was seen as a key site. "Immigrants come here to work, more than anything, and that's where the injustice takes place," said Lorenzo, an undocumented immigrant with fourteen years in the U.S. "The boss pays whatever they want, and sometimes they don't even pay the wages, and if one keeps demanding their wage, they threaten to call *la migra* [ICE]." I asked what he and other migrants might do in this situation. He spoke softly, as if ashamed: "We're the ones that have the most to lose. So, we keep quiet." Increasingly draconian immigration laws have subjected many undocumented U.S. immigrants to a life "in the shadows" characterized by fears of being "found out" and apprehended—or, worse yet, deported and separated from family (Abrego and Menjívar 2011). Many undocumented immigrants fear speaking out when they are exploited in the workplace, and employers are well aware of their concerns. Most established immigrants I spoke to had, at some point in time, worked a job in the U.S. that was hazardous to their health, physically strenuous, or low-paying, or one that exposed them to verbal abuse from supervisors.

Although men and women alike recounted experiences of mistreatment on the job, undocumented men were more likely to say they had experienced harassment in public while working or in search of work. This is due to the racialized and gendered labor hierarchy. Both men and women held the most backbreaking and isolating jobs in the U.S. economy. But women often worked jobs, such as housekeeping and childcare, that required them to labor in private homes and outside the public eye. Men were often day laborers, which frequently meant searching for work in highly visible locations. In between jobs and looking to earn extra money, Josue, a legal resident with eleven years in the U.S., would spend his days alongside other day laborers in the parking lot of a Home Depot in Commerce, a majority-Latino neighborhood. One day, he said, he was harassed by a security guard.

> I was in Home Depot . . . and there was a security guard. He looked White, but I'm not sure if he was gringo. We were outside in the parking lot, you know, looking for work, and he walked over and tried to kick us out. I was eating and didn't

hear him, so he walks right up to me and yells at me to leave. I
stood up for myself, and it pissed him off so much that he tried
to handcuff me, so I ran. He caught up to me and called the
cops. They arrested me, and I spent an entire day locked up
and got fined $300.

Migrants are easy targets for security guards and police in
public spaces, and day laborers may spend long hours waiting for
work. Day-laborer hiring sites are commonly associated with undocumented status, and it is common for police to racially profile
Latino men in such areas (Herrera 2016). In his study of an Oakland day-laborer site, Juan Herrera found that federal immigration
officials targeted certain places they read as "illegal" and associated all Latinos in that given space with illegality. In fact, Home
Depot security guards have been accused of violence and of threatening to call immigration authorities to obtain compliance from
day laborers. This made headlines as recently as 2018, when, describing mistreatment by security guards, day laborers called on
Home Depot to end its contract with a particular security company that operated in certain stores. Although the City of Los Angeles now requires Home Depot stores to include a designated site
for day laborers in its parking lots and to thus not allow security
guards to harass workers waiting for jobs, the targeting of Latino
men at these sites continues.

Gender differences accounted for some of the variation in long-
term immigrants' experiences with discrimination in ways similar to the recent arrivals discussed in Chapter 3. Many immigrant
women in this study were expected to fulfill traditional family re-
sponsibilities. Even those who fully participated in the labor market spent most of their free time caring for children, keeping up
with medical appointments, cooking, cleaning the house, running

errands, or looking in on extended family members in need of care. These spaces did not subject them to the same level of public harassment by authorities that men experienced. However, schools, health-care facilities, and other neighborhood institutions were sometimes sites of discriminatory treatment that they interpreted as rooted in their Mexican and immigrant status.

White-majority neighborhoods were also spaces of threat. Very few immigrants generally ventured into wealthy White neighborhoods like Santa Monica and Beverly Hills, and those who did felt unwelcome. Rodrigo recalled:

> One time, I was at the Santa Monica Pier, just looking at the stuff vendors were selling, and it's really crowded and you have to keep walking along the boardwalk. Back then, I wore my hair long, and, well, I was distracted window-shopping and was heading toward a White lady. And I don't know what it was—maybe my looks?—and she got scared and clutched her purse and ran the other way. I don't know what kind of experiences she's had, maybe with someone who looked like me, but that made me feel really bad.

In addition to particular locations, linguistic differences shape migrants' perceptions of discrimination. Carol has lived in the U.S. over twenty-two years. She migrated at the age of twenty-five. She doesn't speak English and is undocumented. She told me she never experienced discrimination in Mexico but affirmed she had generally experienced discrimination in the U.S. because of her lack of English language proficiency. As she said, "you're treated worse" if you don't speak English. She recalled her experiences with a state agent when she needed to cancel her husband's business license after the Great Recession led him to close his cleaning business. "The person who attended me was [White] American and didn't speak Spanish. She got really frustrated with me because, well, I understand English but don't speak it. The very first thing she said to me was 'Don't you know that in this country we speak English, not Spanish?' . . . To me, that was discrimination. I felt so small."

Marcos also recounted an experience of discrimination based on English proficiency shortly after he arrived in the U.S., when he didn't speak any English. He found a job as a gardener. His manager was a French man who would constantly scold him and the other Mexican gardeners because they didn't understand him. "He would yell at me. It felt like he was going to hit us. He did this for many years. Once I fixed my [immigration] papers and joined the union, I told them that he was discriminating against me. The union talked to him and said that if I don't understand English, he has to provide an interpreter or else it's discrimination. He calmed down after that." For Marcos, legal status that allowed him to join the union, where he could file a formal complaint, coincided with his increasing English skills. He said over the years it gave him the confidence to stand up for himself. "Now if I go someplace and they don't speak Spanish," he asserted, "I don't just stand there. I make sure they understand me, even in my broken English."

For some established immigrants, other Mexicans (both U.S.-born and immigrant) might be a source of discrimination because of their perceived failure to assimilate to White America. Los Angeles is highly segregated, and immigrants often interact far more with other Latinos, Black Americans, and Asians than with White Americans. For instance, Marta spends most of her time in her majority-Latino community, where her main reference group is other Mexicans. She said that it was not "los Americanos" who subject her to discrimination but "other Latinos just like me." She explained that other Latinos think they're better than she is "because they've spent more time here and have accomplished little things, and now they have the latest-model cars." Whereas in Mexico class divisions and skin color were identified as the most common basis for Mexican-on-Mexican discrimination, respondents in the U.S. spoke of discrimination from fellow working-class Mexican immigrants who are either "envious" of one another's financial success or are doing well and "think they're better than the rest."

Pablo alluded to the crabs-in-a-barrel metaphor. "There's a saying that goes like this," he explained. "There are three cans. One has American crabs, the other Japanese crabs, and the third Mexican crabs. The American and Japanese cans are closed with lids, but the Mexican one is open. Why? Because if we open the first two, all the crabs will help each other get out. The Mexican one doesn't even need a lid because if a Mexican crab tries to climb out, the other Mexican crab will pull it back down. Unfortunately, that's how we Mexicans are." Several participants felt that other immigrant and minoritized groups, such as Asians and Jews, did a better job of "sticking together" than Mexicans.

When I asked participants whether they believe they have anything in common with Mexican Americans, I received varied answers. Some said that simply "looking Latino" makes one susceptible to racial discrimination. "In the workplace, the simple fact that you're Latino, they treat you poorly, even if you speak English," said Mario. But most felt less sense of commonality. In addition to the birthright citizenship of Mexican Americans, immigrants pointed to advantages such as English proficiency, access to education, and upward mobility that they as immigrants did not have. U.S. citizenship and language were important boundaries, particularly when referring to Mexican Americans who did not speak Spanish and who did not make visible efforts to interact with immigrants in public spaces. Immigrants' sentiment that U.S.-born Latinos sometimes disassociate themselves from immigrant co-ethnics is supported by Tomás Jiménez's (2008, 176) study of Mexican American assimilation, where he argues the "recent and heavy influx of Mexican immigrants" reinforces intergroup boundaries between Mexican immigrants and Mexican Americans, who attempt to distance themselves from stigma attached to a racialized Mexican immigrant identity. "They're the same race as us," explained Juan, "but instead of helping us out, sometimes our own people are against us."

Respondents also felt that Asian Americans sometimes treated them in discriminatory ways. Many of the shops that my respondents frequented are Korean- and Chinese-owned. "Some are really good people, but they can also be very racist," said Marcos. "I've been in lots of stores owned by *Chinos*, and they see me and it's like I'm not even there. But when a [White] American comes in, they practically help carry their bags out." Marcos felt he received unequal treatment because he is Latino. (His use of "Chinos" is at best ignorant; Korean shop owners, of course, do not identify with the term.)

Eva described her interactions with Asian American merchants as follows:

Sometimes when you're looking to buy something but end up not buying it, they get upset. When you buy from them, it's expensive. But when you sell to them, they want everything super cheap. That's what I've realized. They set high prices and get upset when you don't buy from them. They're taking ownership of everything here [in the U.S.]. I'm telling you, they're owning everything; even everywhere in Puebla [Mexico] you

see Chinese. My daughter [who lives in Mexico] tells me they
have their Chinese restaurants and stuff.

There was a marked difference in how established immigrants
spoke of anti-immigrant discrimination by Whites compared with
other groups, however. For established and recent immigrants
alike, White Americans almost exclusively represented U.S. institutions and practices believed to target immigrant groups. Juanita
put it this way:

> When it comes out [on the news] that they deport people,
> it's almost always Whites doing that. I've never seen a per-
> son of color deporting people. I think it's mostly Whites. . . .
> Some Blacks discriminate too, I won't lie. They can say re-
> ally offensive things to you, but I've never seen them at [anti-
> immigrant] protests.

When immigrants described discrimination by Black Americans,
Asians, and U.S.-born Latinos, these anecdotes tended to involve
direct encounters occurring at the neighborhood level, in public
spaces, or at work. However, as Juanita's quote implies, White racism was described as both personal and systemic in nature.

This was the case for Isabel, a thirty-nine-year-old naturalized
citizen who believed that immigration laws are discriminatory
against Mexican and other Latino immigrants. She said:

> In my twenty-two years living in the U.S., I've seen that the
> law has changed. It's harder for the undocumented to find
> jobs, so things have changed in that regard. Before, they
> didn't ask you for a social security number to get your license

or ID. Before, lots of [undocumented] people would file taxes and make up social security numbers, and it wasn't a problem. Now the government is making things a lot harder for immigrants, and the laws are going to get worse.

Latinos Are Made in the USA: Shifting Racial Identities

Mexican immigrants in my study did not define themselves according to traditional U.S. racial categories, such as White, Black, or even Latino. About half of my long-term immigrant respondents preferred to identify as "*raza Mexicana*" exclusively or in combination with "Latino" or "*Hispano*." Their experiences aligned with sociologist Julie Dowling's (2014) findings that U.S. racial categories are foreign to many Mexican immigrants, as is the very act of identifying with a "racial" group. Living in Mexico had not made respondents accustomed to checking a race on a form with any regularity, as the decennial census is typically the only time they would answer the race question in Mexico. As Dowling notes, paperwork for school, employment, housing, and medical care elicits racial category in the United States but not in Mexico (2014, 81). What it means to be "Latino," therefore, is firmly rooted in U.S. racialization experiences (Suárez-Orozco and Páez 2002). In other words, Latino identity is "made in the USA," and when Mexicans come to the U.S., they must contend with what this new identity means to them and to American society more broadly.

When I asked established immigrants, "What race are you?" they were more likely than recent arrivals to have a ready answer, but when I followed up with "When you were in Mexico, how did you respond to the race question?" they looked at me with confusion. Juanita, for example, had been in the U.S. for twenty-two years. "What race?" she repeated back to me, as if looking for clarification. "No, you didn't really hear that [question] in Mexico.

You would only hear things like 'Where are you from?' [To which I might respond,] 'Oh, I'm *Chilango*, from D.F. [the Federal District in Mexico City],'" she explained. Juanita's insistence that people in Mexico don't commonly ask one another about their race alludes to the country's "raceless" ideology of *mestizaje*, in which all Mexicans are considered mestizo. Instead, as she explains, differentiation is established by the region of Mexico one hails from (and its associated ethnic and class markers).

Given the stark contrasts between Latin American and U.S. racial classification systems, it is not surprising that most studies examining transnational migration and race tend to focus on racial identity (Roth 2012; Joseph 2015). Racial identity formation is key to understanding how individuals assess their status position within a hierarchical society like the U.S. As Omi and Winant (1994) theorize, individuals come to learn what "race" they are based on a combination of society's treatment and labeling of the group in question and how the group sees itself. The case of immigrant groups in the U.S. is especially illustrative of this racial formation because newcomers arrive with their own understandings of race and racial identity originating in their home countries. In line with this, pan-ethnic Latino identity, much like Asian American and Middle Eastern identities, is very much a product of U.S. racialized systems.

Over the course of their time in the U.S., established immigrants had become quite familiar with *Latinidad* discourse, the idea that Latin American immigrants and their descendants in the U.S. make up a unifying and broadly defined Latino group with a common heritage and culture. Spanish-language television networks, such as the ever-popular Univision, began promoting the idea of Latinidad to national audiences in the 1980s, when the U.S. government started counting Latinos in the census (Mora 2014).

Nine of the thirty longtime immigrant respondents continued to identify exclusively with the term "raza Mexicana," but this did not correlate with the length of time they had lived in the U.S. Marcos specified, *"Pues soy Mexicano, ciudadano Americano"* ("I'm a Mexican, with American citizenship"). Another ten respondents, including Juanita, relied on "Latino" or *"Hispano"* as their primary racial identification. This signals a shift, given that non-migrant respondents in Mexico overwhelmingly told me they identified as "raza Mexicana." As discussed in Chapter 1, this common understanding of Mexican racial identity reflects the hegemonic national discourse of Mexico as a racially unified mestizo nation free of racism. Thus, the adoption of a Latino or Hispano identity suggests that some Mexicans may be incorporating into a U.S. racial classification system. Five respondents identify with both "raza Mexicana" and a pan-ethnic Latino or Hispano identity. The experiences of these few align with Dowling's (2014) and Roth's (2012, 85) findings that immigrants do not merely shed old racial schemas. Rather, they had learned and adapted U.S. racial schemas and applied them differently according to the context or situation. One respondent identified as *"indio,"* another three as "mestizo," and still another declined to answer. Perhaps suggesting that they recognize their exclusion from U.S. society, none of my respondents identified as "Americano/a" (American), in spite of citizenship, or "Blanco/a" (White), even those whose phenotypical features might lead others to classify them as such.

Shifting Racial Attitudes

Generally speaking, immigrants who have lived in the U.S. for longer periods of time had more varied experiences with different racial and ethnic groups, including through interactions with police officers, schoolteachers, medical professionals, and employers. A longer time in the U.S., however, was not directly associated with more positive attitudes toward other groups. Greater social contact and physical proximity with African Americans, for example, did not always result in increased acceptance of the group. Moreover, some immigrants' social networks remained limited to co-ethnic immigrants and thus resulted in fewer opportunities for meaningful cross-racial encounters of any kind.

It seems likely that one reason long-term immigrants had not developed actual friendships across racial lines is that their English fluency remained limited. Only two out of thirty long-term immigrants said they spoke English "well" or "very well." Others felt that their limited English skills prohibited them from gaining greater familiarity with the American way of life and forming cross-racial relations. Miriam, a thirty-five-year-old undocumented immigrant with ten years in the U.S., remarked on this:

> I think it's happened to most of us [immigrants], when you don't know the [English] language and you want to have a conversation with someone but you can't. You feel very limited in your ability, as if you're not on their level. And you need it—because, like, with Blacks, they can be explosive, but then all of a sudden you meet someone Black who compliments you or your child, and your fear starts to diminish. But all you can say is "Oh, thank you." There's so many times when you wish you could say certain things, but you have to learn the system here, what things you can say and what you can't.

Manuel, a permanent resident with twenty-eight years in the U.S., was one of two respondents who spoke fluent English. When he was a young man living in Guanajuato, Mexico, he used to sell picture frames to American retirees living in San Miguel de

Allende, a popular retirement area for North Americans. When he first arrived in the U.S. at the age of twenty-three, he enrolled in adult school English classes almost immediately. "I was a very dedicated student. I learned to read and write in English, but it took me a long time to learn to speak it." Manuel worked for over twenty years at a gas station in Huntington Park, where nearly everyone spoke Spanish, including his Mexican American boss. One day he was transferred to a Hollywood station, where he started interacting with people of different races. "In Hollywood I was forced to learn English. I was a bit scared but also liked that I was able to learn." In his early years, before learning English, he said, he didn't get along well with African American customers who would come to his gas station. He credits his English-speaking skills for helping him get along well with African Americans, who he says are some of the nicest people he has met in his new country.

Still, there were a few long-term immigrants, particularly those who had had a violent encounter with a Black person early on, who had not budged in their anti-Black biases. Many times, it was these immigrants who reinforced their anti-Black prejudices when engaging in race brokering and attempting to "school" newcomers about the local rules of race. Limited English-speaking proficiency also prevents many long-term immigrants from forming and sustaining cross-racial relations that could challenge preexisting negative racial attitudes. At the same time, acculturating to U.S. racial norms over time can also familiarize immigrants to the horrific injustices Black Americans have faced, from slavery through modern-day "lynchings" by police and the criminal justice system. Indeed, some immigrants' views about the relative privilege of Black Americans overlapped with the opinion that Black people, much like them, also contend with the burden of White racism.

The presence of U.S.-born children in the household can powerfully influence immigrants' racial perceptions of African Americans in particular (Hondagneu-Sotelo and Pastor 2021). A majority of the immigrants I interviewed migrated to the U.S. as young adults and did not experience a U.S. education. Thus, those with kids born in the U.S. learned about America through their children's local public school teachings, and both Katy and Judith expressed nuanced views because of their children's experiences with Black friends in their neighborhoods.

Katy was particularly impressed by lessons her kids' teachers imparted about the Civil Rights Movement. A homemaker in her early forties living in South L.A., she had two children who were in elementary school at the time of the interview.

> They learn about discrimination in school simply because they interact with the *morenitos* [Black kids] and they learn about Martin Luther King from a young age. So my kids will say, "It's due to the color of their skin that Blacks were discriminated against and treated poorly." They bring home school assignments and talk with me about it. My daughter tells me White people were very mean and would beat up Blacks.

Katy never got past the fifth grade in Mexico, but the notion of a Black social movement for equal rights and representation was virtually unheard of in Mexico until long after she migrated. Most respondents admitted that they were unfamiliar with the particularly violent history of Black enslavement by White Americans and Black Americans' ongoing struggle for full citizenship.[3] Mexican public education textbooks, in fact, dedicate no more than a few paragraphs to U.S. slavery and the Civil Rights Movement.[4]

Given that Mexican immigrants arrive with very little knowledge of U.S. Black politics, it is unsurprising that African American respondents in Niambi Carter's (2019) study of Black public
opinion on immigration felt strongly that Latino immigrants' lack
of historical understanding hinders the possibility of Black and
Brown racial solidarity. Indeed, research shows that immigrant
Latinos hold more negative views of Black Americans than their
U.S.-born children, who are socialized in the U.S. racial system
and tend to express a common fate with Black Americans (Flores-
González 2017; Hondagneu-Sotelo and Pastor 2021). U.S. public
education may play a role in this.

In Judith's case, social proximity in her son's school, rather
than curriculum, drove her views. She had developed a meaningful relationship with her Black neighbors across the street, in large
part because of her teenage son. "Our kids get along great," she
said. The relationship she described was one of reciprocity, trust,
and cultural exchange if not precisely friendship. "When they have
family parties, they bring me a plate of food, and I do the same.
They make a lot of barbecue, but they eat a lot of Mexican food too,
even the spicy stuff." I asked if she had ever been inside their house
or invited the parents to hers. She said, "Now that I think about it,
the only time they've come to my house was when their car broke
down and they borrowed mine. I trust them." The relationship was,
in Judith's telling, both a symptom and a driver of her positive feelings toward Black people in recent years. Judith said she was afraid
of her Black neighbors when she first arrived in South L.A. from
Guanajuato and would avoid contact in an effort to "not start any
problems." She said that the change came when she relocated to a
solidly lower-middle-class neighborhood in a different part of the
city. "I would walk my son to school every day, and you really get
to know your neighborhood that way, and that's when I'd see them

[Black neighbors] taking their kids to school. That's how I got to know them, ever since our kids were little. And look at [our kids] now, hanging out in my house like usual," she said, pointing to her front door as we sat outside in her garden.

Pablo said he understands that longtime Black residents might initially resist the demographic changes taking place in their neighborhood, but ultimately he feels accepted by his new neighbors. "Us Mexicans, or Latinos, we forget that we are buying our homes in what has been their grandparents' [neighborhood] for their entire lives. . . . They learn to accept us because we're in their midst," he explained, noting Black Americans' generally positive reception of Mexican newcomers compared with White Americans' explicitly racist segregationist practices.

Indeed, many respondents pointed out the obvious absence of White people in their neighborhoods. For some, this was evidence that Whites harbor anti-immigrant and anti-Black sentiment and prefer to self-segregate from both groups. In fact, the majority of interactions described by respondents that involved White people took place in the context of Mexicans working for, or serving, White Americans. Even immigrants who had lived in the U.S. several decades and were naturalized citizens generally lacked meaningful relationships with White Americans. For example, Pablo and his wife run a *taquero* business on weekends, primarily for house parties. A friend referred him to his first White customer, which he describes as a positive experience.

It was the first time we went to a White neighborhood, and I felt really uncomfortable. There was nothing but White people around. When we arrived and asked if we had the right party, they came out and right away started helping unload my truck. "How can we help?" When I turned around, this guy was carrying the tortillas, that guy had brought the cart out. They helped me set up. They loved the food and were very welcoming, offering us a beer and wine. *La verdad si nos han tratado bien los gabachos. Gracias a Dios.* ["Truthfully, Whites have treated us really well. Thank God."]

Similar to what Jazmín Muro (2016) found in her study of Latino and White relations in Los Angeles, respondents characterized their interactions with White people as mainly surface-level conversations that were polite, civil, and even enjoyable, yet rarely deeply meaningful. Rosario, an established immigrant living in South L.A., put it this way:

Well, more than anything, Mexicans and Whites don't have relations with each other. Many times it's related to issues with work. Because supposedly Mexicans come to invade the United States, the White man's country. And that's a lie, because the United States has gained a lot from the immigrant. . . . There are Whites who, like I said, are friendly. And there are Whites who also help Mexicans. But it's always and only when Mexicans are serving Whites.

Similarly, Nico, a long-term legal resident, explained:

I try to relate to them, to get to know them. But they need to get to know us too, how we truly are. Anglo-Saxon Americans make us feel like we're beneath them. They don't want us Mexicans, Latinos—because we come here to work hard and for a better life and to do many things. We all come here and start at the bottom and improve ourselves. How many Mexicans have businesses and restaurants who started as dishwashers or janitors and now own their own businesses in the United States? And the Anglo-Saxons don't want to accept that. They don't want us to improve our status . . . they don't want us to triumph like they have in this country.

By and large, established immigrants were indistinguishable from non-migrants and recent arrivals in terms of their attitudes about White Americans: they saw White Americans as kind, friendly, or benevolent, as arrogant and entitled, or as hostile and racist. However, regardless of whether immigrants felt positively or negatively about White Americans, Whites were overwhelmingly perceived as "true" Americans who yield disproportionate power in society and are largely responsible for the country's increasingly hostile anti-immigrant climate. In fact, the general perception that White society was not very welcoming of those who "look" Mexican was held by established immigrants of all legal statuses.

Positive shifts in some long-term immigrants' perceptions of Black Americans notwithstanding, most did not want their children to marry Black people and said they would not date Black people themselves. It was common to espouse color-blind rhetoric such as "Love is love" when asked about this, and parents understood that they could not control who their children fall in love with. Some said they would not have a problem if their child dated a Black person so long as the child were treated well. But immigrants like Alicia, a long-term immigrant living in Watts, spoke of significant "cultural differences" between Mexicans and African Americans that would be too difficult to overcome in a marriage, yet did not seem to feel this would be an issue in intermarriage with Whites. Citing "cultural differences" as a reason to disapprove of intermarriage can be a racially coded way of saying that one is against racial mixing—particularly with Black Americans

(Dowling 2014). Other scholars have reported similar findings, explaining that stigmatization of intermarriage with African Americans and a preference for White or lighter-skinned partners among Latinos in the U.S. context may well be an extension of the whitening or *blanqueamiento* ideology from Latin America that denigrates dark skin and Blackness (Feliciano, Lee, and Robnett 2011; Morales 2012; Vasquez-Tokos 2017; Sue 2013). One study found that Latino immigrants impart racialized messages to their U.S.-born children discouraging intimate contact with Black people and that Latinas are more likely than their male counterparts to be sanctioned for dating African American men (Morales 2012).

White Power, Black Privilege, and Immigrant Disadvantage

How long-term immigrants understand and experience their racialization is much more complex than a simple ranking of White and Black Americans above noncitizen immigrants. Immigrants' experience of race in the U.S. is as much about perceptions of their own privilege and disadvantage relative to other racialized groups as it is a question of discrimination. Immigrants positioned Black Americans as racially subordinate to White Americans yet above themselves along the axes of citizenship and belonging. Immigrants' impressions of being at the bottom of the socioracial hierarchy relative to other groups is powerfully linked to the social exclusion and legal vulnerability respondents contend with on a daily basis in the United States.

I asked Azusena, an undocumented street vendor who sells tamales, whether she believed that African Americans and Latinos suffer from similar injustices. Azusena replied, "No. I think that . . . Latinos have more to lose than Blacks [from being here illegally]. . . . Since [Blacks] have papers, well, obviously they have better jobs, be it a bus driver or whatever, but it's something better. . . .

They are not discriminated against in the same way. I think we are treated as 'less than human' more so than they are." Azusena explained that her opinion stemmed from an encounter with a Black police officer who approached her while she was selling tamales outside a storefront. "The officer was being very forceful in demanding that I speak English to her and insisting that I must carry an ID at all times or should not be in this country if I don't have papers." A passerby noticed Azusena struggling to communicate in English and stopped to translate, ultimately helping her to avoid arrest. However, the experience made her feel that citizenship would have been the ultimate insulation against danger. The fact that a Black person could be the agent of the state in this case reinforced her view.

Although most immigrants endorsed society's stereotype of the immigrant work ethic that makes them superior workers compared with "lazy" African Americans, they also sensed that African Americans can avoid the hardest work if they want to because citizenship gives them options unavailable to undocumented workers. Raul, a worker at a local Mexican bakery, was one of the only respondents who had worked alongside a Black American. "I got along well with the man, and he did good work, but . . . he didn't last longer than a few weeks. Baking bread is a tough job. You have to wake up very early, sometimes at 3 a.m., and work with really hot ovens," he said.

Raul asserted that African Americans who had been hired at his bakery "couldn't hang on the job" very long. He admitted that the job is strenuous and that if he could find a better one, he would. He also noticed that the majority of his coworkers who stayed on the job were other immigrants. Raul felt strongly that tenuous and exploitable labor in the United States has been strictly reserved for undocumented immigrants for whom the threat of deportation has long been used as a tool for compliance. He believed that citizenship status afforded his Black coworker the choice to quit an undesirable job in search of a "less strenuous" one, a privilege he noted he lacked due to his undocumented status. Although immigrants recognized that both groups struggle to find good jobs, they attributed this to differences in the behavior of "lazy" Black Americans versus the structural barrier of the legal status facing Mexicans.

At the same time, respondents recognized that White Americans do not regard Black Americans as "true" Americans. For example, several respondents expressed that White Americans do not like immigrants coming to "their" country. Immigrants may be sensing Black Americans' second-class citizenship status. Their tendency to compare their own "opportunities," or stymied incorporation, to the condition of Black Americans may reflect an understanding that African Americans are, at least, closer to them in the U.S. socioracial hierarchy than Whites.

In theorizing where Latinos fit into the U.S. racial order, sociologist Eduardo Bonilla-Silva (2004) suggests that the U.S. is undergoing a transition from a binary Black-White racial order into a "complex and loosely organized tri-racial stratification system" more similar to Latin American racial systems. Although both regions uphold White supremacy, Bonilla-Silva argues, certain Latinos in the U.S.—those with light skin and high education and income levels—are positioned as intermediary "honorary Whites." Others, like Mexican immigrants with dark skin and "illegal" immigrant status, he notes, will form part of a "collective Black" and be relegated to the bottom of the racial hierarchy along with Black Americans (Bonilla-Silva 2004, 938). My interviews, however, offer evidence of a potentially different outcome. Like Bonilla-Silva (2004) predicted, study participants are experiencing heightened levels of social and legal exclusion that powerfully relegate them to the lower rungs of the racial hierarchy.

In fact, some immigrants considered Black Americans as being far closer, culturally speaking, to White Americans than to Latinos and thus more powerful and influential than themselves. Sergio, an established immigrant living in South L.A., asserted:

The majority of [African Americans] are American citizens, and the majority of us [Mexican immigrants] are not citizens. That is the main difference. . . . A Black American is North American in his way of thinking. You see his North Americanness reflected culturally. It could be a White person, a Black person, but it's a North American at the end of the day.

By drawing the boundary around a "North American way of thinking," Sergio situates Anglo Americanness as the very cultural essence that unifies White and Black American citizens and distinguishes them from Mexicans and Latin Americans more broadly. Similar feelings were reported among Brazilians in Boston, who situated Black Americans as real "Americans" with greater political power by virtue of their birthright claims to citizenship and as less discriminated against compared with Latino immigrants, who, as one respondent put it, "all came from another country" (Marrow 2003).

Asians—whether U.S.-born or immigrants—were rarely mentioned in discussions of American identity, citizenship, and legality. Most references to Asians were specific to Korean, Chinese, and sometimes Filipino immigrant bosses and store merchants, rarely as neighbors or coworkers. Although Mexican immigrants positioned Asians above themselves in terms of socioeconomic status, it was less clear where they placed Asians racially. Immigrants for the most part did not regard Asian groups as White or even approximating Whiteness, but neither did they position Asians on the lower rungs of the racial hierarchy. Immigrants did, however, subscribe to long-standing racial stereotypes of Asians as forever foreigners and model minorities ("They help each other out and stick together" was a common phrase, typically in reference to Asian immigrants). Although Asian Americans have been in the U.S. for multiple generations, not once did Mexican immigrants reference Asians in our discussions of "Americans," suggesting that Mexicans, like much of the U.S., continue to view Asians as foreigners in America.

Still, instances in which immigrants felt that Black Americans, Mexican Americans, or Asian Americans exhibited anti-immigrant prejudice rarely, if ever, rested on the notion that these groups were in a position to perpetrate restrictionist immigration policy. Yet, contrary to the literature suggesting that a shared status as oppressed minorities will foster racial solidarity, a far more nuanced and multifaceted dynamic emerged in the interviews. For example, recognition that Black Americans are also targets of White racism did not, in and of itself, serve as grounds for commonality with these groups. Rather, significant feelings of disempowerment informed immigrants' views that despite occupying an inferior position to White people, groups like Black Americans and U.S.-born Latinos were relatively better positioned than they were.

Race, Illegality, and Emerging Socioracial Hierarchies

Notions of Americanness, U.S. citizenship, and the stigma of perceived illegality powerfully shaped how the established immigrants I interviewed made sense of the U.S. racial hierarchy. Although Carla (mentioned in the opening vignette), together with her Mexican immigrant husband, managed to achieve the pinnacle of the American Dream, homeownership, her sense of belonging in America remained in question. Carla, like many immigrants in the U.S. today, belongs to a mixed-status family, in which some members have legal status and others do not. Although Carla has earned U.S. citizenship status, she describes being heartbroken over the legal liminality and suffering her undocumented daughter has endured due to legal status. Despite being brought over to the U.S. as a little girl, Carla's daughter has been unsuccessful in her quest for legalization. For others, being perceived as "illegal" and targeted on the job or in public spaces go to the heart of immigrants' beliefs that they are situated below not only White Americans but also Black Americans, albeit for qualitatively different reasons. Although most immigrants I interviewed recognized that the U.S. racial hierarchy positions African Americans below White Americans, they also saw Black Americans as occupying a "privileged" position, albeit a tenuous one, relative to themselves.

How immigrants conceive of Americanness is tied to questions of belonging and who can or cannot make claims for membership, rights, and resources. Ultimately, being perceived as "illegal" by those considered to be "true" Americans has profound effects on how immigrants experience being treated by others and how they view racism and discrimination in the U.S. American citizenship is a highly coveted social and legal status among the immigrants I interviewed. Some respondents gave citizenship more weight than race, skin color, or class status in shaping their fate in U.S. society, a far cry from their assessment of Mexican ethnoracial hierarchies.

Social scientists studying Mexican immigrant incorporation have long been concerned with how the U.S. context of reception shapes immigrants' prospects for full inclusion in U.S. society and institutions. In the past decade, the rise of anti-immigrant policy at both the federal and state levels has created significant barriers to inclusion, leading to what some scholars suggest is an emerging U.S. society strongly stratified by citizenship and legal status (Marrow 2020). Intensifying enforcement practices have in recent years only worsened the climate of anxiety and fear of being apprehended by police, put in detention, or facing deportation. I pick up where these studies left off by examining how the growing social and legal marginalization and exclusion of Mexican immigrants shape their racial attitudes and understanding of their position in the socioracial hierarchy relative to other racialized groups, namely African Americans.

To be sure, Mexicans and Mexican Americans have long been viewed and treated as racially inferior by White America and have faced enduring racialization and racial violence since the American military invasion of Mexico, resulting in the 1848 Treaty of Guadalupe Hidalgo, in which Mexico ceded half of its territory to the U.S. and thousands of Mexicans living there were given naturalized American citizenship. Since then, as documented by Leo Chavez in his book *The Latino Threat* (2008), Mexican immigrants who have crossed the border in search of work have been racialized as a disposable labor force occupying the bottom rung of the U.S. labor market (Gómez 2020). Even after multiple generations in the United States, the children and grandchildren of Mexican immigrants face enduring social, political, and racial exclusion (Telles and Ortiz 2008).

Sociologists of race have portrayed immigrant racial attitudes, and anti-Black prejudice in particular, as clear evidence of a long history of immigrants' efforts to achieve upward mobility via proximity to Whiteness. My interviews with long-term immigrants living in Los Angeles, however, reveal a far more nuanced, sometimes contradictory, and relational nature to how immigrants position themselves vis-à-vis Black Americans and other groups.[5]

Indeed, although some immigrants expressed more positive attitudes toward White people than Black people, their racial experiences tell a different story than in the previous literature, which has suggested that immigrants view the social boundaries separating themselves from White people as more permeable than those with Black Americans (Marrow 2009; McClain et al. 2006). Instead, immigrants saw White people as the main perpetrators of anti-immigrant discrimination, at both the individual and institutional levels. Put plainly, immigrants understood that Anglo Americans—at least those with economic and political power—were the architects of their precarious legal and economic circumstances, even though actual White people were rarely present in their neighborhoods.

Experiencing anti-immigrant discrimination from White America, however, was not a sufficient impetus to create a sense of racial solidarity with Black Americans. Although many immigrants did not explicitly view Black people as discriminatory toward Latinos—some even described group relations as friendly—neither did they view Black Americans as subject to the same barriers to upward mobility. Even in cases when immigrants, such as Judith and Katy, recognized similar experiences of oppression with Black Americans, they felt that the causes were different. The master status of illegality featured prominently in immigrants' understandings of their place in the U.S. racial hierarchy. This was the case even for those who were, by most standards, incorporated into U.S. social institutions.

As sociologist Vanessa Ribas (2016, 27) reminds us, relations between subordinated groups are best understood as "pragmatic engagements," whereby groups encounter one another "in a field of racial positions characterized by white dominance." In her study of workers at a slaughterhouse in the U.S. South, Ribas (2016) found that highly exploited immigrant laborers became "embittered sub-ordinates" who believed that there is a "cost to being Latino" and that it is "worth it" on the job to be African American. A similar study found that although both Latino (U.S.-born and immigrant) and African American workers at a Mississippi poultry plant experienced similar workplace abuses, immigrants believed that both Black and White supervisors treated Black workers better than Latino immigrants (Stuesse 2016). Those I interviewed echoed a similar sentiment that Black Americans had advantages in U.S. contexts because they believed Black Americans' citizenship status granted them access to better, more-secure job opportunities. Ribas astutely points out that immigrants' belief that there is a value to being Black in America—despite the fact that Blackness has been historically devalued—is a paradox that powerfully illustrates how immigrants make sense of their place in the racial hierarchy in relation to not only Whites but also other racialized groups. Neither of these studies examined beliefs about African American citizenship among Mexican immigrants with decades in the U.S., which I found was the main reason even established immigrants in my study—who, in some cases, had worked hard to become naturalized U.S. citizens—viewed Black citizens as comparatively privileged.

Of course, not all of my respondents placed Black citizens squarely above them in the status chain. Anti-Black prejudice was evident when it came to views about dating preferences and interracial marriage between Mexicans and Black Americans. White people, on the other hand, are overwhelmingly perceived as the quintessential American group most hostile toward Latino immigrants and most threatened by their presence. However, even in light of ample evidence pointing to a history of systemic racism against Black Americans in nearly all facets of life, immigrants' vulnerability as racialized "illegals" significantly shaped their perceptions of subordination to African Americans, particularly regarding "opportunities" for upward mobility (De Genova 2004; Ribas 2016). In fact, the findings presented in this chapter suggest that the entrenchment of social illegality that racializes even established immigrants who earned naturalized citizenship as "illegal" may be the primary reason that immigrants are constructing symbolic boundaries with Black Americans—and perhaps even certain segments of American-born Latinos. As I have argued, racialized illegality powerfully shapes Mexican immigrants' understanding of the U.S. racial stratification system and their lowly place within it. Thus, contrary to scholars' suggestion that immigrants' quest for Whiteness is the main impediment to African American and Latino racial solidarity, it is America's structural racism and nativist xenophobia that, in the words of Vanessa Ribas (2016, 183), "cast a dubious shadow on the potential for Latina/o workers to extend solidarity to their African American counterparts."

From Mestizo to Minority

A S SOCIOLOGIST JULIE DOWLING (2014) asserts in her book *Mexican Americans and the Question of Race*—and which the stories in this book echo—when newcomers arrive in the U.S. they are tasked with adapting new ways of understanding their unique racial position. Indeed, the Mexicans in this study often took for granted that they were part of the "Mexican mainstream" in their home country, where mestizos make up the demographic majority. This privilege often translated into lack of awareness of the blatant racial discrimination taking place all across Mexico. As discussed in Chapter 1, mestizaje ideology has so effectively homogenized the Mexican population into a single mestizo "race" that it works to downplay racism, even among mestizos who themselves experience colorism. In fact, the belief that racism does not exist in Mexico is so entrenched that until fairly recently, race and ethnic relations had received little attention from social scientists (Sue 2013). Even in cases when mestizo respondents challenged this prevailing notion by acknowledging discrimination in Mexico, it was typically attributed to Indigenous Mexicans, not themselves. Other mestizos simply denied the existence of racism outright, expressing instead the idea that the discrimination they witness around them is due to class, not race.

To date, scholars of immigrant racialization have tended to focus on immigrants' experiences with race almost exclusively in the U.S., *after* migration. Yet to not examine how race and difference are constructed in the immigrant sending society is to render incomplete our understanding of the racial lens that newcomers arrive with—and, most importantly, how they negotiate their place within a distinctly American racial landscape. I argue throughout this book that immigrants are not clean slates when they arrive in the U.S.; rather, their lifelong socialization with race begins in their country of origin, and they consequently bring this racial baggage with them to their new place of settlement. The racial baggage immigrants carry over into the U.S. does not simply travel in one direction; transnational social ties and globalized media ensure that U.S. hegemonic racial—and racist—ideologies also make their way into Mexico, exposing would-be migrants to distinctly American racial discourse and practices long before they set foot in the U.S. This racial baggage has consequences for how newcomers subsequently negotiate socioracial boundaries in their Los Angeles neighborhoods.

The transnational lives of Mexican immigrants, and of many other immigrant groups in the U.S., play a key role in facilitating the exchange of racial ideas across borders. Immigrants regularly make phone calls to loved ones back home and, in some cases, return to their hometowns for visits and annual fiestas. Recent technological advancements like social media platforms Instagram and WhatsApp further enable American popular culture—and the racial ideologies it carries with it—to travel across borders with unprecedented ease. I found that these transnational racial exchanges are often imbued with U.S. anti-Black stereotypes characterizing African Americans as boisterous, aggressive, and criminal and are especially consequential for how immigrants relate to Black Americans when they arrive.

Once in the U.S., Mexicans undergo a unique process of racialization that marks them as simultaneously a racialized minority and "illegal" outcast. Indeed, it is precisely their mestizaje—that which conferred a relative privilege in the Mexican context—that has historically deemed Mexicans a racially inferior "mongrel" race in America (Gómez 2015). U.S. racial ideology, much like mestizaje ideology, homogenizes all (non-Indigenous) Mexicans into one "race," but as Mexican newcomers became acquainted with the American racial and legal landscape, they learn that to be Mexican in the U.S. context is to be relegated to an inferior social, racial, and legal status. When viewed through a transnational lens, it is clear that the racialization of the "illegal" immigrant is a distinctly U.S. brand of racialization that, although relatively nonexistent in understandings of inequality in Mexico, features prominently in the transnational racial journey of immigrants—even those who have lived in the U.S. for decades. Ultimately, there is a consensus among Mexican immigrants that they occupy a distinct racial position vis-à-vis Black and White Americans, illustrating a clear departure from both Mexico's so-called raceless society and the United States' long-standing Black-White color line. Thus, racialization is a transnational process that complicates the notions of race that newcomers bring with them; the pigmentocracy of Mexican society, in which skin color and mestizo identity may have afforded more privileges, collides with the American racial system, in which Mexican immigrants are positioned on the lower rungs of society.

A transnational lens further highlights the ways in which immigrants' new racial encounters affect not only their lives in the U.S. but potentially also race relations in the sending community.[1] For example, a recent arrival in Los Angeles may have a negative experience with a Black neighbor. When that individual returns to Mexico or communicates this experience to loved ones back home—in the form of a racial remittance—it may subsequently set the tone for how those individuals respond to the presence of Black Americans in Mexico. Consider this insight from Agustín, a non-migrant factory worker in Guadalajara:

> There are Mexican people who migrate to the U.S. and something happens to them there, and they come back with negative ideas about Blacks, and when they see Blacks they discriminate against them even here [in Mexico]. . . . They see a Black person and get scared, and now they're in their own country and feel like, "If they did that to me in their country, well, I'm going to do it to them in my country."

In this excerpt, we see how transnational analyses can generate critical insights into the ways racial meanings circulate and generate new forms of racialization. That a Black visitor to Mexico can become a target of discrimination based on the racial encounters of immigrants in the U.S. illustrates the powerful reach of racial remittances and the relevance of transnational processes of racialization in shaping racial attitudes and behaviors abroad. Given the strength of transnational ties in the Mexican immigrant community and the steady replenishment of Mexican immigrants (Jiménez 2008), along with the cultural ideas about race they bring with them, the transnational racialization of Black Americans and other racialized groups is likely to continue.

Of course, the same mechanism that facilitates the transnational racialization of Black Americans may also facilitate the exchange of anti-racist strategies leading to the development of a radical Black political movement among Afro-Mexicans and a growing awareness of structural racism among the general Mexican population similar to that brought on by Black Lives Matter protests in the U.S. There is growing evidence to suggest that this is already happening. In 2020, George Floyd protests "went global," including in places like Mexico City and Guadalajara, where my research took place (Klebnikov 2020). There, massive demonstrations demanded justice for the fatal police beating of thirty-year-old construction worker Giovanni Lopez, with protesters holding up signs expressing solidarity with BLM and denouncing racism and police brutality in the U.S. and Mexico. Reverend Flaviano Cisneros, a member of the Afro-Mexican pastoral commission and coordinator of the nonprofit *Mexico Negro*, also remarked that the current wave of demonstrations has encouraged Black Mexicans to keep pressing for their civil rights at home (Campos Lima 2020).

Mexicans' understandings of race "here and there" are not static; they can be renegotiated or transformed. Whether and how racial attitudes may change are largely a result of factors that can vary across region and time, including the nature of interactions with different racial and ethnic groups at work and in the neighborhood, experiences with discrimination, exposure to global media, and, for immigrants in particular, the coming-of-age of U.S.-born children who may relate positively to Black Americans. To be sure, some immigrants eventually gain more nuanced understandings of Black America as well as White America, which at times fosters warmer sentiments toward the groups. On some occasions, new experiences with race in America altogether challenged previously held attitudes and stereotypes, particularly of Black Americans.

My interviews further reveal that notions of citizenship were central to how Mexicans perceive their racial status in the U.S.[2] Immigrants believed that their group overall is distinctly disadvantaged relative to those—of any race—whom they perceive as rightful Americans and privileged U.S. citizens. This is not new, however. In America, the term "illegal immigrant" has never been race-neutral. It once referred specifically to Mexicans, but due to rising numbers of Central American migrants, the term has broadened to encompass all Latinos (Molina 2014; Flores and Schachter 2018). Fox News and other conservative media outlets are notorious for stoking anti-immigrant sentiment by plastering "illegal immigrant" or, worse, "alien" on their headlines and marquees (Chavez 2013). Everyday Americans rely on these powerful stereotypes to classify Latino immigrants, specifically Mexicans, as "illegal" regardless of actual documentation status, a condition that sociologists René Flores and Ariela Schachter (2018) refer to as "social illegality." The majority of Mexican immigrants featured in this study experienced the negative effects of social illegality, even after decades of living in the U.S. Immigrants like Carla, in Chapter 4, who had earned their status as naturalized U.S. citizens and in some cases had achieved the epitome of the American Dream by becoming homeowners, expressed feelings of exclusion and denigration by American society similar to those of their undocumented peers. Feelings of anti-immigrant and anti-Latino prejudices, stereotypes, and discrimination among those who might otherwise be deemed "incorporated" into U.S. society reinforced the view that Mexican immigrants were not only on the margins of the American mainstream but also inferior to it. Thus, the United States' increasingly hostile anti-immigrant climate appears to be working to solidify social boundaries between immigrants and American citizens. Immigrants simply believed that Black and White Americans alike had very little in common with the Latino immigrant struggle, and this, I argue, bears important implications for enduring racial hierarchies—even as that society is rapidly "Browning" (Bonilla-Silva and Dietrich 2008).

There is evidence to suggest that for Mexican immigrants, Whitening—and the trappings of White privilege—is no longer a viable strategy for upward mobility, if it ever was. Instead, Anglo-White supremacist structures that render certain groups in the U.S. context "illegal" powerfully shape how Mexican immigrants articulate social boundaries in relation not only to the dominant White group but also racially subordinate groups like Black Americans and Asian Americans (Ngai 2004). My findings challenge the assertion by some that Mexicans are being absorbed into an inclusive White racial boundary and contest the zero-sum notion that for Mexicans, drawing social boundaries between themselves and Black Americans goes hand in hand with feelings of closeness with White Americans or a desire to achieve Whiteness. This line of thinking tends to center Whiteness in our understanding of Latino immigrant experiences with race and is no longer fruitful for theorizing Latino racialization in the U.S.

Latino Immigrants and Evolving U.S. Race Relations

While Mexico is beginning to reckon with the fact that Blackness is, and has always been, a part of the social fabric of Mexico, in the U.S., debates rage on about whether Latinos are becoming "White." An article published by Slate Magazine in 2014 was headlined "Will Today's Hispanics Be Tomorrow's Whites?: How Hispanics perceive themselves may shape the future of race in America" (Bouie 2014). This and other similar headlines signaled a growing preoccupation with the Latino "race question" in media and scholarly circles. This is not surprising, considering that Latinos are in fact transforming race in the U.S. in ways that are challenging the dominant Black-White paradigm. In the past decade alone, Latinos have single-handedly surpassed African Americans as the nation's largest "minority group" and, according to the 2020 census, account for more than half of the nation's growth (U.S. census 2020).

The painful history of immigrant assimilation in the U.S. teaches us that the Latino race question is as much a question about the fate of Black (and thus White) America as it is a preoccupation with Latino identity. In her 1993 essay "On the Backs of Blacks," Toni Morrison reminds us that the process of immigrant incorporation, long synonymous with "becoming American," has long been predicated on learning contempt for Black Americans. Demonstrating loyalty and attachment to America, she argues, requires immigrants to "surrender to whiteness" and embrace the existing racial order that places Black Americans on the lowest rungs. Although the racial estrangement from Black Americans became common practice among European immigrants who could pass for White, Morrison warns us, the "shade of the newcomers' skin" no longer matters, alerting us to the notion that immigrants of color could very well follow in the anti-Black footsteps of European immigrants before them.

Controversial events involving the killing of unarmed Black Americans have only intensified the Latino racial debate. Was the killing of Trayvon Martin, a Black teenage boy fatally attacked while walking home by civilian George Zimmerman, who is half-White and half-Peruvian, a case of White racial violence against Black bodies or a new manifestation of anti-Black violence by Latinos who align themselves with Whiteness? The 2016 shooting and killing of unarmed Philando Castile in Minnesota by Latino police officer Jeronimo Yanez also raised questions about the possibility of a new configuration of Latino anti-Blackness—this time at the hands of Latino law enforcement. At the same time, police continue to racialize and target Latino men, such as Sean Monterrosa, a twenty-two-year-old from Vallejo, California, who was shot and killed in June of 2020 while kneeling with his hands up, and Adam Toledo, a thirteen-year-old boy who was fatally shot by Chicago police. These, along with several other more recent killings of Black and Latino men and women, have sparked national outrage and protests over state-sanctioned killings and racial injustice. But this time it isn't only White people who are being held accountable.

Despite clear evidence that Latinos of all hues are racialized as inferior by the White majority, there is a growing notion that "White-passing" Latinos stand to gain the most from a system of White supremacy and therefore must reckon with their anti-Blackness. This is reflected in, among other things, the increasing visibility of *Las vidas negras importan* (Black Lives Matter) signs in Latino spaces. Led by mostly younger generations of U.S.-born Latinos, including Afro-Latinos, this small but growing movement aims to build a bridge with the Black diaspora across the Americas in the fight against White supremacy. Julio Ricardo Varela, the founder of online media outlet Latino Rebels, states:

> [Latinos] need to just accept the reality that we also come from a racist society that is embedded in white supremacy.... If you look at Latin America in general, we literally carry around that baggage and bring that system with us.

As this book demonstrates, immigrants indeed bring with them anti-Black racial baggage that dates back to the racist logics of the Spanish colonial system in Mexico. But the story doesn't end there. This baggage is further weighed down by distinctly U.S. racist ideologies that make their way into Mexico and across Latin America via global media and racial remittances sent by immigrant loved ones residing in the U.S. This resembles similar processes of

transnational racialization observed by sociologists studying Dominicans and Puerto Ricans (Roth 2012), Brazilians (Joseph 2015),
and Koreans (Kim 2008) in the U.S. In these studies, migrants witnessed and, in some cases, adopted American ideals of White superiority and anti-Blackness. Indeed, there is evidence to suggest
that this dynamic has existed since the first wave of mass migration from Europe (Carter 2019). If we have learned anything from
earlier European immigrants about how to navigate the U.S. racial
hierarchy, it is that success and inclusion in America are predicated
on social distance from Black Americans.

But what might the contours of African American and immigrant solidarity look like if we consider the most disadvantaged immigrant groups, such as Central Americans and Haitians, who encounter exacerbated forms of legal violence and exclusion from U.S.
society and institutions? Some argue that Latino immigrants may
come to reject an "American" identity in favor of one that better reflects the group's experience with racialized exclusion.[3] As immigrants continue to experience the stigma of illegality and blocked
opportunities for upward mobility, many may grow increasingly
disillusioned with the prospects of achieving the so-called American Dream. Sociologist Jennifer Jones (2012, 72) reflects on this
changing dynamic, arguing that many immigrants "no longer believe in the promise of upward mobility through a prism of achiev-
able whiteness . . . they no longer speak of the American Dream,
but rather of the U.S. as a country with a history of racism, of which
they are now the primary targets."

Indeed, growing racial and legal oppression of immigrants can
serve as the impetus for African American and Latino coalition-
building, particularly around issues of racial profiling, detention,
and mass incarceration. Immigrant rights movements, which have
largely focused on issues relating to Latino and Asian immigration,

are beginning to acknowledge that Black immigrants are often the most impacted by anti-immigrant policies and are disproportionately apprehended and deported (Golash-Boza 2015). In 2016, Black Lives Matter adopted a new platform with a list of demands that called for an end to immigration raids and deportations, in a sign of solidarity with immigrants of all racial backgrounds.

The second generation (children of immigrants), who grew up in the U.S. and have more familiarity and meaningful contact with African Americans, could serve as a bridge between their parents and Black Americans. Recent studies found that U.S.-born Latinos express far greater commonality with Black Americans than their immigrant parents do (Flores-González 2017; Hondagneu-Sotelo and Pastor 2021). This generation may be more attuned to how the racial experiences of marginalized groups are profoundly interrelated and thus more likely to see in Black Americans a much-needed ally in the fight against White systemic racism. Although the goal of this book is to focus on how migration transforms conceptions of race, I hope that it has planted the seeds for further exploration of how Latino immigrants—and subsequent generations of their U.S.-born children—define themselves in relation to Black America and the Black diaspora more broadly.

While progressive African American and Mexican alliances have existed in places like South Los Angeles (Rosas 2019), they might have been less likely forty years ago, when the majority of Mexican newcomers hailed from more rural and heavily mestizo central-western parts of the country. Many of the immigrants in this study are part of an older generation who grew up in a very different Mexico, a more traditional and less race-conscious one. In focusing this study on a particular segment of the Mexican population—mestizos from central-western Mexico—I sought to move away from U.S. scholarly approaches to immigrant racialization that tend to limit their analyses of race and identity to singular national-origin groups or, in this case, the "Mexican" experience. "Latino" immigration must be recognized as a multiethnic and multiracial process that reflects the increasing diversity of the Latin American migrant population, which has grown dramatically over the past three decades. Indeed, Indigenous and Black migrants now make up a larger share of the Latino population in the U.S. than ever before (Logan 2010; Fox and Rivera-Salgado 2004; Fox 2006).

Ultimately, I argue, the way in which Mexican immigrants and their children—who are by far the largest Latino group in the U.S.—are received in the host society and the opportunities they have to incorporate into civic, economic, and political life will speak volumes about how the racial boundary-making process unfolds. Under the current political climate, Latino immigrants, particularly those who are poor and Brown, are increasingly subjected to anti-immigrant prejudice and hate crimes that signal to these communities that they are not accepted as part of American society. This, in turn, influences immigrants' views of other racialized groups, not just their own.

Of course, African Americans also have their own opinions about how the growing presence of Latino immigrants shapes their life chances (Carter 2019). In her book *American While Black: African Americans, Immigration, and the Limits of Citizenship*, political scientist Niambi Carter argues that recent waves of immigration present a dilemma for African Americans because immigration— namely the integration of immigrants to the body politic—has served as a reminder of the limited inclusion and second-class-citizenship status of African Americans. Carter points out that although African Americans have long supported social justice for all groups, they are ambivalent and, in some cases, even hold negative attitudes toward migrants because they interpret their own precarious citizenship and racial status through the lens of how well immigrants have fared and the common perception that immigrants undermine their job prospects.

In looking ahead, we must keep in mind that "racial" groups, such as Latinos, Asians, Middle Easterners, and Black people, are not monolithic, and no study of immigrant racialization should treat them as such. Racial ideologies and practices vary by immigrants' country of origin (e.g., Mexico vs. Dominican Republic) and national region (e.g., northern vs. coastal vs. highland). Moreover, certain Latinos, such as those who pass (either in their home country or the U.S.) for White, have different assimilation trajectories than those presumed to be "illegal" based on phenotype, accent, or social class. It is these Latinos (immigrant or not) who experience a particularly racist brand of xenophobia that makes them the primary targets of anti-Latino hate crimes. Even experiences with illegality differ among Latinos (Herrera 2016). For example, Juan Herrera (2016) found that Indigenous Guatemalan migrants in California experienced double marginalization; they were racialized as inferior in Guatemala and again in the U.S. context, where they faced the stigmatization of illegality while being simultaneously racialized as inferior by mestizo immigrants and mainstream society.

Processes of globalization and migration are also generating new meanings of Blackness and Black identity politics (Thomas and Clarke 2006; Clerge 2019; Hamilton 2019). In the U.S., the relationship between Black Americans and Black immigrants is far more complex than existing studies may suggest. Black people are an increasingly heterogeneous group in terms of ethnicity, nationality, and class and legal status and therefore have experienced a stratified ethnoracial incorporation to U.S. society (Itzigsohn 2009; Clerge

2019). Varied incorporation patterns may also affect how Black immigrants position themselves in the socioracial hierarchy vis-à-vis African Americans. The majority of Black immigrants arrived in the U.S. in the post-1965 context, when the country was expanding opportunities for people of color, and they thus do not share the pre-1965 history of chattel slavery, Jim Crow, and lynching that Black Americans experienced (Hamilton 2019, 11). Most recently, growing numbers of Haitian asylum seekers gathering in South Texas, near the Mexico-U.S. border, are facing deportations and deplorable treatment by Border Patrol. Like other immigrant groups, Black immigrants hold a spectrum of racial and political ideologies that shape how they view their racial status, from pro-Black stances to social distancing from an African American identity and culture (Clerge 2019; Waters 2001).

The implications of this study extend beyond the case of Mexican migration to the U.S. As this book has shown, migration—whether at the regional, national, or transnational level—can generate new ideas and experiences of belonging, citizenship, and racial difference. Of course, the direction of the U.S. color line is not only the result of individual attitudes, choices, and actions. The color line is a structural formation shaped by a long history of U.S. imperial and neoliberal policies and practices of territorial expansion, war, military occupation, and economic exploitation (King 2019). Latino racial formation in the U.S. stretches back to American colonialism and hegemony in Latin America (Gómez 2020). Mass migration from Mexico and other Latin American countries is the direct result of U.S. interventionist policies that have caused economic displacement and dispossession of mostly rural and poor populations. Neoliberal economic policies have further exacerbated the massive flow of migrants and refugees we see today. Currently, millions of Central American and Haitian refugees are experiencing legal precarity at the Mexico-U.S. border and across Mexico. The racist and xenophobic contexts of reception facing immigrants of color, which intensified under the Trump administration, are leading to economic hardships and new forms of legal exclusion that will undoubtedly have implications for the well-being of already-marginalized family members remaining in the sending region.

I thus follow the tradition of Bonilla-Silva, Telles, and others[4] in examining the Latin American context for theorizing the U.S. racial hierarchy and call for scholars of migration to engage more seriously in transnational, hemispheric, and global approaches to the study of racial formation. In his theory of the "Latin Americanization" of race in the U.S., sociologist Eduardo Bonilla-Silva posited that the nation was undergoing a reorganization of its racial stratification scheme, shifting from a biracial Black-White structure to a loosely structured triracial system comprising "White," "honorary White," and "collective Black" categories. Although Bonilla-Silva's race predictions have been challenged by some (Murguia and Saenz 2002; Sue 2009), his framework remains useful for reconceptualizing race in the U.S. Similarly, Edward Telles's theorization of Brazilian race relations may provide further insight into how a "Latin Americanization" of race may play out in the U.S., even as it is rapidly "Browning."[5] For example, an emphasis on skin color hierarchies among Latinos could lead to a scenario where "honorary White" Latinos coexist harmoniously with darker-skinned mestizo, Indigenous, and Afro-Latinos as friends, neighbors, and even romantic partners, while structural inequalities that disadvantage Brown and Black Latinos remain intact.[6] Put differently, a "majority-minority" U.S. could look more and more like Brazil, where White supremacy and racism continue to proliferate alongside growing interracial and ethnic coexistence.

Shifting Racial Tides in Mexico

In March of 2020, for the first time in over two centuries, the Mexican government included a Black ancestry question on the national census.[7] This came one year after another historic move toward greater visibility of Afro descendants in Mexico: a constitutional amendment that would extend to Black Mexicans the same rights and recognitions long (formally) given to *"los pueblos indigenas"* (Indigenous peoples). Together, these historic moves represent a major shift in Mexican racial thinking. The official state recognition of Afro descendants breaks with the dominant ideology of mestizaje and the long-standing taboo on discussions of race and racism. Indeed, it was only thirty years ago, during a United Nations convention on racial and ethnic equity, that a Mexican government representative declared, "Racism does not exist in Mexico" (Sue 2013).

The Afro-ancestry question did not come without a fight. It was the result of long-standing collaborative social efforts of Mexican grassroots organizers, scholars, media entities, and governmental institutions. This mirrors what happened in the U.S. three decades prior, in 1980, when the federal government included for the first time a Hispanic question in the national census. Prior to that, it would have been unthinkable to refer to "the Hispanic population" as a group because Puerto Ricans, Mexicans, and Cubans (the three largest Latino groups at the time) identified primarily with their nationality (Mora 2014). Over fourteen million people ended up identifying as Latino on the census.[8] As U.S. law professor Laura Gómez (2020) points out, "The census has always been a primary race-making site for the racial state." Everything from the wording of a race question to the racial categories included—and omitted—speak volumes about how a nation chooses to represent itself to its citizens and the world. Such representation is not static;

changes in census categories and questions are also important social indicators of shifting public perceptions of race. More often
than not, census changes are propelled by grassroots organizers
pushing for equal representation and policies to address racial disparities. The Hispanic question, therefore, did more than just legit-
imize the Latino category in the eyes of the federal government. It
gave visibility and political power to the millions of Latin American descendants who did not see themselves reflected in the existing census categories (Rodríguez-Muñiz 2021). It also transformed the way ordinary Americans thought of Latinos and race in
the U.S. more generally because the Hispanic category challenged
the dominant Black-White racial paradigm of the time.

Similarly, the Afro-Mexican question is about much more than
a straightforward counting of Black residents in Mexico. It rep-
resents a turning point in the symbolic inclusion of a previously
marginalized group whose experiences quite literally did not count
in the national imaginary. For example, the media campaign for
the Mexican census, aptly named #AfroCensoMx, encouraged
Afro descendants to proudly affirm their Black ancestry by checking the "Black" box. According to the 2020 census, there are about
2.5 million Mexicans (out of roughly 126 million people in Mexico) who identify as Afro-descendant, and this is likely an under-
estimate, as official campaigns promoting Black identity are fairly
new. Many, like Monica Moreno Figueroa, scholar and cofounder
of the National Council to Prevent Discrimination (CONAPRED),
are hopeful that these census figures will "make racism visible" and
help catalyze new programs and laws designed to eliminate long-
standing structural inequality (Frias 2020).

For Mexico, the move toward collecting racial data on the Black
population might also signal a growing awareness of structural racism in the mestizo nation. Would the migrants in my study, who

grew up believing that there were no Black people in Mexico, think differently about Blackness had this Black category—and the political efforts made possible by an official category—existed back in the day? As we look into the future, how will Mexico's growing recognition of Blackness transform the way ordinary Mexicans— and perhaps other Latin American countries with large Indigenous and mestizo populations—think of their Afro-descendant compatriots and, by extension, the Black diaspora they will inevitably encounter if and when they join the ranks of the millions of Latin American migrants in the U.S.?

Indeed, as I write this conclusion, Latino activists and scholars are making renewed calls for research exploring the complex relationship between Latin America, U.S. *Latinidad,* mestizaje, Blackness, and Indigeneity—a reflection of how the growing diversity of the U.S. Latino population demands more studies of transnational racialization and inter- and intra-group relations throughout the Americas. More broadly, it is my hope that the stories of my Mexican respondents compel race scholars to extend their analytical lens beyond the geopolitical confines of the U.S. racial state to gain a deeper understanding of the ways in which transnational migration transforms how race is both conceptualized and experienced across multiple borders.

Notes

Introduction. Immigration and Racial Transformation in America

1. New research by sociologist Tahseen Shams (2020) theorizes that migrants engage in the creation and maintenance of social connections not only in societies of origin and destination but also to places beyond them, which she refers to as "elsewheres."

2. The 2020 census figures point to this possibility; the share of Latinos choosing "White" fell from about 53 percent in 2010 to about 20 percent in 2020.

3. The 2020 census shows that just under 2 percent of the population in Jalisco identifies as Afro-descendant.

4. Male migrants have historically outnumbered female migrants. However, the gender gap in migration is closing. In 2011, 53 percent of the immigrant population was male and 47 percent female (Stoney and Batalova 2013).

Chapter 1. Race in Mexico: Mestizo Privilege

1. In Peter Wade's (1993) study of Blackness and race mixture in Colombia, he interprets this paradox (also found in various Latin American nations, including Brazil) as a complex coexistence of *mestizaje* and discrimination.

2. There is a long tradition among U.S. and Latin American scholars alike of using comparisons to the United States to explain the unique contours of race relations in the two regions.

3. Spanish conquistadores first arrived in what is today known as Mexico City in 1519. It would be another two years before they could claim military victory over the Aztec empire, in 1521.

4. During that century, Mexico imported more enslaved Africans than any other colony in the Americas; however, many of the enslaved Africans did not

remain there and were soon after exported to other colonies throughout the Americas (Palmer 1967).

5. Although colorism in the U.S. has roots in slavery, in which enslaved persons with fairer complexions received preferential treatment, enslaved people were nonetheless considered Black. This created a system of racial passing, whereby "White-passing" African Americans could access privileges reserved only for Whites.

6. This is consistent with many other regions in Mexico, where, due to the population's racial mixture of European, Indigenous, and African ancestry, individuals fall within a broad range of phenotypes and skin tones.

7. Similar findings were reported in a study by Telles and PERLA (2014). They found that although Mexicans with light- or medium-colored skin acknowledged that racism exists in Mexico, they suggested that it affects only people darker than themselves.

8. Only 2 percent of the population in Guadalajara identified as Black or Afro descendant in the 2020 Mexican census.

9. Some say that Memín is a Cuban-Mexican boy (Gonzalez 2010).

10. The new image of Nito continues to be problematic, however. The character is a light-skinned Black boy who is wearing jeans and a T-shirt and has an exaggerated Afro hairstyle.

Chapter 2. Racial Border Crossings

1. According to the 2010 Brazilian census, 50.7 percent of the population defines themselves as "Black" or "mixed race," compared with 47.7 percent who label themselves "White."

Chapter 3. First Encounters with Race in *El Norte*

1. As a counterexample, a study of Mexican immigrant fruit vendors in Los Angeles by sociologist Rocío Rosales (2020) found that established immigrants who employed migrants or helped them secure jobs often exploited vulnerable newcomers for their own financial benefit.

2. According to Sam Quinones, an *L.A. Times* journalist who has written extensively about Latino gangs, the Mexican Mafia is "an enormously important institution in the lives of people who live in Latino barrios across Southern California." This is because large organized gangs like the Eme (*M*, for "Mexican Mafia") often tax local businesses like fruit vendors and small cantinas that tend to employ immigrants (L.A. Taco 2015, https://www.lataco.com/gangs-los -angeles-2015-sam-quinones/).

3. Victory Outreach offers weekly Spanish mass and services for gang youth in multiple locations across Southern California.

4. Vasquez-Tokos (2020) compared Latinos in Los Angeles with those in northeastern Kansas and found significant differences in how each group related to the "mainstream" as well as co-ethnics. Whereas L.A. Latinos, as a strategy of social mobility, distanced themselves from co-ethnics they perceived as poor and gang-related, Latinos in Kansas, a majority-White space, downplayed race and racism to fit into the local "mainstream."

Chapter 4. Settling In: Illegality and the U.S. Color Line

1. Mexican American Legal Defense and Education Fund (2014).

2. This was well before Arpaio became even more famous after Donald Trump pardoned him in 2017. Arpaio had been convicted of criminal contempt for ignoring a judge's orders to stop detaining people simply because he suspected them of being undocumented immigrants.

3. A review of current Mexican public education textbooks reveals that in their K-12 schooling, students are taught very little about U.S./African American history. In one example, racial segregation is mentioned in a one-paragraph lesson plan on the U.S. Civil Rights Movement.

4. See, for example, Historia 2 Libro de Secundaria Grado 3, by Comisión de Libros de Texto Gratuitos.

5. Immigrant attitudes toward Black Americans may also be shaped by the belief that Black Americans are anti-immigrant. A study by Sandoval (2010) found that some Black Americans in Chicago, feeling that the U.S. has yet to fulfill its promise of granting full citizenship to African Americans, strategically drew on nativist discourse of citizenship when making claims about who is entitled to resources and jobs and drew boundaries between themselves and undocumented immigrants.

Conclusion. From Mestizo to Minority

1. For a recent empirical study of how U.S. migration transforms race in the immigrant sending region, see Tiffany Joseph's (2015) study of Brazilian return-migrants.

2. Just over half of the respondents reported being undocumented.

3. Massey and Sanchez (2012).

4. See my discussion of Ginetta Candelario, Jorge Duany, and Jose Itzigsohn, among others, in the Introduction.

5. See Telles's book *Race in Another America* (2004) for more about Brazilian race relations and Telles and PERLA (2014) for more on race in Latin America more generally.

6. For more on the social and economic disparities between Latinos who identify as White versus Black, see John Logan (2010).

7. The census question asks Mexican residents if they self-identify as Afro-Mexican, Afro-descendant, or Black.

8. In the U.S., a coalition of Mexican American, Puerto Rican, and Cuban activists and grassroots organizations, governmental institutions, and Spanish-language media networks successfully campaigned for the Latino question to be included on the census. For more, see Christina Mora (2014).

References

Abrego, Leisy, and Cecilia Menjívar. 2011. "Immigrant Latina Mothers as Targets of Legal Violence." *International Journal of Sociology of the Family* 37 (1): 9–26.

Acevedo, Nicole. 2020. "Latinos Must Confront 'Ingrained' Anti-Black Racism amid George Floyd Protests, Some Urge." NBC News, June 12, 2020. https://www.nbcnews.com/news/latino/latinos-must-confront-ingrained -anti-black-racism-amid-george-floyd-n1223696.

Aguirre-Beltrán, Gonzalo. (1946) 1972. *La población negra de México: estudio etnohistórico.* 3ra edición, México DF: Fondo de Cultura Económica.

Alba, Richard D. 2020. *The Great Demographic Illusion: Majority, Minority, and the Expanding American Mainstream.* Princeton, NJ: Princeton University Press.

Alba, Richard D., and Victor Nee. 2003. *Remaking the American Mainstream: Assimilation and Contemporary Immigration.* Cambridge, MA: Harvard University Press.

Almaguer, Tomás. 2008. *Racial Fault Lines: The Historical Origins of White Supremacy in California.* Berkeley: University of California Press.

Andrews, George Reid. 2004. *Afro-Latin America, 1800–2000.* New York: Oxford University Press.

Armenta, Amada. 2017. *Protect, Serve, and Deport: The Rise of Policing as Immigration Enforcement.* Berkeley: University of California Press.

Arredondo, Gabriela F. 2008. *Mexican Chicago: Race, Identity, and Nation, 1916–39.* Chicago: University of Illinois Press.

Baran, Dominika. 2017. *Language in Immigrant America.* New York: Duke University Press.

Barragan, Esteban. 1997. *Con un pie en el estribo: Formación y deslizamientos de las sociedades rancheras en la construcción de México moderno.* Zamora: El Colegio de Michoacan.

Basch, Linda, Nina Glick Schiller, and Cristina Szanton Blanc. 1994. *Nations Unbound: Transnational Projects, Postcolonial Predicaments, and Deterritorialized Nation-State.* London: Gordon and Breach Science Publishers.

Baumgartner, Alice L. 2020. *South to Freedom: Runaway Slaves to Mexico and the Road to the Civil War.* New York: Basic Books.

Bean, Frank D., Susan K. Brown, and James D. Bachmeier. 2015. *Parents Without Papers: The Progress and Pitfalls of Mexican American Integration.* New York: Russell Sage Foundation.

Bonilla-Silva, Eduardo. 2004. "From Bi-racial to Tri-racial: Towards a New System of Racial Stratification in the USA." *Ethnic and Racial Studies* 27 (6): 931–50.

Bonilla-Silva, Eduardo, and David R. Dietrich. 2008. "The Latin Americanization of Racial Stratification in the U.S." In *Racism in the 21st Century*, edited by Ronald E. Hall, 151–70. New York: Springer Science and Business Media.

Bouie, Jamelle. 2014. "Will Today's Hispanics Be Tomorrow's Whites?: How Hispanics Perceive Themselves May Shape the Future of Race in America." *Slate*, April 15, 2014. https://slate.com/news-and-politics/2014/04/americas-future-racial-makeup-will-todays-hispanics-be-tomorrows-whites.html.

Britton, Marcus. 2014. "Latino Spatial and Structural Assimilation: Close Intergroup Friendships Among Houston-Area Latinos." *Journal of Ethnic and Migration Studies* 40 (8): 1192–1216.

Budiman, Abby. 2020. *Key Findings About U.S. Immigrants.* Washington, DC: Pew Research Center. https://www.pewresearch.org/fact-tank/2020/08/20/key-findings-about-u-s-immigrants/.

Burawoy, Michael, et al. 2000. *Global Ethnography: Forces, Connections, and Imaginations in a Postmodern World.* Berkeley: University of California Press.

Campos Lima, Eduardo. 2020. "Black Lives Matter Is Inspiring Demonstrations all over Latin America." *America: The Jesuit Review*, June 22, 2020. https://www.americamagazine.org/politics-society/2020/06/22/black-lives-matter-movement-latin-america-protests.

Candelario, Ginetta. 2007. *Black Behind the Ears: Dominican Racial Identity from Museums to Beauty Shops.* Durham, NC: Duke University Press.

Carter, Niambi. 2007. "The Black/White Paradigm Revisited: African Americans, Immigration, Race, and Nation in Durham." PhD diss., Duke University.

———. 2019. *American While Black: African Americans, Immigration, and the Limits of Citizenship.* Oxford University Press.

Casas, Regina Martínez, Emiko Saldívar, René D. Flores, and Christina A. Sue. 2014. "The Different Faces of Mestizaje: Ethnicity and Race in Mexico." In *Pigmentocracies: Ethnicity, Race, and Color in Latin America,* edited by Edward E. Telles and the Project on Ethnicity and Race in Latin America (PERLA), 36–80. Chapel Hill: University of North Carolina Press.

Chasteen, John Charles. 2001. *Born in Blood and Fire: A Concise History of Latin America.* New York: W. W. Norton and Company.

Chavez, Leo R. 2008. *The Latino Threat: Constructing Immigrants, Citizens, and the Nation.* Palo Alto, CA: Stanford University Press.

Chaudhary, Ali R. 2014. "Racialized Incorporation: The Effects of Race and Generational Status on Self-Employment and Industry-Sector Prestige in the U.S." *International Migration Review* 49 (2): 318–54.

Clerge, Orly. 2019. *The New Noir: Race, Identity & Diaspora in Black Suburbia.* Berkeley: University of California Press.

Cobas, Jose A., Jorge Duany, and Joe R. Feagin. 2009. *How the United States Racializes Latinos: White Hegemony and Its Consequences.* Paradigm Publishers.

Davis, Mike. 2001. "Sunshine and the Open Shop: Ford and Darwin in 1920s Los Angeles." In *Metropolis in the Making: Los Angeles in the 1920s.* Edited by Tom Sitton and William Deverell. Berkeley: University of California Press.

Deggans, Eric. 2020. "'Cops' Show Canceled amid Worldwide Protests Against Police Violence." *NPR,* June 10, 2020. https://www.npr.org/sections/live-updates-protests-for-racial-justice/2020/06/10/873624536/cops-show-canceled-amid-worldwide-protests-against-police-violence.

De Genova, Nicholas P. 2004. "The Legal Production of Mexican/Migrant 'Illegality.'" *Latino Studies* 2 (2): 160–85.

De Genova, Nicolas, and Ana Y. Ramos-Zayas. 2003. *Latino Crossings: Mexicans, Puerto Ricans, and the Politics of Race and Citizenship.* New York: Routledge.

———. 2003. "Latino Racial Formations in the United States: An Introduction." *Journal of Latin American Anthropology* 8 (2): 2–17.

De la Fuente, Alejandro. 2000. *A Nation for All: Race, Inequality, and Politics in Twentieth Century Cuba.* Chapel Hill: University of North Carolina Press.

DePalma, Anthony. 1995. "The World; Racism? Mexico's in Denial." *New York Times,* June 11, 1995.

Desmond, Matthew. 2014. "Relational Ethnography." *Theoretical Sociology* 43: 547–79.

Dowling, Julie. 2014. *Mexican Americans and the Question of Race.* Austin: University of Texas Press.

Duany, Jorge. 1998. "Reconstructing Racial Identity: Ethnicity, Color, and Class Among Dominicans in the United States and Puerto Rico." *Latin American Perspectives* 25 (3): 147–72.

———. 2005. "Neither White nor Black: The Representation of Racial Identity Among Puerto Ricans on the Island and in the U.S. Mainland." In *Neither Enemies nor Friends: Latinos, Blacks, Afro-Latinos,* edited by Anani Dzidzienyo and Suzanne Oboler, 173–88. New York: Palgrave Macmillan.

Dulitzky, Ariel E. 2005. "A Region in Denial: Racial Discrimination and Racism in Latin America." In *Neither Enemies nor Friends: Latinos, Blacks, Afro-Latinos,* edited by Anani Dzidzienyo and Suzanne Oboler, 39–59. New York: Palgrave Macmillan.

Duquette-Rury, Lauren. 2019. *Exit and Voice: The Paradox of Cross-Border Politics in Mexico.* Berkeley: University of California Press.

Dzidzienyo, Anani, and Suzanne Oboler, eds. 2005. *Neither Enemies nor Friends: Latinos, Blacks, Afro-Latinos.* New York: Palgrave Macmillan.

Ebert, Kim, and Sarah M. Ovink. 2014. "Anti-Immigrant Ordinances and Discrimination in New and Established Destinations." *American Behavioral Scientist* 58 (13): 1784–1804.

Farr, Marcia. 2006. *Rancheros in Chicagoacán: Language and Identity in a Transnational Community.* Austin: University of Texas Press.

Feagin, Joe R. 2013. *The White Racial Frame: Centuries of Racial Framing and Counter-Framing.* New York: Routledge.

Feliciano, Cynthia, Rennie Lee, and Belinda Robnett. 2011. "Racial Boundaries Among Latinos: Evidence from Internet Daters' Racial Preferences." *Social Problems* 58 (2): 189–212.

FitzGerald, David Scott, and David Cook-Martín. 2014. *Culling the Masses: The Democratic Origins of Racist Immigration Policy in the Americas.* Cambridge, MA: Harvard University Press.

Flamming, Douglas. 2006. *Bound for Freedom: Black Los Angeles in Jim Crow America.* Berkeley: University of California Press.

Flippen, Chenoa A., and Emilio A. Parrado. 2015. "Perceived Discrimination Among Latino Immigrants in New Destinations: The Case of Durham, North Carolina." *Sociological Perspectives* 58 (4): 666–85.

Flores-González, Nilda. 2017. *Citizens but Not Americans: Race and Belonging Among Latino Millennials.* New York: New York University Press.

Flores, René, and Edward Telles. 2012. "Social Stratification in Mexico: Disentangling Color, Ethnicity, and Class." *American Sociological Review* 77 (3): 486–94.

Flores, René D., and Ariela Schachter. 2018. "Who Are the 'Illegals'? The Social Construction of Illegality in the United States." *American Sociological Review* 88 (5): 839–68.

Forman, Tyrone, Carla Goar, and Amanda E. Lewis. 2004. "Neither Black nor White?: An Empirical Test of the Latin Americanization Thesis." *Race & Society* 5 (1): 65–84.

Fox, Jonathan. 2006. "Reframing Mexican Migration and a Multi-Ethnic Process." *Latino Studies* 4: 39–61.

Fox, Jonathan, and Gaspar Rivera-Salgado. 2004. *Indigenous Mexican Migrants in the United States.* Boulder, CO: Lynne Rienner Publishers.

Frank, Reanne, Ilana R. Akresh, and Bo Lu. 2010. "Latino Immigrants and the U.S. Racial Order: How and Where Do They Fit In?" *American Sociological Review* 75 (3): 378–401.

Frias, Sebastian. 2020. "Mexicans of African Descent Are Being Counted in Historic 2020 Census." W. K. Kellogg Foundation, March 20, 2020. https://everychildthrives.com/mexicans-of-african-descent-are-being-counted-in-historic-2020-census/.

Fujioka, Yuki. 1999. "Television Portrayals and African-American Stereotypes: Examination of Television Effects when Direct Contact Is Lacking." *Journalism & Mass Communication Quarterly* 76 (52): 52–75.

Gans, Herbert. 1999. "The Possibility of a New Racial Hierarchy in the Twenty-First-Century United States." In *The Cultural Territories of Race: Black and White Boundaries,* edited by Michèle Lamont, 371–90. Chicago: University of Chicago Press.

Garcia Bedolla, Lisa. 2005. *Fluid Borders: Latino Power, Identity, and Politics in Los Angeles.* Berkeley: University of California Press.

Golash-Boza, Tanya. 2006. "Dropping the Hyphen? Becoming Latino(a)-American Through Racialized Assimilation." *Social Forces* 85 (1): 27–56.

———. 2015. *Deported: Immigrant Policing, Disposable Labor and Global Capitalism*. New York: New York University Press.

Golash-Boza, Tanya, and William Darity. 2008. "Latino Racial Choices: The Effects of Skin Colour and Discrimination on Latinos' and Latinas' Racial Self-Identifications." *Ethnic and Racial Studies* 31 (5): 899–934.

Golash-Boza, Tanya, and Pierrette Hondagneu-Sotelo. 2013. "Latino Immigrant Men and the Deportation Crisis: A Gendered Racial Removal Program." *Latino Studies* 11 (3): 271–92.

Gómez, Laura E. 2007. *Manifest Destinies: The Making of the Mexican American Race*. New York: New York University Press.

———. 2015. "Opposite One-Drop Rules: Mexican Americans, African Americans and the Need to Reconceive Turn-of-the-Twentieth-Century Race Relations." In *How the United States Racializes Latinos: White Hegemony and Its Consequences*, edited by José A. Cobas, Jorge Duany, and Joe R. Feagin. United Kingdom: Taylor & Francis.

———. 2020. *Inventing Latinos: A New Story of American Racism*. New York: The New Press.

Gonzalez, Anita. 2010. *Afro-Mexico: Dancing Between Myth and Reality*. Austin: University of Texas Press.

Gonzalez, Roberto. 2016. *Lives in Limbo: Undocumented and Coming of Age in America*. Berkeley: University of California Press.

Gordon, Milton. 1964. *Assimilation in American Life: The Role of Race, Religion, and National Origins*. United Kingdom: Taylor & Francis.

Griffith, Kati L., and Shannon Gleeson. 2019. "Trump's 'Immployment' Law Agenda: Intensifying Employment-Based Enforcement and Un-Authorizing the Authorized." *Southwestern Law Review* 48 (2): 475–501.

Guan, Shu-Sha Angie, Afaf Nash, and Marjorie Faulstich Orellana. 2016. "Cultural and Social Processes of Language Brokering Among Arab, Asian, and Latin immigrants." *Journal of Multilingual & Multicultural Development* 37 (2): 150–66.

Hagan, Jacqueline. 1998. "Social Networks, Gender, and Immigrant Incorporation: Resources and Constraints." *American Sociological Review* 63 (1): 55–67.

Haller, William, and Patricia Landolt. 2005. "The Transnational Dimensions of Identity Formation: Adult Children of Immigrants in Miami." *Ethnic and Racial Studies* 28 (6): 1182–1214.

Hamilton, Tod G. 2019. *Immigration and the Remaking of Black America*. New York: Russell Sage Foundation.

Haney López, Ian F. 2003. *Racism on Trial: The Chicano Fight for Justice.* Cambridge, MA: Harvard University Press.

Harris, Paul. 2007. "Gang Mayhem Grips L.A." *Guardian,* March 17, 2007. https://www.theguardian.com/world/2007/mar/18/usa.paulharris.

Hartigan, John. 2013. "Mexican Genomics and the Roots of Racial Thinking." *Cultural Anthropology* 28 (3): 372–95.

Hernández Cuevas, Marco Polo. 2004. *African Mexicans and the Discourse on Modern Nation.* University Press of America, Inc.

Hernandez, Tanya K. 2007. "Roots of Anger: Longtime Prejudices, Not Economic Rivalry, Fuel Latino-Black Tensions." *Los Angeles Times,* January 7, 2007. https://www.latimes.com/archives/la-xpm-2007-jan-07-op
-hernandez7-story.html

Herrera, Juan. 2016. "Racialized Illegality: The Regulation of Informal Labor and Space." *Latino Studies* 14, 320–43.

Hoffmann, Odile. 2006. "Negros y afromestizos en Mexico: Viejas y nuevas lecturas de un mundo olvidado." *Revista Mexicana de sociología* 68 (1): 103–35.

Hondagneu-Sotelo, Pierrette, and Manuel Pastor. 2021. *South Central Dreams: Finding Home and Building Community in South L.A.* New York: New York University Press.

Hooker, Juliet. 2017. *Theorizing Race in the Americas: Douglass, Sarmiento, Du Bois, and Vasconcelos.* Oxford: Oxford University Press.

Huante, Alfredo. 2021. "A Lighter Shade of Brown? Racial Formation and Gentrification in Latino Los Angeles." *Social Problems* 68 (1): 63–79.

Innis-Jiménez, Michael. 2013. *Steel Barrio: The Great Mexican Migration to South Chicago, 1915–1940.* New York: New York University Press.

Instituto Nacional de Estadística y Geografía (INEGI). 2010. "Censo de Población y Vivienda 2010." https://www.inegi.org.mx/programas/ccpv/2010/.

Itzigsohn, Jose. 2009. *Encountering American Faultlines: Race, Class, and the Dominican Experience in Providence.* New York: Russell Sage Foundation.

Itzigsohn, Jose, Carlos Dore Cabral, Esther Hernandez Medina, and Obed Vazquez. 1999. "Mapping Dominican Transnationalism: Narrow and Broad Transnational Practices." *Ethnic and Racial Studies* 22 (2): 316–39.

Jerry, Anthony R. 2014. "Chasing Blackness: Re-Investing Value and Mexico's Changing Racial Economy." PhD diss., University of Illinois at Urbana-Champaign.

Jiménez, Tomás R. 2008. "Mexican-Immigrant Replenishment and the Continuing Significance of Ethnicity and Race." *American Journal of Sociology* 113 (6): 1527–67.

Jones, Jennifer A. 2012. "Blacks May Be Second Class, but They Can't Make Them Leave: Mexican Racial Formation and Immigrant Status in Winston-Salem." *Latino Studies* 10 (1/2): 60–80.

———. 2013. "'Mexicans Will Take the Jobs that Even Blacks Won't Do': An Analysis of Blackness and Invisibility in Contemporary Mexico." *Ethnic and Racial Studies* 36 (10): 1564–81.

———. 2019. *The Browning of the New South*. Chicago: University of Chicago Press.

Jones, John Curtis, and Edison J. Trickett. 2005. "Immigrant Adolescents Behaving as Cultural Brokers: A Study of Families from the Former Soviet Union." *The Journal of Social Psychology* 145 (4): 405–27.

Jones-Correa, Michael. 2013. "Commonalities, Competition, and Linked Fate." In *Just Neighbors: Research on African American and Latino Relations*, edited by Edward Telles, Mark Q. Sawyer, and Gaspar Rivera-Salgado, 63–95. New York: Russell Sage Foundation.

Joseph, Tiffany D. 2015. *Race on the Move: Brazilian Migrants and the Global Reconstruction of Race*. Stanford: Stanford University Press.

———. 2015. "'US Blacks Are Beautiful but Brazilian Blacks Are Not Racist': Brazilian Return Migrants' Perceptions of US and Brazilian Blacks." In *Re-Positioning Race: Prophetic Research in a Postracial Obama Age*, edited by Sandra Barnes, Zandria Robinson, and Earl Wright II, 151–72. Albany: State University of New York Press.

Katzew, Ilona. 2004. *Casta Painting: Images of Race in Eighteenth-Century Mexico*. New Haven, CT: Yale University Press.

Kim, Nadia Y. 2008. *Imperial Citizens: Koreans and Race from Seoul to LA*. Stanford: Stanford University Press.

King, Katrina Quisumbing. 2019. "Recentering U.S. Empire: A Structural Perspective on the Color Line." *Sociology of Race and Ethnicity* 5 (1): 11–25.

Kirkham, Chris, and Tiffany Hsu. 2015. "Few California Workers Win Back Pay in Wage-Theft Cases." *Los Angeles Times*, April 6, 2015. https://www.latimes.com/business/la-fi-wage-theft-20150407-story.html.

Klebnikov, Sergei. 2020. "Floyd Protests Go Global—from Mexico, London, Germany and France—and Sometimes Violent." *Forbes*, June 6, 2020. https://www.forbes.com/sites/sergeiklebnikov/2020/06/06/floyd-protests-go-global-from-mexico-london-germany-and-france-and-sometimes-violent/?sh=58eb2e4b4921.

Knight, Alan. 1990. "Racism, Revolution, and Indigenismo: Mexico 1910–1940." In *The Idea of Race in Latin America, 1870–1940*, edited by Richard Graham, 71–113. Austin: University of Texas Press.

Lamont, Michèle, and Virág Molnár. 2002. "The Study of Boundaries Across the Social Sciences." *Annual Review of Sociology* 28, 167–95.

Lee, Jennifer, and Frank D. Bean. 2010. *The Diversity Paradox: Immigration and the Color Line in Twenty-First Century America*. New York: Russell Sage Foundation.

Levitt, Peggy. 1998. "Social Remittances: Migration Driven Local-Level Forms of Cultural Diffusion." *International Migration Review* 32 (4): 926–48.

———. 2001. *The Transnational Villagers*. Berkeley: University of California Press.

Levitt, Peggy, and Deepak Lamba-Nieves. 2011. "Social Remittances Revisited." *Journal of Ethnic and Migration Studies* 37 (1): 1–22.

Lewis, Laura A. 2000. "Blacks, Black Indians, Afromexicans: The Dynamics of Race, Nation, and Identity in a Mexican 'Moreno' Community (Guerrero)." *American Ethnologist* 27 (4): 898–926.

Light, Michael T., Jingying He, and Jason P. Robey. 2020. "Comparing Crime Rates Between Undocumented Immigrants, Legal Immigrants, and Native-Born US Citizens in Texas." *Proceedings of the National Academy of Sciences* 117 (51): 32340–47.

Loewen, James W. 1988. *The Mississippi Chinese: Between Black and White*. Long Grove, IL: Waveland Press.

Logan, John R. 2010. "How Race Counts for Hispanic Americans." In *The Afro-Latino Reader: History and Culture in the United States*, edited by Miriam Jiménez Román and Juan Flores, 471–84. Durham, NC: Duke University Press.

Logan, John R., and Richard N. Turner. 2013. "Hispanics in the United States: Not Only Mexicans." Brown University: US 2010 Project Report. https://s4.ad.brown.edu/Projects/Diversity/Data/Report/report03202013.pdf.

Lomnitz, Claudio. 2001. *Deep Mexico, Silent Mexico: An Anthropology of Nationalism*. Minneapolis: University of Minnesota Press.

Lomnitz-Adler, Claudio. 1992. *Exits from the Labyrinth: Culture and Ideology in the Mexican National Space*. Berkeley: University of California Press.

Marciniak, Katarzyna. 2013. "Legal/Illegal: Protesting Citizenship in Fortress America." *Citizenship Studies* 12 (2): 260–77.

Marrow, Helen. 2003. "To Be or Not to Be (Hispanic or Latino): Brazilian Racial and Ethnic Identity in the United States." *Ethnicities* 3 (4): 427–64.

———. 2008. "Hispanic Immigration, Black Population Size, and Intergroup Relations in the Rural and Small-Town South." In *New Faces in New Places: The Changing Geography of American Immigration*, edited by Douglas S. Massey, 211–48. New York: Russell Sage Foundation.

————. 2009. "New Immigrant Destinations and the American Colour Line."
Ethnic and Racial Studies 32 (6): 1037–57.

————. 2020. "Hope Turned Sour: Second-Generation Incorporation and Mobility in U.S. New Immigrant Destinations." *Ethnic and Racial Studies* 43 (1): 99–118.

Martínez-Echazábal, Lourdes. 1998. "Mestizaje and the Discourse of National/Cultural Identity in Latin America, 1845–1959." *Latin American Perspectives* 25 (100): 21–42.

Massey, Douglas S. 2014. "The Racialization of Latinos in the United States." In *The Oxford Handbook of Ethnicity, Crime, and Immigration,* edited by Sandra M. Bucerius and Michael Tonry, 21–40. New York: Oxford University Press.

Massey, Douglas S., and Magaly R. Sanchez. 2012. *Brokered Boundaries: Creating Immigrant Identity in Anti-Immigrant Times.* New York: Russell Sage Foundation.

Mau, Steffen. 2010. *Social Transnationalism: Lifeworlds Beyond the Nation-State.* New York: Routledge.

McClain, Paula D., Niambi M. Carter, Victoria M. DeFrancesco Soto, Monique L. Lyle, Jeffrey D. Grynaviski, Shayla C. Nunnally, Thomas J. Scotto, J. Alan Kendrick, Gerald F. Lackey, and Kendra Davenport Cotton. 2006. "Racial Distancing in a Southern City: Latino Immigrants' Views of Black Americans." *The Journal of Politics* 68 (3): 571–84.

Menchaca, Marcha. 1995. *The Mexican Outsiders: A Community History of Marginalization and Discrimination in California.* Austin: University of Texas Press.

Menjívar, Cecilia, and Leisy Abrego. 2012. "Legal Violence: Immigration Law and the Lives of Central American Immigrants." *American Journal of Sociology* 117 (5): 1380–1421.

Mindiola, Tatcho Jr., Yolanda Flores Niemann, and Nestor Rodríguez. 2002. *Black-Brown Relations and Stereotypes.* Austin: University of Texas Press.

Molina, Natalia. 2014. *How Race Is Made in America: Immigration, Citizenship, and the Historical Power of Racial Scripts.* Berkeley: University of California Press.

Molina, Natalia, Daniel Martinez HoSang, and Ramón A. Gutierrez. 2019. *Relational Formations of Race: Theory, Method, and Practice.* Berkeley: University of California Press.

Montejano, David. 1987. *Anglos and Mexicans in the Making of Texas, 1836–1986.* Austin: University of Texas Press.

Mora, G. Cristina. 2014. *Making Hispanics: How Activists, Bureaucrats, and the Media Constructed a New American.* Chicago: University of Chicago Press.

Morales, Erica. 2012. "Parental Messages Concerning Latino/Black Interracial Dating: An Exploratory Study Among Latina/o Young Adults." *Latino Studies* 10 (3): 314–33.

Moreno Figueroa, Monica. 2008. "Historically Rooted Transnationalism: Slightedness and the Experience of Racism in Mexican Families." *Journal of Intercultural Studies* 29 (3): 283–97.

———. 2010. "Distributed Intensities: Whiteness, Mestizaje and the Logics of Mexican Racism." *Ethnicities* 10 (3): 387–401.

Moreno Figueroa, Monica, and Emiko Saldívar Tanaka. 2016. "'We Are Not Racists, We Are Mexicans': Privilege, Nationalism and Post-Race Ideology in Mexico." *Critical Sociology* 42 (4/5): 515–33.

Morris, Aldon. 2015. *The Scholar Denied: W. E. B. Du Bois and the Birth of Modern Sociology.* Berkeley: University of California Press.

Muñoz, Edgardo. 2009. "The Legal Construction of Racial Discrimination in Mexico: Celebrating 200 Years of Independence?" *Mexican Law Review* 2 (2): 109–24.

Murguia, Edward, and Rogelio Saenz. 2002. "An Analysis of the Latin Americanization of Race in the United States: A Reconnaissance of Color Stratification Among Mexicans." *Race and Society* 5, 85–101.

Muro, Jazmín A. 2016. "'Oil and Water'? Latino-White Relations and Symbolic Interaction in a Changing California." *Sociology of Race and Ethnicity* 2 (4): 516–30.

Nelson, Laura J. 2019. "L.A. Is Hemorrhaging Bus Riders—Worsening Traffic and Hurting Climate Goals." *Los Angeles Times*, June 27, 2019. https://www .latimes.com/local/lanow/la-me-ln-bus-ridership-falling-los-angeles-la -metro-20190627-story.html.

Ngai, Mai. 2004. *Impossible Subjects: Illegal Aliens and the Making of Modern America.* Princeton, NJ: Princeton University Press.

Nteta, Tatishe. 2006. "Plus ça Change, Plus C'est La Même Chose? An Examination of the Racial Attitudes of New Immigrants in the U.S." In *Transforming Politics, Transforming America: The Political and Civic Incorporation of Immigrants in the United States,* edited by Taeku Lee, Karthick Ramakrishnan, and Ricardo Ramírez, 194–216. Charlottesville: University of Virginia Press.

Oboler, Suzanne, and Anani Dzidzienyo. 2005. "Flows and Counterflows: Latinas/os, Blackness, and Racialization in Hemispheric Perspective." In

Neither Enemies nor Friends: Latinos, Blacks, Afro-Latinos, edited by Anani Dzidzienyo and Suzanne Oboler, 3–35. New York: Palgrave Macmillan.

O'Brien, Eileen. 2008. *The Racial Middle: Latinos and Asian Americans Living Beyond the Racial Divide.* New York: New York University Press.

Ocampo, Angie N., and Chenoa A. Flippen. 2021. "Re-evaluating Intergroup Dynamics in the South: Racial Attitudes Among Latino Immigrants in Durham, NC." *Social Science Research* 94 (2021): 3–15.

Ochoa, Gilda. 2004. *Becoming Neighbors in a Mexican American Community: Power, Conflict, and Solidarity.* Austin: University of Texas Press.

Oliver, Eric J., and Janelle Wong. 2003. "Intergroup Prejudice in Multiethnic Settings." *American Journal of Political Science* 47 (4): 567–82.

Oliver, Mary Beth. 2003. "African American Men as 'Criminal and Dangerous': Implications of Media Portrayals of Crime on the 'Criminalization' of African American Men." *Journal of African American Studies* 7 (2): 3–18.

Omi, Michael, and Howard Winant. 1994. *Racial Formation in the United States: From the 1960s to the 1990s.* New York: Routledge.

Orgad, Shani. 2012. *Media Representation and the Global Imagination.* Malden, MA: Policy Press.

Palmer, Colin A. 1976. *Slaves of the White God: Blacks in Mexico, 1570–1650.* Cambridge, MA: Harvard University Press.

Park, Robert. 1950. *Race and Culture.* Glencoe, IL: Free Press.

Passel, Jeffrey S., and D'Vera Cohn. 2008. *Trends in Unauthorized Immigration: Undocumented Inflow Now Trails Legal Inflow.* Washington, DC: Hispanic Trends, Pew Hispanic Center. www.pewhispanic.org/s008/10/01/trends-in-unauthorized-immigration/.

Pinedo-Turnovsky, Carolyn. 2019. *Daily Labors: Marketing Identity and Bodies on a New York City Street Corner.* Philadelphia: Temple University Press.

Portes, Alejandro, and Rubén G. Rumbaut. 2006. *Immigrant America: A Portrait.* Third edition, Berkeley: University of California Press.

Prieto, Greg. 2018. *Immigrants Under Threat: Risk and Resistance in Deportation Nation.* New York: New York University Press.

Rendón, María G. 2019. *Stagnant Dreamers: How the Inner City Shapes the Integration of the Second Generation.* New York: Russell Sage Foundation.

Ribas, Vanesa. 2016. *On the Line: Slaughterhouse Lives and the Making of the New South.* Berkeley: University of California Press.

Rios, Victor, and Cid Martinez. 2014. "Conflict, Cooperation, and Avoidance." In *Just Neighbors: Research on African American and Latino Relations*, edited by Edward Telles, Mark Q. Sawyer, and Gaspar Rivera-Salgado. New York: Russell Sage Foundation.

Rodríguez, Clara E. 2000. *Changing Race: Latinos, the Census and the History of Ethnicity in the United States.* New York: New York University Press.

———. 2018. *America, as Seen on TV: How Television Shapes Immigrant Expectations Around the Globe.* New York: New York University Press.

Rodríguez-Muñiz, Michael. 2021. *Figures of the Future: Latino Civil Rights and the Politics of Demographic Change.* Princeton, NJ: Princeton University Press.

Rosales, Rocío. 2020. *Fruteros: Street Vending, Illegality, and Ethnic Community in Los Angeles.* Berkeley: University of California Press.

Rosas, Abigail. 2019. *South Central Is Home: Race and the Power of Community Investment in Los Angeles.* Stanford: Stanford University Press.

Roth, Wendy D. 2009. "'Latino Before the World': The Transnational Extension of Panethnicity." *Ethnic and Racial Studies* 32 (6): 927–47.

———. 2012. *Race Migrations: Latinos and the Cultural Transformation of Race.* Stanford: Stanford University Press.

Roth, Wendy, and Nadia Y. Kim. 2013. "Relocating Prejudice: A Transnational Approach to Understanding Immigrants' Racial Attitudes." *International Migration Review* 47 (2): 330–73.

Sandoval, Claudia. 2010. "Citizenship and the Barrier to Black and Latino Relations in Chicago." *NACLA Report on the Americas* 43 (6): 36–45.

Sawyer, Mark. 2005. "Racial Politics in Multiethnic America: Black and Latina/o Identities and Coalitions." In *Neither Enemies nor Friends: Latinos, Blacks, Afro-Latinos*, edited by Anani Dzidzienyo and Suzanne Oboler, 265–79. New York: Palgrave Macmillan.

Shams, Tahseen. 2020. *Here, There, and Elsewhere: The Making of Immigrant Identities in a Globalized World.* Stanford: Stanford University Press.

Stepan, Nancy. 1991. *In The Hour of Eugenics: Race, Gender, and Nation in Latin America.* Cornell University Press.

Stuesse, Angela. 2016. *Scratching Out a Living: Latinos, Race, and Work in the Deep South.* Berkeley: University of California Press.

Stoney, Sierra, and Jeanne Batalova. 2013. "Mexican Immigrants in the United States." February 28, 2013. Washington, DC: Migration Policy Institute. https://www.migrationpolicy.org/article/mexican-immigrants-united -states-2011#top.

Suárez-Orozco, Marcelo, and Mariela Páez. 2002. *Latinos Remaking America.* Berkeley: University of California Press.

Sue, Christina. 2009. "An Assessment of the Latin Americanization Thesis."
Ethnic and Racial Studies 32(6): 1058–70.

Sue, Christina A. 2013. *Land of the Cosmic Race: Race Mixture, Racism, and Blackness in Mexico*. New York: Oxford University Press.

Sue, Christina A., and Tanya Golash-Boza. 2009. "Blackness in Mestizo America: The Cases of Mexico and Peru." *Latino(a) Research Review* 7 (1/2): 30–58.

Taberski, Dan. 2019. "What 'Running from Cops' Learned from 'Cops.'" June 12, 2019. *Running from Cops*. Podcast. https://www.wnycstudios.org /podcasts/otm/episodes/onthemedia-what-running-cops-learned-cops.

Tamir, Christine. 2021. *The Growing Diversity of Black America*. Washington, DC: Pew Research Center.

Telles, Edward E. 2004. *Race in Another America: The Significance of Skin Color in Brazil*. Princeton, NJ: Princeton University Press.

Telles, Edward E., and Christina A. Sue. 2019. *Durable Ethnicity: Mexican Americans and the Ethnic Core*. New York: Oxford University Press.

Telles, Edward E., Mark Q. Sawyer, and Gaspar Rivera-Salgado, eds. 2013. *Just Neighbors: Research on African American and Latino Relations*. New York: Russell Sage Foundation.

Telles, Edward E., and PERLA. 2014. *Pigmentocracies: Ethnicity, Race, and Color in Latin America*. Chapel Hill: University of North Carolina Press.

Telles, Edward E., and Tianna Paschel. 2014. "Who Is Black, White, or Mixed Race? How Skin Color, Status, and Nation Shape Racial Classification in Latin America." *American Journal of Sociology* 120 (3): 864–907.

Telles, Edward E., and Vilma Ortiz. 2008. *Generations of Exclusion: Mexican Americans, Assimilation, and Race*. New York: Russell Sage Foundation.

Thomas, Deborah A., and Kamari Maxine Clarke. 2006. "Introduction: Globalization and the Transformations of Race." In *Globalization and Race: Transformations in the Cultural Production of Blackness*, edited by Kamari Maxine Clarke and Deborah A. Thomas, 1–34. Duke University Press.

Treviño Rangel, Javier. 2008. "Racismo y nacion: comunidades imaginadas en Mexico." *Estudios Sociologicos* XXVI, 78.

Tse, Lucy. 1996. "Language Brokering in Linguistic Minority Communities: The Case of Chinese- and Vietnamese-American students." *Bilingual Research Journal* 20 (3/4): 485–98.

United States Census Bureau. 2015. "QuickFacts." Accessed July 18, 2020. http://www.census.gov/quickfacts/table/RHI725215/0673080,00.

Vasconcelos, José. 1925. *The Cosmic Race, La Raza Cósmica*. Baltimore: Johns Hopkins University Press.

Vasquez, Jessica M. 2011. *Mexican Americans Across Generations: Immigrant Families, Racial Realities*. New York: New York University Press.

Vasquez-Tokos, Jessica M. 2017. *Marriage Vows and Racial Choices*. New York: Russell Sage Foundation.

———. 2020. "Do Latinos Consider Themselves Mainstream?: The Influence of Region." *Sociological Perspectives* 63 (4): 571–88.

Vaughn, Bobby. 2005. "Afro-Mexico: Blacks, Indígenas, Politics, and the Greater Diaspora." In *Neither Enemies nor Friends: Latinos, Blacks, Afro-Latinos*, edited by Anani Dzidzienyo and Suzanne Oboler, 117–36. New York: Palgrave Macmillan.

———. 2013. "Mexico Negro: From the Shadows of Nationalist Mestizaje to New Possibilities in Afro-Mexican Identity." *Journal of Pan African Studies* 6 (1): 227–40.

Villarreal, Andres. 2010. "Stratification by Skin Color in Contemporary Mexico." *American Sociological Review* 75 (5): 652–78.

Wade, Peter. 1993. *Blackness and Race Mixture: The Dynamics of Racial Identity in Colombia*. Baltimore: Johns Hopkins University Press.

Waldinger, Roger. 2013. "Immigrant Transnationalism." *Current Sociology Review* 61 (5/6): 756–77.

Waters, Mary. 2001. *Black Identities: West Indian Immigrant Dreams and American Realities*. New York: Russell Sage Foundation.

Wimmer, Andreas, and Nina Glick Schiller. 2002. "Methodological Nationalism and Beyond: Nation-State Building, Migration and the Social Sciences." *Global Networks* 2 (4): 301–34.

Yancey, George A. 2003. *Who Is White? Latinos, Asians, and the New Black/Non-black Divide*. Boulder, CO: Lynne Rienner Publishers.

Zamora, Sylvia. 2016. "Racial Remittances: The Effect of Migration on Racial Ideologies in Mexico and the United States." *Sociology of Race and Ethnicity* 2 (4): 466–81.

———. 2018. "Mexican Illegality, Black Citizenship, and White Power: Immigrant Perceptions of the U.S. Sociracial Hierarchy." *Journal of Ethnic and Migration Studies* 44 (11): 1897–1914.

Zepeda-Millán, Chris, and Sophia J. Wallace. 2013. "Racialization in Times of Contention: How Social Movements Influence Latino Racial Identity." *Politics, Groups, and Identities* 1 (4): 510–27.

Index

accent (speech), 31, 32, 45, 52, 61, 127, 184. *See also* language; proficiency, English

activism, 13, 48, 49, 189, 194n8. *See also* Black Lives Matter; protests

adaptation, 17, 24, 102, 105, 117, 172; to racial systems, 133–34, 139, 154

African Americans. *See* Black Americans

Africans, 22, 40, 65, 191n4

Afro descendants, 33, 38, 49, 50, 63; communities, 44; immigrants, 12; Latin Americans, 189; populations, 23

Afro-Mexicans, 23, 32, 41, 44, 51, 99, 189; cultural representation of, 63; disadvantaged condition of, 68; in ethnoracial hierarchy, 70; marginalization of, 141; in Mexican census, 48, 49, 187, 188, 191n3, 192n8, 194n7; Mexican understandings of, 65, 66; migration to the U.S., 69; political movements, 175, 176; racial mixing of, 11, 64

aggressiveness, inherent, 43, 74, 89, 90, 101, 131, 173

American Dream, 167, 177, 181

Americanization, 8, 34, 73, 124

Americano/a, 75, 82, 142, 148, 154

Americanos, los, 33, 34, 75, 82, 142, 148, 154

ancestry, 40, 64, 67, 192n6; Black, 11, 48, 49, 65, 187, 188; Indigenous, 22; Mexican, 30; Spanish, 22, 41, 61

Anglos, 1–2, 17, 18, 27, 160–61, 169; Americanness, 165; Anglo-American colonialism, 22; Anglo-American cultural norms, 40; Anglocentrism, 38; Anglo nation, 43, 106; arrogance of, 44; vs. racially Mexican, 34; settlers, 42; supremacism, 105, 139, 178

Anglosajón, 34

Anglo supremacy. *See* White supremacy

anti-Blackness, 9, 15, 39, 74, 86, 180, 181; Latino, 179; White, 21

anti-immigrant sentiment, 7, 13, 14, 159; climate of, 161, 177; discrimination, 151, 169; harassment, 142; hostility, 35; nativist xenophobia, 3; police practices, 20; policies, 28,

Candelario, Ginetta, xi, 11, 12

capital, 3–4; cultural, 57; social, 8, 12, 118

Caribbean, 17, 64

Carter, Niambi, 158, 183

casta/castizo, 41

census, Brazil, 48, 192n1

census, Mexican, 48, 187, 191n3, 192n8, 194n7; counts Afro-Mexicans, 49; media campaign for, 188; race question on, 44, 152

census, Puerto Rico, 72

census, U.S., 13, 153, 178–79, 187–88, 191n2, 194n8

Central Americans, 10, 83, 126, 128, 177, 181, 185

Central Europeans, 17

central-western Mexico, 34, 182

Chapala, Mexico, 96, 99

Chavez, Leo, 20, 168

Chinatown, L.A., California, 24

Chinese, 96, 106–7, 114, 115, 116, 121; as bosses, 117, 165; migrants, 14; shop owners, 150–51

cholos, 118, 124, 125, 126, 134. *See also* gangs

Cisneros, Flaviano, 176

citizenship, 98, 143, 162, 183, 185; advantages of, 141, 163, 164, 167, 177; birthright, 36, 149, 165; of Black Americans, 157, 170, 193n5; liminal stage precedes, 138; Mexican, 5, 101; of migrants, 3, 20; naturalized, 18, 139, 168, 171; notions of, 176; precarious, 184; in racial hierarchy, 104, 140, 166; and racial identification, 154

civil rights, 66, 96, 157, 176, 193n3

Civil Rights Movement, 96, 157, 193n3

class, 40, 52, 149; disparity, 51, 53; hierarchy, 54; intermediate, 42; markers, 153; social, 54, 55, 184; status, 24, 53, 55, 133, 167; structure, 114; underclass, 6, 125

coalitions, viii–ix, 181, 194n8

Colombia, 191n1

colonialism, x, 22, 41, 44, 58; Spanish, 99, 102, 180; U.S., 185

colonias, 24, 107. *See also* neighborhoods

colonization, 6, 14, 15, 18, 38, 45, 72; of Indigenous people, 22

colorism, 172, 192n5

color lines, 14, 136, 185; Black-White, 5, 11, 13, 38, 102, 174

communities, immigrant, vii, x, 20, 88, 110, 175

conflict, viii, 1, 70, 93, 115, 123; in American movies, 78; with Black people, 89; strategies to minimize, 130–34; White-Black, 90, 91. *See also* tension, racial

cosmic race, 43, 70

Costa Chica, Mexico, 33

country of origin, 7, 15, 30, 34, 35, 74, 191n1; racial ideologies and, 184; social boundary lines and, 127; socialization with race and, 173. *See also* sending region

crack epidemic, vii, 27, 76, 109, 136. *See also* drugs

crime, 28, 68, 76, 80, 92, 101; drug-related, 78; gang-related, 124; hate, 14, 183, 184; rate, 125; violent, 136

criminality, 20, 78, 87

criminal justice system, 13, 156
cross-border social ties, 69, 86, 87
Cuba, 38, 72
Cubans, 64, 66, 187, 194n8
culture, 30, 49, 63, 123, 153; African
    American, 26, 71, 80, 185; global,
    70, 73; Indigenous peoples, 69;
    Mexican, 23, 45, 66; popular, 7, 66,
    77, 79, 101, 173; U.S., 6, 8, 15, 17, 40,
    43, 118
customs, sociocultural, 3–4, 139

Davis, Mike, 25
day laborers. *See* workers/laborers
demographics, 12, 30, 38, 114; change,
    vii, ix, 13, 107, 159; of Jalisco, Mex-
    ico, 23; local, 125, 135; in Mexico,
    172; Mexico vs. U.S., 22
denial of racism, 46–49, 68
deportation, 74, 119, 142, 151, 163, 182,
    185; fear of, 145, 168
detention (imprisonment), 119, 168,
    181, 193n2. *See also* apprehension
    (police)
discourse, viii, 20, 63; anti-Black, 66,
    93, 96; anti-Mexican, 20; *Latini-
    dad*, 153; of Mexicanness, 45; Mex-
    ico's, 39, 154; nativist, 193n5; racial,
    4, 9, 32, 70, 79, 147, 173; U.S., 73, 99
discrimination, 1, 5, 18, 142–43, 149,
    191n1; anti-immigrant, 151, 169;
    anti-Mexican, 21, 84, 100, 123, 142;
    class, 52; denials, 46–47; ethnic,
    34; against *morenos*, 142, 157; skin
    color, 58; structural, 60; in the
    U.S., 9, 79, 147, 167. *See also* racial
    discrimination
disparities, 13, 51, 53, 188

diversity, 23, 63, 69, 114, 183, 189
documents, 2, 21, 141, 148, 162, 163. *See
    also* undocumented immigrants
dominance, 26, 47, 126, 141; of
    Spanish-speaking Latinos, 122;
    White, 18, 169, 178
Dominican Republic, 8, 73, 86, 184
Dominicans, 9, 10, 11, 86, 181, 184; mi-
    grants, 8, 12, 73
Dowling, Julie, 12, 18, 152, 154, 172
downtown L.A., viii, 25, 97, 125, 130
driver's licenses, 19, 109
drugs, 28, 75; addiction, vii, 76, 77,
    110; crack, vii, 27, 76, 109, 136;
    crimes, 78; use, 68, 101, 137
Duany, Jorge, xi
Dzidzienyo, Anani, xi, 39

Eagle Pass, Texas, 43
East L.A., California, 106, 124, 125
economic remittances, 4, 8, 72, 73.
    See also racial remittances; social
    remittances
economics, 45, 132, 183; advantages,
    68; challenges, 17; context, 111; de-
    velopment, 40; differences, 52;
    disadvantages, 42; effects on legal
    status, 135; hardships, 186; institu-
    tions, 86; Mexico-U.S. intertwin-
    ing, 4; mobility, 56, 140; neglect,
    27–28; opportunity, 133; policies,
    74, 185; power, 169; residential seg-
    regation, 24; restructuring, 2, 25;
    standing, 41; structures, 38; trans-
    formation, 138; U.S., 145; world, 6
education, 31, 42, 138; access to, 149;
    association with light skin, 55, 164;
    bilingual, 45; level, 24, 29, 30, 69;

gangs, 3, 28, 136; Blacks portrayed as, 78; Latino, 118, 124, 125, 126, 192n2, 193n3, 193n4; shootings, ix; violence, 2, 111. *See also* cholos

Garcia Bedolla, Lisa, 124

gender, 20, 49, 105, 128, 133, 134; differences, 146; equality, 8; expression, 69; gap in migration, 191n4; labor hierarchy, 145; network structures, 129; norms, 73; recreational activities, 130. *See also* men; women

generations: fourth, 10, 18; second, 15, 33, 124, 182; third, 33

geopolitical borders, 3, 6, 28, 72, 100, 189

globalization, 3–4, 28, 99–100, 184; of media, 7, 173; neoliberal, 6; processes of, 184

global media, 7, 8, 67, 73, 173, 176; expose U.S. racism, 9, 16, 74, 86, 180; racial remittances via, 84, 87, 100; transnationalism through, 75–76

Gómez, Laura, 19, 66, 187

Gonzalez, Roberto, 141

Gordon, Milton, 18

government, Latin American, 46

government, Mexico, 37, 44, 48, 49, 66, 69, 187

gringo/a, 34, 90, 95, 96, 123, 145

Guadalajara, Mexico, 1, 22–23, 28, 56, 84, 90, 113; American tourists in, 96, 97, 98; interactions with Afro-Mexicans, 76; lack of Afro-Mexican culture, 63; media in, 71–72, 78, 176; non-migrants in, 4, 29, 112, 175; perspectives in, 3; phenotypes in, 50; race relations in, 39;

racial identity in, 192n8; return migrants in, 123; views of U.S. race relations, 80; views on Afro-Mexicans, 64, 65, 66; views on Indigenous people, 59, 61

Guanajuato, Mexico, 23, 155, 158

Guatemalans, 126, 184

Güereca, Sergio Adrián Hernández, 84

Guerrero, Mexico, 40, 48

Guerrero, Vicente, 42, 44

Hagan, Jacqueline, 129

Haitians, 181, 185

hate crimes, 14, 183, 184

Hawaii, 13

health care, 13, 19, 147, 152

hegemony, x, 19, 68, 154; racial ideologies, 8–9, 17, 47, 86, 133, 173

heritage, 45, 48, 153

Herrera, Juan, 146, 184

Highland Park, California, ix

Hispano, 152, 154

Hollywood (U.S. cinema), 4, 72, 75–76, 78, 80, 97; depictions, 79, 87; stereotypes, 95. *See also* movies

Hollywood, California, 156

Home Depot, 145, 146

homeownership, 26, 138, 167, 177. *See also* American Dream

honorary White status, 14, 19, 122, 123, 164, 186

hostility, 27, 94, 95, 113, 133; anti-immigrant, 35, 105, 143, 161, 170, 177

host society/country, 3, 5, 12, 36, 73; reception in, 183; transition to, 16, 17, 108

Immigration Reform and Control Act
(IRCA), 139
inclusion. *See* exclusion/inclusion
income, 24, 25, 109, 123, 138, 164. *See
also* employment/unemployment
incorporation, immigrant, 19, 137, 141,
167, 185; race and, 15–16, 35, 105,
179; theories of, 17
incorporation, racial, 17, 118, 184
incorporation, social, 17
Indigeneity, x, 22, 39, 59, 189
Indigenous Mexicans, 45, 53, 57, 172,
174
indio/india/indito, 45, 46, 57, 58, 59,
154
inequality, 25, 36, 37, 105, 141, 174; income, 24; Mexicans' understand-
ing of, 3; racial, 39, 46, 50; social,
9, 34, 39, 46, 50, 51; structural,
186, 188
inferiority, 134, 166; of dark-skinned
Mexicans, 53, 57; of Indigenous
Guatemalan migrants, 184; of Indigenous in Mexico, 46, 134; legal, 21, 139, 141; of mestizaje, 6; of
Mexican immigrants, 84, 85, 166,
168, 174, 177; racial, 18, 19, 21, 47,
168, 174, 180
Instagram, 7, 173
institutions, 60, 181; cultural, 45; economic, 86; governmental, 8, 73,
187, 194n8; Mexican Mafia, 192n2;
neighborhood, 147; social, 169;
U.S., 139, 151, 167
insults/epithets, 45, 55, 59, 117
integration, 26, 135, 183
interactions, 94, 106, 122, 127, 144, 154,
159; Afro-Mexicans in Guadala-
jara, 76; with Asian Americans,

150; cross-racial, 130, 134; ethnic,
132, 134; negative, 117; neighborhood, 6, 176; positive, 131; with racialized "others," 135; social, 54,
74, 86, 93, 111; with White people, 160
intermarriage, 18, 161, 162. *See also* racial mixing
Italians, 17, 18
Itzigsohn, Jose, xi

Jackson, Jesse, 66
Jalisco, Mexico, 1, 28, 29, 30, 57; demo-
graphics of, 23; mestizo identity
in, 50; perspectives of Mexicans
in, 3; racial identity in, 191n3; rac-
ism denial in, 49
Jim Crow, 1, 3, 26, 37, 60, 96, 185
Jiménez, Tomás, 150
Jones, Jennifer, 14, 181
Joseph, Tiffany, 9, 11, 99

Kim, Nadia, 9, 86
King, Rodney, 27, 82
Knight, Alan, 45, 51
Koreans, 114, 150, 165, 181; perceptions
of African Americans, 9; society,
9; in South L.A., 27; transnational
migration, 86

laborers. *See* workers/laborers
language, 69, 111, 124, 133; accent,
31, 32, 45, 52, 61, 127, 184; barriers, 105, 119, 120, 134; boundary of,
149; brokering, 118; English proficiency, 144, 147, 148, 155, 156; Indigenous, 45, 62; remedial skills,
121; Spanish, 31, 45, 62, 121, 153
la Sierra Madre Occidental, 50, 59

New York City, 8, 9, 115
non-Blackness, 38
non-racism, 21, 38
norms, 105; racial, 16, 40, 105, 139, 156; social, 31
North Carolina, 14, 16, 166

Oakland, California, 146
Oaxaca, Mexico, 40
Obama, Barack, 7, 80, 81–82, 142
Oboler, Suzanne, 39
occupation, 29, 30, 69. *See also* employment/unemployment
Ochoa, Gilda, 123
one-drop rule, 5, 41, 66
oppression, 45, 83, 166, 169, 181
Orozco, José Clemente, 43

paisas, 120–21
papers. *See* documents
phenotypes, 29, 61, 154, 184, 192n6;
    Afro, 42, 53, 56, 57; Black, 32, 64, 65; discrimination based on, 52; European, 23; Indigenous, 41, 56; Mexican, 31, 50
pigmentocracy, 41, 56, 68, 174
pinche indio/a, 45, 58, 59
Pinedo-Turnovsky, Carolyn, 115
police, 20, 41, 63, 77, 78, 85, 109, 111;
    brutality, viii, 7, 27, 82, 83, 91, 176; hyper-policing, 28; shooting, 180; surveillance, vii, viii, 2, 27
policies, 5, 54, 75; to address racial disparities, 188; anti-immigrant, 167, 182; economic, 74; immigration, 14, 19, 166, 182; interventionist, 185; racially segregationist, 72; racist, 28; reform, 49

politics, 37, 189; challenges, 17; climate, 183; connection, 7; divider, 20; dynamics of East L.A., 124; effects of legal status, 135; exclusion, 6, 46, 168; figures, 43; ideas, 8; ideologies, 185; institutions, 86; intertwining of Mexico and U.S., 4; involvement in hometown associations, 72; landscape, 4; movements, Black, 175; power, 165, 169, 188; representation of Latinos, 13; status of illegality, 140; system, 118; transformation, 2, 44, 138; upheaval, 43
poorness. *See* poverty
popular culture, 7, 66, 77, 79, 101, 173
post-migration hypothesis, 14, 15
poverty, 24, 76, 185, 193n4; among Black Americans, 111; among immigrants, 20; among Indigenous people, 62; among Mexicans, 53, 55, 68; and Latino immigrants, 183; Latinos associated with, 125; legal status and, 135; in Los Angeles, 134; in Mexico, 69, 107; neighborhoods, 80; social distancing from, 123; in South L.A., 27, 109; in Watts, vii; working, 25. *See also* wealth
power, 8, 95; anti-Black schemas, 92–93; of migrants, 70, 73; national Black movement, 48; political, 169, 188; of race brokers, 134; of racial remittances, 100, 175; of racism, 111, 133, 135; of racist messages, 86; of television, 76; U.S., 37, 97; White, 91, 97, 161, 162, 165

Printed in the USA
CPSIA information can be obtained
at www.ICGtesting.com
JSHW021902050923
47771JS00001B/2